# Technical Manual and Dictionary of
## Classical Ballet

# Technical Manual and Dictionary of
# Classical Ballet

## Third Revised Edition

### Gail Grant

**ILLUSTRATED BY THE AUTHOR**

## Dover Publications, Inc.
**NEW YORK**

This third edition, first published by Dover Publications,
Inc., in 1982, is a new thorough revision starting out from
the second edition, first published by Dover in 1967. That
1967 version was itself a thoroughly revised republication,
with regard to both text and illustrations, of the work first
published by Kamin Dance Publishers, New York, in 1950.
The Prefaces to the Second and Third Editions, the Pronunciation Guide and the Bibliography are completely new
features of the Dover editions.

*International Standard Book Number: 0-486-21843-0*
*Library of Congress Catalog Card Number: 67-26481*

Manufactured in the United States of America
Dover Publications, Inc., 31 East 2nd Street, Mineola, N.Y. 11501

*TO W. J. R.*

# Preface to the Third Edition

This new 1982 Dover edition of Gail Grant's *Technical Manual and Dictionary of Classical Ballet* has been completely revised, and over 300 new terms have been added, all of them alphabetized into the text.

Four new books have been added to the bibliography as sources for the revisions and the additional terms.

WALTER J. RYAN

*Boca Raton, Florida*

# Preface to the Second Edition

The first edition of Gail Grant's *Technical Manual and Dictionary of Classical Ballet* was published in 1950. This new and revised 1967 Dover edition has so considerably broadened the scope of her original work that it should find even readier acceptance by students, teachers, choreographers, dance directors and balletomanes.

Augmenting Miss Grant's initial effort are these new and valuable adjuncts:

**1.** Nearly 100 additional terms have been incorporated.

**2.** All terms are now in one complete alphabetical listing, including all the newly added terms and those formerly added in an appendix.

**3.** Each foreign-language term is followed by an improved phonetic aid to pronunciation which will be immediately useful even to those readers who may know little or nothing of the French and Italian languages. The general guide to this phonetic aid is to be found on page xiii.

**4.** New and revised illustrations have been added. All illustrations are now located in one section of the book for ease of reference.

**5.** A bibliography has been added.

**6.** There are three distinct schools of ballet technique—the classic Italian (Cecchetti method), the graceful French and the strong Russian. The fundamental principles of classical technique are the same in all three. However, certain steps, exercises, poses and movements are performed in different ways and different names are given to similar steps and positions by these three schools. This edition has completely cross-referenced these dissimilarities and the resultant terminological deviations. The new typographic arrangement makes for effortless reading and quick references.

By vastly improving her original text and format, Miss Grant has fashioned a manual and dictionary that has every opportunity for acceptance as the official textbook of classical ballet for all dance associations and institutions.

WALTER J. RYAN

*Toledo, Ohio*
*January 1967*

# List of Illustrations

# Pronunciation Guide

Since most of the terms used in classical ballet are French (a few are Italian), we have provided a phonetic aid to pronunciation immediately following each foreign-language key word. Naturally, these simplified pronunciations are only approximate, but you will not go far wrong if you remember the following rules of thumb:

| LETTER(S) | AS IN | SHOULD BE PRONOUNCED |
|---|---|---|
| a | ba-law-NAY | Except when shown in the combinations "ah," "ahn," "aw," "awn" and "ay" (the next five items on this list), the "a" in the phonetic aids should always be pronounced like the *a* in *cat*, never like any other kind of *a*. |
| ah | rwah-YAL | As in English, but not drawn out. |
| ahn | tahn | Like *ah* in English, but pronounced very strongly "through the nose." |
| aw | vaw-LAY | Like the *aw* in *tawdry*, but not drawn out. |
| awn | rawn | Like the *aw* in *tawdry*, but pronounced very strongly "through the nose." |
| ay | ra-ma-SAY | Like *ay* in *play*, but not drawn out. |
| e, eh | peer-WET; eh-fa-SAY | Like the *e* in *met*. |

| | | |
|---|---|---|
| ee | w*ee*t | As in English. |
| e͞n | pw*en*t | Like the *a* in *cat*, but pronounced very strongly "through the nose." |
| e̲w̲ | ba-T*E̲W̲* | To make this sound, round your lips as if to say *oo*, then (without moving your lips!) say *ee*. |
| g | g*r*a͞hn | Like the *g* in *good*. |
| oh | s*oh*-TAY | As in English, but not drawn out. |
| oo | *oo*-VEHR | Like the *oo* in *food*, but not drawn out. |
| r | feh*r*-MAY | May be rolled with the tip of the tongue. The Parisian *r*, made at the back of the mouth, resembles the sound of gargling. |
| s, ss | s*ee*s*s* | Like the *s* in *sit*. |
| uh | p*uh*-TEE | Like the *e* in *battery*, this is a weak, vague sound. Any syllable in which it appears is generally pronounced very quickly, so that *puh-TEE* is practically like *p-tee*. |
| u̲h̲ | d*u̲h̲*-ZYEM | To make this sound, round your lips as if to say *oh*, then (without moving your lips!) say *eh*. |
| u͞hn | *u͞hn* | This is the same as the preceding sound (*u̲h̲*) but pronounced very strongly "through the nose." |
| zh | *zh*a͞hnb | Like the *z* in *azure*. |

All other sounds are as in English.

Syllables printed in capital letters receive more stress (although stress in French words is generally not as strong as in most English words).

The phonetic pronunciation is always given in the normal word order. For instance, the phonetic pronunciation for the key word "Battement, grand" is given as if for "Grand battement": *grahn bat-MAHN*.

# Bibliography

Albertieri, Luigi. *The Art of Terpsichore.* New York, 1923.
Beaumont, Cyril W. *Dictionary of Technical Terms Used in Classical Ballet.* London, 1939.
——. *A Primer of Classical Ballet.* London, 1941.
——. *The Theory and Practice of Classical Theatrical Dancing.* London, 1940.
Bourgat, Marcelle. *Technique de la Danse.* Paris, 1946.
Bruhn, Eric, and Moore, Lillian. *Bournonville and Ballet Technique.* London, 1961.
Craske, Margaret, and Beaumont, Cyril W. *The Theory and Practice of Allegro in Classical Ballet (Cecchetti Method).* London, 1930.
——. *The Theory and Practice of Advanced Allegro in Classical Ballet (Cecchetti Method).* London, 1956.
Espinosa, Eduard. *Technical Dictionary of Dancing.* London, 1935.
French, Ruth, and Demery, Felix. *Advanced Steps in Ballet.* London, 1950.
——. *First Steps in Ballet.* London, 1934.
——. *Intermediate Steps.* London, 1947.
Guillot, Genevieve, and Prudhommeau, Germaine. *The Book of Ballet.* Englewood Cliffs, N.J., 1976.
Kersley, Leo, and Sinclair, Janet. *A Dictionary of Ballet Terms.* London, 1952.
Kirstein, Lincoln, and Stuart, Muriel. *The Classic Ballet.* New York, 1952.
Kostrovitskaya, Vera, and Pisarev, A. *School of Classical Dance.* Moscow, 1978.
Lawson, Joan. *Classical Ballet, Its Style and Technique.* London, 1960.
Legat, Nadine Nicolaeva-. *Ballet Education.* London, 1947.
——. *Preparation for Ballet.* London, 1953.
Lifar, Serge. *Lifar on Classical Ballet.* London, 1951.
Mara, Thalia. *The Language of Ballet.* Cleveland, 1966.
Messerer, Asaf. *Classes in Classical Ballet.* New York, 1975.
Meunier, Antonine. *La Danse classique.* Paris, 1931.

Noverre, Jean-Georges. *Lettres sur la danse, et sur les ballets.* Lyons, 1760.
Vaganova, Agrippina. *Fundamentals of the Classic Dance.* New York, 1946. (Reprinted by Dover, with additions and corrections, as *Basic Principles of Classical Ballet.*)
Wilson, G. B. L. *A Dictionary of Ballet.* London, 1957.

# Technical Manual and Dictionary of
## Classical Ballet

# Technical Manual and
# Dictionary of Classical Ballet

**Abstract ballet.** A ballet without a plot. A composition of pure dance movement expressed for its own sake.

**Adage, Adagio** [French: *a-DAHZH*]. Adage is a French word derived from the Italian *ad agio*, meaning at ease or leisure. English ballet teachers use "adage," the French adaptation, while Americans prefer the original Italian. In dancing it has two meanings: (1) A series of exercises following the centre practice, consisting of a succession of slow and graceful movements which may be simple or of the most complex character, performed with fluidity and apparent ease. These exercises develop a sustaining power, sense of line, balance and the beautiful poise which enables the dancer to perform with majesty and grace. The principal steps of adagio are pliés, développés, grand fouetté en tournant, dégagés, grand rond de jambe, rond de jambe en l'air, coupés, battements tendus, attitudes, arabesques, preparations for pirouettes and all types of pirouettes. (2) The opening section of the classical pas de deux, in which the ballerina, assisted by her male partner, performs the slow movements and enlèvements in which the danseur lifts, supports or carries the danseuse. The danseuse thus supported exhibits her grace, line and perfect balance while executing développés, pirouettes, arabesques and so on, and achieves combinations of steps and poses which would be impossible without the aid of her partner.

**Ailes de pigeon** [*el duh pee-ZHAWN*]. Pigeon's wings. The dancer performs a cabriole devant, then the legs change and beat again, then change once more before the dancer lands on the leg he or she jumped from, leaving the other leg extended in the air. Also known as "pistolet."

**Air, en l'** [*ahn lehr*]. In the air. Indicates: (1) that a movement is to be made in the air; for example, rond de jambe en l'air; (2) that the working leg, after being opened to the second or fourth position à terre, is to be raised to a horizontal position with the toe on the level of the hip.

**Alignment.** *See* Directions or body alignment.

**Allégro** [*a-lay-GROH;* Italian: *al-LAY-groh*]. Brisk, lively. A term applied to all bright and brisk movements. All steps of elevation such as the entrechat, cabriole, assemblé, jeté and so on, come under this classification. The majority of dances, both solo and group, are built on allégro. The most important qualities to aim at in allégro are lightness, smoothness and ballon.

**Allongé, allongée** [*a-lawn-ZHAY*]. Extended, outstretched. As, for example, in arabesque allongée.

**Angle of the leg in the air.** In the Russian School the angle formed by the legs in relation to the vertical axis of the body is measured in general terms. For example, 45 degrees for half height (demi-hauteur), 90 degrees for a horizontal position with the toe at hip height (à la hauteur) and 135 degrees for any position considerably above hip height. *See* Positions soulevées.

**Aplomb** [*a-PLAWN*]. Assurance, poise. This term applied to the dancer means that he or she has full control of body and limbs with the weight correctly centered during a movement.

**Arabesque** [*a-ra-BESK*]. One of the basic poses in ballet, arabesque takes its name from a form of Moorish ornament. In ballet it is a position of the body, in profile, supported on one leg, which can be straight or demi-plié, with the other leg extended behind and at right angles to it, and the arms held in various harmonious positions creating the longest possible line from the fingertips to the toes. The shoulders must be held square to the line of direction. The forms of arabesque are varied to infinity. The Cecchetti method uses five principal arabesques; the Russian School (Vaganova), four; and the French School, two. Arabesques are generally used to conclude a phrase of steps, both in the slow movements of adagio and the brisk, gay movements of allégro.

THE CECCHETTI ARABESQUES (see illustrations, p. 126)

*First arabesque:* The body is held upright from the waist and is supported on a straight leg with the other leg extended and at right angles to the supporting leg. The shoulders are held square to the line of direction with the arms extended, palms down, so that the extended fingertips of the forward arm (which is the one on the same side as the supporting leg) are in a line with the centre of the space between the eyes, and the extended back arm slightly lowered so that the arms are in one straight line. The forward hand should be slightly turned outward.

*Second arabesque:* The arms are reversed so that the forward arm is the opposite to the supporting leg. The head is slightly inclined and turned toward the audience.

*Third arabesque:* Both arms are extended forward to the side of the supporting leg. The fingertips of the arm farther from the audience are in a line with the centre of the space between the eyes while the arm nearer the audience is in a line with the shoulder.

*Fourth arabesque:* The supporting leg is nearer the audience and is in demi-plié. The arms and head are held as in the first arabesque with the arm on the side of the raised leg being forward.

*Fifth arabesque:* The arms and head are held as in the third arabesque with the arm farther from the audience being the higher. The supporting leg is the leg nearer the audience and is in demi-plié.

The fourth and fifth arabesques are usually taken facing the right front corner of the room or stage if the supporting leg is the left, or facing the left front corner if the supporting leg is the right. In the illustrations the position is shown sideways for the sake of clearness.

THE FRENCH ARABESQUES (see illustrations, p. 127)

*Arabesque ouverte:* The body is supported on a straight leg with the other extended and at right angles to the supporting leg, the extended leg being nearer the audience. The body leans forward with the arm on the side of the supporting leg held in front and the other taken well back and held parallel to the extended leg.

*Arabesque croisée:* The position is the same as the above but the supporting leg is the leg nearer to the audience, the arm on the side of the supporting leg held forward.

THE RUSSIAN ARABESQUES (VAGANOVA) (see illustrations, p. 128)

*First arabesque:* The body is supported on one leg with the other lifted at a right or greater angle to the supporting leg. The body is inclined forward from the waist with a strongly arched back. The arm on the side of the supporting leg is extended forward and the other taken out to the side a little behind the second position.

*Second arabesque:* The body and legs are the same as in the first arabesque but the arms are reversed. That is, the arm on the side of the supporting leg is taken back far enough to be seen behind the body while the other arm is extended forward. The head is turned toward the audience.

*Third arabesque:* This arabesque faces diagonally toward the audience. The supporting leg is nearer the audience with the other raised in croisé derrière at right angles to the supporting leg. The body is inclined forward with the arm opposite the supporting leg extended forward on a level with the shoulder and the other arm extended to the side. The head is turned toward the forward arm.

*Fourth arabesque:* The legs are in the same position as in the third arabesque but the arms are reversed and held at shoulder level. The arm on the side of the supporting leg is brought forward and the other arm taken back far enough to be seen behind the back. The body is half turned away from the audience by the strong arching of the back, with the head turned toward the audience.

**Arabesque, en** [*ah na-ra-BESK*]. In arabesque, that is, in an arabesque position. As, for example, in pirouette en arabesque.

**Arabesque à deux bras** [*a-ra-BESK a duh brah*]. Arabesque with two arms. This arabesque is taken in profile with the extended leg nearest the audience. Both arms are extended forward with the arm on the side of the supporting leg held slightly higher. The head may be held in profile or turned to the audience.

**Arabesque à la demi-hauteur** [*a-ra-BESK a lah duh-MEE-oh-TUHR*]. Arabesque at half-height. A term of the French School. In this arabesque the foot is raised to a position halfway between the position à terre and a horizontal position in the air.

**Arabesque à la hauteur** [*a-ra-BESK a lah oh-TUHR*]. Arabesque at the height. A term of the French School. An arabesque in which the working leg is raised at right angles to the hip. Also termed arabesque allongée.

**Arabesque à la lyre** [*a-ra-BESK a lah leer*]. Arabesque with the lyre. This position resembles the arabesque à deux bras (third arabesque Cecchetti) but both palms are held up and the elbows are slightly curved as if the dancer were holding a lyre.

**Arabesque allongée** [*a-ra-BESK a-lawn-ZHAY*]. Extended or out-stretched arabesque. The line required for this arabesque is a horizontal one. *See* Arabesque à la hauteur.

**Arabesque allongée à terre** [*a-ra-BESK a-lawn-ZHAY a tehr*]. Arabesque extended on the ground. In this arabesque the body is supported on one leg which is completely bent in plié while the other leg is extended in the back with the foot well turned out and on the ground. The arms may be held en attitude, en couronne and so on. This lunge position may be taken en face, croisé or ouvert.

**Arabesque à terre** [*a-ra-BESK a tehr*]. Arabesque on the ground. The arms and body are in arabesque but the leg, usually raised, is extended in the fourth position back, pointe tendue.

**Arabesque croisée** [*a-ra-BESK krwah-ZAY*]. Arabesque crossed. This arabesque presents a three-quarter view of the body and faces a front corner of the stage. The supporting leg is the leg nearer the audience. The arms may be held in a variety of positions. See illustration, p. 127.

**Arabesque de face** [*a-ra-BESK duh fahss*]. Arabesque facing. An arabesque facing the audience. The arms may be held in a variety of positions. (De face = en face.)

**Arabesque effacée** [*a-ra-BESK eh-fa-SAY*]. Arabesque shaded. This is the first arabesque (all schools) taken in an effacé direction.

**Arabesque en promenade** [*a-ra-BESK ahn prawm-NAD*]. Arabesque, walking. An arabesque is said to be en promenade when a slow turn is made either en dedans or en dehors in an arabesque position. This is a temps d'adage. *See* Promenade, tour de; Tour lent.

**Arabesque en tournant** [*a-ra-BESK ahn toor-NAHN*]. Arabesque, turning. An arabesque is said to be en tournant when a pivot is made on the supporting foot.

**Arabesque épaulée** [*a-ra-BESK ay-poh-LAY*]. Arabesque shouldered. This is an arabesque in which the dancer stands at an oblique angle to the audience. The raised leg and forward arm are nearest the audience and the shoulders are turned so that the dancer's back is visible. *See* Épaulé.

**Arabesque étirée** [*a-ra-BESK ay-tee-RAY*]. Arabesque stretched or drawn out. A term of the French School. This is a neoclassical arabesque in which the ballerina, on point and supported by her partner, shifts her axis backward so that her supporting leg is oblique and her free leg held very high (as in a split).

**Arabesque fondue** [*a-ra-BESK fawn-DEW*]. Arabesque, sinking down. An arabesque in which the knee of the supporting leg is bent. Also called "arabesque pliée."

**Arabesque inclinée** [*a-ra-BESK en-klee-NAY*]. Arabesque inclined. A term of the French School. A neoclassical arabesque in which the ballerina, on point and supported by her partner, shifts her axis forward so that her supporting leg is oblique. Because of the slant of the supporting leg the free leg will be held at an angle of less than 90 degrees. Also called "arabesque poussée."

**Arabesque ouverte** [*a-ra-BESK oo-VEHRT*]. Open arabesque. A term of the French School. This arabesque is taken in profile to the audience. The leg nearer the audience is raised and the arm on the side of the supporting leg extended forward. The head is in profile. *See section on* "The French arabesques" *under* Arabesque.

**Arabesque penchée** [*a-ra-BESK pahn-SHAY*]. Arabesque, leaning. An arabesque in which the body leans well forward in an oblique line, the forward arm and the head being low and the foot of the raised leg the highest point.

**Arabesque pliée** [*a-ra-BESK plee-AY*]. Arabesque with a bent knee. Same as arabesque fondue.

**Arabesque poussée** [*a-ra-BESK poo-SAY*]. Arabesque pushed. A term of the French School. Same as arabesque inclinée.

**Arabesque voyagée** [*a-ra-BESK vwah-yah-ZHAY*]. Arabesque, traveling. This is a series of small hops in an arabesque position. The supporting knee is bent and the instep of the supporting foot does not stretch. The arabesque may be traveled forward or backward. *See* Voyagé.

**Arqué** [*ar-KAY*]. Arched (bowlegged). Very few people have perfectly straight legs and nearly every dancer conforms to one of the two types arqué and jarreté (*q.v.*). When the arqué, or bowlegged, dancer stands in the first position there is a space between the knee joints. This type of dancer is usually strongly built but stiff. Their extensions are never high but they have great power and ballon and sharp brilliant beats.

**Arrière, en** [*ah na-RYEHR*]. Backward. Used to indicate that a step is executed moving away from the audience. As, for example, in glissade en arrière. See floor plan illustration, p. 125.

**Arrondi, arrondie** [*a-rawn-DEE*]. Rounded, curved. As, for example, in battement arrondi.

**Assemblé** [*a-sahn-BLAY*]. Assembled or joined together. A step in which the working foot slides well along the ground before being swept into the air. As the foot goes into the air the dancer pushes off the floor with the supporting leg, extending the toes. Both legs come to the ground simultaneously in the fifth position. If an assemblé is porté it requires a preparatory step such as a glissade to precede it. If an assemblé is en tournant it must be preceded by a preparatory step. Assemblés are done petit or grand according to the height of the battement and are executed dessus, dessous, devant, derrière, en avant, en arrière and en tournant. They may be done en face, croisé, effacé or écarté. Assemblé may also be done with a beat for greater brilliance. In the Cecchetti assemblé both knees are bent and drawn up after the battement so that the flat of the toes of both feet meet while the body is in the air.

**Assemblé, double** [*doob la-sahn-BLAY*]. Double assemblé. A term of the Russian School. This step consists of two assemblés to the second position at 45 degrees; the first assemblé is done without changing the position of the legs and the second with a change.

**Assemblé, grand** [*grahn ta-sahn-BLAY*]. Big assemblé. The jump is higher and the working leg is swept into the air into a horizontal position or à la hauteur. The legs join in the fifth position in the air before coming to the ground.

**Assemblé, petit** [*puh-TEE ta-sahn-BLAY*]. Little assemblé. The working leg is swept into the air with a battement to a point midway between a position of the foot à terre and its equivalent en l'air. This position is called demi-position in the Cecchetti method or demi-hauteur in the French School.

**Assemblé battu** [*a-sahn-BLAY ba-TEW*]. Assemblé beaten. Assemblés dessus, dessous and en tournant may be done with beats.

*Assemblé dessus battu:* Fifth position R foot back. Demi-plié, brush the R leg to the side and push off the floor with the L foot. On the return to fifth position the R leg beats the L in the back, opens slightly and comes to the ground simultaneously with the L leg in the fifth position R foot front. The beat is made with the calves.

*Assemblé dessous battu:* The working leg beats in the front and closes in the back.

*Assemblé battu en tournant:* This assemblé is done dessus. The working leg beats in the back, and finishes in the fifth position front. *See* Assemblé en tournant, grand.

**Assemblé coupé** [*a-sahn-BLAY koo-PAY*]. Cut assemblé. This is a term of the Cecchetti method for an assemblé started from one foot. The working leg may be sur le cou-de-pied or pointe tendue or raised en l'air. The working leg closes into the fifth position without a brush.

**Assemblé coupé derrière** [*a-sahn-BLAY koo-PAY deh-RYEHR*]. Assemblé cut behind. A term of the Cecchetti method. Stand on the R foot with the L foot sur le cou-de-pied derrière or pointed in the fourth position derrière à terre or en l'air. Demi-plié and spring off the R foot. Come to the ground in demi-plié in the fifth position L foot back.

**Assemblé coupé devant** [*a-sahn-BLAY koo-PAY duh-VAHN*]. Assemblé cut in front. A term of the Cecchetti method. Stand on the R foot with the L foot sur le cou-de-pied devant or pointed in the fourth position devant à terre or en l'air. Demi-plié and spring off the R foot. Come to the ground in demi-plié in the fifth position L foot front.

**Assemblé derrière** [*a-sahn-BLAY deh-RYEHR*]. Assemblé in back. Fifth position R foot back. The R foot slides out to the second position en l'air and at the completion of the assemblé closes in the fifth position back.

**Assemblé dessous** [*a-sahn-BLAY duh-SOO*]. Assemblé under. Fifth position R foot front. The R foot slides out to the second position en l'air and at the completion of the assemblé is closed in the fifth position back. Also called "assemblé en remontant" or "assemblé en reculant."

**Assemblé dessus** [*a-sahn-BLAY duh-SEW*]. Assemblé over. Fifth position R foot back. Demi-plié and slide the R foot to the second position en l'air. Push from the ground with the L foot, extending the toes. Both feet return to the ground simultaneously, landing in the fifth position R foot front, with a soft demi-plié. The tips of the toes reach the ground first, then the heels. Also called "assemblé en descendant."

**Assemblé de suite** [*a-sahn-BLAY duh sweet*]. Continuous assemblé. A term from the Cecchetti method used when assemblés are executed in a series without straightening the knees at the conclusion of each assemblé.

**Assemblé devant** [*a-sahn-BLAY duh-VAHN*]. Assemblé in front. Fifth position R foot front. The R foot slides out to the second position en l'air and at the completion of the assemblé is closed in the fifth position front.

**Assemblé élancé** [*a-sahn-BLAY ay-lahn-SAY*]. Assemblé, darting. An assemblé dessus traveled to the side. *See* Assemblé porté.

**Assemblé en arrière** [*a-sahn-BLAY ah na-RYEHR*]. Assemblé backward. Fifth position R foot back. The R foot slides backward to the fourth position en l'air and at the completion of the assemblé closes in the fifth position back. This assemblé may be done in place or traveling backward.

**Assemblé en avant** [*a-sahn-BLAY ah na-VAHN*]. Assemblé forward. Fifth position R foot front. The R foot slides forward to the fourth position en l'air and at the completion of the assemblé closes in the fifth position front. This assemblé may be done in place or traveling forward.

**Assemblé en descendant** [*a-sahn-BLAY ahn day-sahn-DAHN*]. Assemblé coming down or moving downstage. A term of the French School. Same as assemblé dessus.

**Assemblé en remontant or en reculant** [*a-sahn-BLAY ahn ruh-mawn-TAHN* (or) *ahn ruh-kew-LAHN*]. Assemblé going up or drawing back (moving upstage). A term of the French School. Same as assemblé dessous.

**Assemblé en tournant, grand** [*grahn ta-sahn-BLAY ahn toor-NAHN*]. Big assemblé, turning. This assemblé is done in the same manner as grand assemblé. It is taken only dessus cr derrière. It is traveled directly to the side, on a diagonal traveling upstage, in a circle, etc. It is usually preceded by a pas couru or a chassé. The battement at 90 degrees to the second position is taken facing upstage, then the dancer completes the turn en dedans and finishes the assemblé facing the audience.

**Assemblé porté** [*a-sahn-BLAY pawr-TAY*]. Assemblé carried. This assemblé requires a preparatory step to precede it and during the actual assemblé the body is carried in the air from one spot to another in the desired direction. Assemblés devant, derrière, dessus and dessous may be porté.

**Assemblé porté et battu** [*a-sahn-BLAY pawr-TAY ay ba-TEW*]. This assemblé is traveled and done with a beat.

**Assemblé soutenu (Cecchetti method)** [*a-sahn-BLAY soot-NEW*]. Assemblé sustained. In the Cecchetti method an assemblé is said to be soutenu when the knees are straightened and another demi-plié is made before executing the next assemblé.

**Assemblé soutenu de face** [*a-sahn-BLAY soot-NEW duh fahss*]. Assemblé sustained and facing the audience. This assemblé is not a jumping step. It is done on the pointes or demi-pointes and may be performed dessus, dessous, derrière, devant, en avant and en arrière. For assemblé soutenu dessus, stand in the fifth position R foot back. Demi-plié, sliding the R foot to the second position pointe tendue à terre; draw the R leg into the fifth position front, springing on the pointes or demi-pointes, then lower the heels in demi-plié in the fifth position. Also called "assemblé soutenu sur les pointes."

**Assemblé soutenu en tournant (demi-tours)** [*a-sahn-BLAY soot-NEW ahn toor-NAHN (duh-mee-TOOR)*]. Assemblé sustained in turning (half-turns).

*En dedans:* Fifth position R foot back. Fondu on the L leg and at the same time slide the R foot to the second position à terre, pointe tendue (dégagé). Draw the R foot into the fifth position front, rising on the demi-pointes. Pivot a half-turn to the left (demi-détourné) to face the back of the room, finishing with the L foot front. Lower the heels in demi-plié.

*En dehors:* Still facing the back of the room with the L foot front, fondu on the R leg and at the same time slide the L foot to the second position à terre, pointe tendue (dégagé). Draw the L foot into the fifth position back, rising on the demi-pointes. Pivot a half-turn to the left (demi-détourné) to face the front of the room, finishing with the L foot front. Lower the heels in demi-plié.

**Assemblé soutenu en tournant en dedans** [*a-sahn-BLAY soot-NEW ahn toor-NAHN ahn duh-DAHN*]. Assemblé sustained and turning inward. Fifth position R foot back. Fondu on the L leg and at the same time slide the R foot to the second position à terre, pointe tendue. Draw the R foot into the fifth position front, rising on the demi-pointes and turning en dedans (to the left) to face the back of the room with the feet in the fifth position, R foot front. Pivot a half-turn to the left (demi-détourné) to face front, finishing with the L foot front. Lower the heels in demi-plié. This is the method of the Russian School. The French School begins the step with a demi-rond de jambe à terre en dedans instead of drawing the working foot straight in to the fifth position from the second position.

**Assemblé soutenu en tournant en dehors** [*a-sahn-BLAY soot-NEW ahn toor-NAHN ahn duh-AWR*]. Assemblé sustained and turning outward. Fifth position R foot front. Fondu on the L leg and at the same time slide the R foot to the second position à terre, pointe tendue. Draw the R foot into the fifth position back, rising on the demi-pointes and turning en dehors (to the right) to face the back of the room with the feet in the fifth position, R foot back. Pivot a half-turn to the right (demi-détourné) to face front, finishing with the R foot front. Lower the heels in demi-plié. This is the method of the Russian School. The French School begins the step with a demi-rond de jambe à terre en dehors instead of drawing the working foot straight in to the fifth position from the second position.

**Assemblé soutenu sur les pointes** [*a-sahn-BLAY soot-NEW sewr lay pwent*]. Assemblé sustained on the points. Same as assemblé soutenu de face.

**Attitude** [*a-tee-TEWD*]. A particular pose in dancing derived by Carlo Blasis from the statue of Mercury by Giovanni da Bologna. It is a position on one leg with the other lifted in back, the knee bent at an angle of 90 degrees and well turned out so that the knee is higher than the foot. The supporting foot may be à terre, sur la pointe or sur la demi-pointe. The arm on the side of the raised leg is held over the head in a curved position while the other arm is extended to the side. There are a number of attitudes according to the position of the body in relation to the audience: for example, attitude croisée, attitude effacée, attitude de face. See illustrations, p. 129.

**Attitude, demi-** [*duh-MEE-a-tee-TEWD*]. Half attitude. A term of the French School. An attitude with the raised leg à la demi-hauteur. The arms are held in the same position as in attitude.

**Attitude, en** [*ah na-tee-TEWD*]. In attitude, that is, in an attitude position. As, for example, in pirouette en attitude.

**Attitude à deux bras** [*a-tee-TEWD a duh brah*]. Attitude with two arms. The same position as the Blasis attitude but with both arms en couronne (raised above the head).

**Attitude à terre** [*a-tee-TEWD a tehr*]. Attitude on the ground. The arms are in attitude and the foot which is usually raised is extended with the toe pointed on the ground in the fourth position back.

**Attitude croisée derrière** [*a-tee-TEWD krwah-ZAY deh-RYEHR*]. Attitude crossed in back. The dancer stands facing a front corner of the stage (croisé direction; see floor plan, p. 125) with the supporting leg nearest the audience. The raised leg is held at 90 degrees and crossed behind the body with the knee bent at a right angle and the foot held parallel or slightly below the raised knee. The body presents a three-quarter view to the audience.

**Attitude croisée derrière (Cecchetti method)** [*a-tee-TEWD krwah-ZAY deh-RYEHR*]. In this method, the body is held upright with a straight back, shoulders aligned and well pressed down. The head is turned with the eyes looking up into the palm of the raised hand. See illustration, p. 129.

**Attitude croisée derrière (French School)** [*a-tee-TEWD krwah-ZAY deh-RYEHR*]. The body is bent toward the supporting leg with the shoulder of the raised arm lifted slightly higher than the other shoulder. The head is turned toward the front shoulder.

**Attitude croisée derrière (Russian School)** [*a-tee-TEWD krwah-ZAY deh-RYEHR*]. The body inclines forward with a well-arched back. The shoulders are aligned and pressed down with the head turned toward the front shoulder. The Russian School also uses a high croisé position in which the foot is raised higher than the knee. See illustration, p. 129.

**Attitude croisée devant** [*a-tee-TEWD krwah-ZAY duh-VAHN*]. Attitude crossed in front. This is the position croisé devant, but the raised leg is bent with the knee pressed outward and the foot raised as high as possible. The arms are held en attitude with the high arm on the same side as the supporting leg and the head slightly inclined toward the low arm. See illustration, p. 129.

**Attitude de face** [*a-tee-TEWD duh fahss*]. Attitude facing. A term of the French School for an attitude facing the audience.

**Attitude effacée derrière** [*a-tee-TEWD eh-fa-SAY deh-RYEHR*]. Attitude shaded in back. The dancer stands facing a front corner of the stage (effacé direction; see floor plan, p. 125). The raised arm and leg are nearer the audience with the leg in a half-bent position so that the audience sees the arched line of the entire leg from hip to toe. The body presents a three-quarter, almost profile view to the audience. The French School terms this the "attitude ouverte" (*q.v.*).

**Attitude effacée derrière (Cecchetti method)** [*a-tee-TEWD eh-fa-SAY deh-RYEHR*]. In this method, the body is held upright with a straight back and the dancer leans slightly back toward the raised leg. The head is turned toward the audience and inclined toward the raised arm.

**Attitude effacée derrière (Russian School)** [*a-tee-TEWD eh-fa-SAY deh-RYEHR*]. The torso is tilted forward toward the supporting leg with the back held upright and both shoulders level. The head is turned toward the audience. The Russian School also uses a high effacé position in which the thigh is raised so that the foot is held higher than the knee at approximately 135 degrees.

**Attitude en promenade** [*a-tee-TEWD ahn prawm-NAD*]. Attitude, walking. When a slow turn is made en dedans or en dehors in an attitude position, the attitude is said to be en promenade. This is a temps d'adage. *See* Promenade, tour de; Tour lent.

**Attitude en tournant** [*a-tee-TEWD* $\overline{ahn}$ *toor-N$\overline{AHN}$*]. Attitude, turning. An attitude is said to be en tournant when a pivot is made on the supporting leg. *See* Pirouette en attitude.

**Attitude épaulée** [*a-tee-TEWD* *ay-poh-LAY*]. Attitude "shouldered." This attitude is executed in the same manner as the Cecchetti attitude croisée but is taken facing either one of the upper corners of the room (corners 3 or 4; see illustration, p. 138) and presents a three-quarter rear view to the audience. If the pose is taken on the L foot, the dancer faces corner 3. See illustration, p. 129.

**Attitude grecque** [*a-tee-TEWD* *grek*]. Greek attitude. In this attitude the heel of the working foot touches the ankle or knee of the supporting leg. The toe is pointed and the thigh opened to the second position. One arm is curved opposite the waistline and the arm on the side of the supporting leg is curved over the head. The head is turned in profile and the body leans toward the raised leg. This attitude may be taken en face, croisée or effacée. Pirouettes may also be done in this position but in this case the head does not "spot."

**Attitude ouverte** [*a-tee-TEWD* *oo-VEHRT*]. Open attitude. This is the French School's term for the attitude effacée derrière. The body leans slightly forward toward the supporting leg with the shoulder of the raised arm held slightly higher than the other shoulder and the head turned toward the audience.

**Attitude penchée** [*a-tee-TEWD* $\overline{pahn}$*-SHAY*]. Attitude, leaning. In this attitude the body leans forward with a well-arched back and the raised foot held high.

**Autour de la salle** [*oh-TOOR* *duh* *lah* *sal*]. A term of the Cecchetti method. *See* Salle, autour de la.

**Avant, en** [*ah* *na-V$\overline{AHN}$*]. Forward. A direction for the execution of a step. Used to indicate that a given step is executed moving forward, toward the audience. As, for example, in sissonne fermée en avant. See floor plan, p. 125.

**Balancé** [*ba-$\overline{lahn}$-SAY*]. Rocking step. This step is very much like a pas de valse and is an alternation of balance, shifting the weight from one foot to the other. Balancé may be done crossing the foot either front or back. Fifth position R foot front. Demi-plié, dégagé the R foot to the second position and jump on it lightly in demi-plié, crossing the L foot behind the R ankle and inclining the head and body to the right. Step on the L demi-pointe behind the R foot, slightly lifting the R foot off the ground; then fall on the R foot again in demi-plié with the L foot raised sur le cou-de-pied derrière. The next balancé will be to the left side. Balancé may also be done en avant or en arrière facing croisé or effacé and en tournant.

**Balancé de côté** [*ba-lahn-SAY duh koh-TAY*]. Rocking step to the side. Same as balancé.

**Balancé en tournant** [*ba-lahn-SAY ahn toor-NAHN*]. Balancé, turning. The turn may be done with quarter or half-turns.

**Balançoire, en** [*ahn ba-lahn-SWAHR*]. Like a seesaw. This term is applied to an exercise, a series of grands battements executed with a continuous swinging motion through the first position to the fourth position front and back. As the leg is thrown forcefully forward, the body leans backward, then as the leg is thrown backward, the body leans forward. *See* Battement jeté balancé, grand; Battement jeté balançoire, grand.

**Ballabile** [*bahl-LAH-bee-lay* (Italian)]. "Danceable." From the Italian *ballare*, to dance. A dance for a group or corps de ballet without solos.

**Ballerina** [*bahl-lay-REE-nah* (Italian)]. A principal female dancer in a ballet company. In the days of the Russian Imperial Theatres the title was given to the outstanding soloists who danced the chief classical roles. At the Maryinski Theatre in St. Petersburg the ballet company consisted of ballerinas, premiers danseurs, first and second soloists, coryphées and corps de ballet.

**Ballerina assoluta, prima** [*PREE-mah bahl-lay-REE-nah ahs-soh-LOO-tah* (Italian)]. First ballerina absolute. This title was bestowed only twice in the two-hundred-year history of the Russian Imperial Theatres, to the two ballerinas Pierina Legnani and Mathilde Kschessinska.

**Ballerina, prima** [*PREE-mah bahl-lay-REE-nah* (Italian)]. A title for an outstanding soloist or first principal female dancer of a ballet company.

**Ballet** [*ba-LAY*]. A theatrical work or entertainment in which a choreographer has expressed his ideas in group and solo dancing to a musical accompaniment with appropriate costumes, scenery and lighting.

**Ballet blanc** [*ba-LAY blahn*]. White ballet. This is a term applied to any ballet in which the dancers wear the traditional long white costumes designed by Eugène Lami for Marie Taglioni in the ballet *La Sylphide* in 1830. Examples are the second act of *Giselle* and the ballet *Les Sylphides*.

**Ballet classique** [*ba-LAY kla-SEEK*]. *See* Classical ballet.

**Ballet d'action** [*ba-LAY dak-SYAWN*]. A ballet with a plot or story. For example, *The Sleeping Beauty*.

**Ballet d'école** [*ba-LAY day-KAWL*]. Ballet of the school. The academic dance based on the turn-out and the five positions of the feet.

**Ballet master, ballet mistress.** The person in a ballet company whose duty is to give the daily company class and to rehearse the ballets in the company repertoire. *See* Maître or maîtresse de ballet.

**Balletomane.** A ballet fan or enthusiast. The word was invented in Russia in the early nineteenth century.

**Balletomania.** A mania for ballet. The word was introduced to the

English-speaking public by Arnold Haskell with his book of that title published in 1934.

**Ballet romantique** [*ba-LAY raw-mahn-TEEK*]. *See* Romantic ballet.

**Ballon** [*ba-LAWN*]. Bounce. Ballon is the light, elastic quality in jumping in which the dancer bounds up from the floor, pauses a moment in the air and descends lightly and softly, only to rebound in the air like the smooth bouncing of a ball.

**Ballonné, coupé** [*koo-PAY ba-law-NAY*]. Ballonné cut. A term of the Russian School. It consists of a coupé dessous followed by a fouetté movement with a temps levé on the supporting leg. *See* Coupé fouetté raccourci.

**Ballonné, pas** [*pah ba-law-NAY*]. Ball-like or bouncing step. A step in which the dancer springs into the air extending one leg to the front, side or back and lands with the extended leg either sur le cou-de-pied or retiré. There are two kinds of ballonné: ballonné simple, which may be performed petit or grand; and ballonné composé, which is a compound step consisting of three movements (see these terms). Ballonné may be executed in all the directions of the body.

**Ballonné arrondi** [*ba-law-NAY a-rawn-DEE*]. Ballonné rounded or curved. This is a series of ballonnés simples devant executed on a diagonal. The first ballonné is performed in the direction effacé en avant with the front foot, immediately followed by the second ballonné with the same foot in the direction écarté en avant.

**Ballonné à trois temps** [*ba-law-NAY a trwah tahn*]. Ballonné in three movements. A term of the Cecchetti method consisting of ballonné, chassé, coupé. The step is executed the same way as the ballonné composé except that the dancer executes a coupé on the last movement instead of closing in the fifth position. It may be performed en avant, en arrière and de côté in all the directions of the body. *See* Ballonné composé.

**Ballonné battu** [*ba-law-NAY ba-TEW*]. Ballonné beaten. Execute a ballonné simple with the R leg to the second position; before closing the leg sur le cou-de-pied derrière, beat the L leg behind the R at the height of the jump. *See* Fouetté battu.

**Ballonné composé** [*ba-law-NAY kawn-poh-ZAY*]. Composite ballonné. A term of the French School. This is a compound step and consists of a ballonné simple, chassé and a close to the fifth position. It may be performed en avant, en arrière and de côté in all the directions of the body. *See* Ballonné à trois temps.

**Ballonné devant sur la pointe** [*ba-law-NAY duh-VAHN sewr lah pwent*]. Ballonné in front on point. *See* Ballonné sur la pointe.

**Ballonné simple** [*ba-law-NAY SEN-pluh*]. Simple ballonné. This may be performed either petit or grand. In petit ballonné, the leg is extended to the second or fourth position at 45 degrees; then the knee is bent and the foot brought sur le cou-de-pied. In grand ballonné, the leg is extended at 90 degrees and finished with the foot at the knee.

**Ballonné simple de côté** [*ba-law-NAY S̄EN-pluh duh koh-TAY*]. Ballonné simple to the side. Fifth position R foot front. Demi-plié, sliding the R foot along the ground to the second position en l'air at 45 degrees; push off the floor with the L foot, toes extended, traveling to the right; land in demi-plié on the L foot, bringing the R foot sur le cou-de-pied, either devant or derrière. This ballonné is performed traveling in the direction écarté en avant, écarté en arrière or de côté.

**Ballonné simple derrière** [*ba-law-NAY S̄EN-pluh deh-RYEHR*]. Ballonné simple in back. Ballonné simple derrière is performed in the same manner as ballonné simple devant (*q.v.*) The working foot glides along the floor to the fourth position derrière en l'air at 45 degrees. The step travels in the direction effacé en arrière or croisé en arrière.

**Ballonné simple devant** [*ba-law-NAY S̄EN-pluh duh-VAHN*]. Ballonné simple in front. Fifth position R foot front. Demi-plié, sliding the R foot along the floor to the fourth position devant en l'air at 45 degrees; push off the floor with the L foot, toes extended, traveling to the right; land in demi-plié on the L foot, at the same time bringing the R foot sur le cou-de-pied devant. This ballonné is performed effacé en avant or croisé en avant with the body and arms placed according to the direction of the movement. The body and arms do not move during the step, but remain in the pose.

**Ballonné sur la pointe** [*ba-law-NAY sewr lah pwent*]. Ballonné on point. This is a relevé on point with the working leg opening at 45 degrees on the musical accent. It is executed in the directions croisé, effacé and écarté, traveling forward or backward.

*Ballonné devant sur la pointe:* Fifth position croisé R foot front. Demi-plié on the upbeat, raising the R foot sur le cou-de-pied devant and turning the body effacé. Relevé on the L pointe, opening the R leg effacé devant at 45 degrees. Lower the L heel in fondu, bringing the R foot sur le cou-de-pied devant. Continue on the same foot, traveling forward on each relevé.

**Ballotté** [*ba-law-TAY*]. Tossed. This step consists of coupé dessous and coupé dessus performed in a series with a rocking, swinging movement. The step may be performed with straight knees at 45 degrees or with développés at 90 degrees. The direction of the body is effacé with the body inclining backward or forward with each change of weight. In the Russian School, ballotté is performed traveling forward on ballotté en avant and backward on ballotté en arrière to the place from which the first jump began. In the French School and the Cecchetti method, ballotté is performed on one spot.

**Ballotté en arrière (Cecchetti method)** [*ba-law-TAY ah na-RYEHR*]. Ballotté backward. At the finish of ballotté en avant (*q.v.*) the R leg is raised in effacé devant. The movement is then reversed by springing off the L foot, drawing the legs up with the feet in the fifth position and landing on the R foot with a fondu in the place vacated by the L foot while the L leg does a développé à la quatrième derrière in effacé, body leaning forward.

**Ballotté en avant (Cecchetti method)** [*ba-law-TAY ah na-VAHN*]. Ballotté forward. Fourth position L foot back, pointe tendue. Raise the L foot slightly off the ground; demi-plié on the R foot; spring into the air, bending the knees and drawing the feet up into the fifth position with toes well pointed. Come to the ground on the L foot with a fondu in the place vacated by the R foot and développé the R leg à la quatrième devant, body effacé and leaning backward.

**Barre** [*bar*]. The horizontal wooden bar fastened to the walls of the ballet classroom or rehearsal hall which the dancer holds for support. Every ballet class begins with exercises at the bar. *See* Exercices à la barre; Side practice.

**Bas, en** [*ahn bah*]. Low. Used to indicate a low position of the arms. As, for example, in fifth position en bas, Cecchetti method.

**Battement** [*bat-MAHN*]. Beating. A beating action of the extended or bent leg. There are two types of battements, grands battements and petits battements. The petis battements are: Battements tendus, dégagés, frappés and tendus relevés: stretched, disengaged, struck and stretched-and-lifted.

**Battement, grand** [*grahn bat-MAHN*]. Large battement. An exercise in which the working leg is raised from the hip into the air and brought down again, the accent being on the downward movement, both knees straight. This must be done with apparent ease, the rest of the body remaining quiet. The function of grands battements is to loosen the hip joints and turn out the legs from the hips. Grands battements can be taken devant, derrière and à la seconde. To execute a *grand battement à la quatrième devant* start in the fifth position R foot front. In one sweeping movement, slide the R foot to the fourth position front (fourth position croisé), pointe tendue, raise the foot to the fourth position front en l'air, lower the foot to the fourth position pointe tendue and slide the foot back to the fifth position front. *Battements à la seconde* and *à la quatrième derrière* are done in the same manner. In the execution of grands battements à la seconde the working leg closes alternately in the fifth position front and back.

**Battement, petit** [*puh-TEE bat-MAHN*]. Small battement. This is another term for a battement tendu. It is also a term for any small beating action of the foot or leg.

**Battement arrondi** [*bat-MAHN a-rawn-DEE*]. Battement rounded. A term of the French School. The toes of the working foot describe a semicircle in the air on an oblique plane at 45 degrees, either en dedans or en dehors. For en dehors, extend the working leg forward and carry it around to the back and finish in the fifth position. For en dedans, reverse the movement.

**Battement arrondi, grand** [*grahn bat-MAHN a-rawn-DEE*]. Large battement rounded. A term of the French School. This is a grand battement circled from the fifth position to the fifth position passing through all the open positions in the air at 90 degrees. The highest point of the battement is reached when the leg passes through the second position in the air. The battement is performed either en dedans or en dehors. Also known as "grand battement en rond."

**Battement arrondi en dedans, grand** [*grahn bat-MAHN a-rawn-DEE ahn duh-DAHN*]. Large battement rounded inward. The working foot starts in the fifth position back and in one sweeping movement passes through the positions à la quatrième derrière en l'air, à la seconde en l'air, à la quatrième devant en l'air, and closes in the fifth position front.

**Battement arrondi en dehors, grand** [*grahn bat-MAHN a-rawn-DEE ahn duh-AWR*]. Large battement rounded outward. In this battement the working foot starts in the fifth position front and in one sweeping movement passes through the positions à la quatrième devant en l'air, à la seconde en l'air, à la quatrième derrière en l'air, and closes in the fifth position back.

**Battement battu** [*bat-MAHN ba-TEW*]. Battement beaten. The R foot is placed in the position sur le cou-de-pied devant or derrière and the R toe beats against the L ankle with a series of quick little taps, using the lower part of the leg from the knee down. Battements battus are performed as an exercise at the barre on the point or demi-pointe. They are also performed by the danseuse on point supported by her partner.

**Battement dégagé** [*bat-MAHN day-ga-ZHAY*]. Disengaged battement. A term of the Cecchetti method. The battement dégagé is similar to the battement tendu but is done at twice the speed and the working foot rises about four inches from the floor with a well-pointed toe, then slides back into the the first or fifth position. Battements dégagés strengthen the toes, develop the instep and improve the flexibility of the ankle joint. Same as battement tendu jeté (Russian School), battement glissé (French School).

**Battement développé** [*bat-MAHN dayv-law-PAY*]. Battement developed. From the fifth position the working foot glides up to the retiré position and forcefully opens in the required direction. On reaching the extreme point the leg is lowered into the fifth position. This exercise is usually done en croix.

**Battement développé tombé** [*bat-MAHN dayv-law-PAY tawn-BAY*]. Battement developed and falling down. This battement is done as an exercise at the bar or in the center adagio. It is done en avant, en arrière and de côté in the directions croisé, effacé and écarté. Fifth position R foot front; développé the R leg to the fourth position front, rising on the L demi-pointe: fall forward into a deep lunge on the R leg with the L leg extended back on the floor pointe tendue; transfer the weight back to the L foot and repeat the exercise in the desired direction.

**Battement divisé en quarts** [*bat-MAHN dee-vee-ZAY ahn kar*]. Battements divided in quarters. A term of the Russian School for an exercise of the centre practice. *See* Relevé d'adage par quart de tour.

**Battement en cloche, grand** [$\overline{grahn}$ *bat-*$\overline{MAHN}$ $\overline{ahn}$ *klawsh*]. Large battement like a bell. A term of the French School and the Cecchetti method. Grands battements en cloche are continuous grands battements executed from the fourth position front or back en l'air to the fourth position back or front en l'air, passing through the first position. Same as grand battement jeté balancé, but the body remains upright as the leg swings.

**Battement en cloche, petit** [*puh-TEE* *bat-*$\overline{MAHN}$ $\overline{ahn}$ *klawsh*]. Small battement like a bell. Same as battement tendu jeté balancé.

**Battement en croix, grand** [$\overline{grahn}$ *bat-*$\overline{MAHN}$ $\overline{ahn}$ *krwah*]. Large battement in the form of a cross. First a grand battement is done en quatrième devant, followed by a grand battement à la seconde closing in the fifth position back. Then a grand battement à la quatrième derrière, followed by a grand battement à la seconde closing in the fifth position front.

**Battement en rond, grand** [$\overline{grahn}$ *bat-*$\overline{MAHN}$ $\overline{ahn}$ $\overline{rawn}$]. Same as grand battement arrondi.

**Battement fini piqué, grand** [$\overline{grahn}$ *bat-*$\overline{MAHN}$ *fee-NEE pee-KAY*]. Large battement finished in piqué. A term of the French School. This battement begins with a grand battement but the foot does not return to the fifth position. The extended leg is lowered to the floor pointe tendue in either the second or fourth position. The foot is raised from this position and continues the movement, returning to the fifth position at the completion of the last battement. Also called "grand battement jeté pointé."

**Battement fondu** [*bat-*$\overline{MAHN}$ *fawn-D*$\underline{EW}$]. Battement, sinking down. This is an exercise in which the supporting leg is slowly bent in fondu with the working foot pointing on the ankle. As the supporting leg is straightened, the working leg unfolds and is extended to point on the floor or in the air. The movement is done devant, derrière and à la seconde. In fondu forward, the conditional position sur le cou-de-pied devant is used. In fondu back, the basic position sur le cou-de-pied derrière is used.

**Battement fondu, double** [*DOO-bluh bat-*$\overline{MAHN}$ *fawn-D*$\underline{EW}$]. Double battement fondu. A term of the Russian School. The step consists of two fondus. The first fondu and relevé is taken with the working foot sur le cou-de-pied, then the working leg stretches in the given direction at 45 or 90 degrees while the supporting leg bends in demi-plié and straightens with a rise to the demi-pointe.

**Battement fondu développé** [*bat-*$\overline{MAHN}$ *fawn-D*$\underline{EW}$ *dayv-law-PAY*]. Battement fondu developed. This is performed in the same manner as battement fondu simple (*q.v*). As the supporting leg straightens, the working leg does a développé at either 45 or 90 degrees. If the développé is at 45 degrees, the working leg opens from sur le cou-de-pied. If the développé is at 90 degrees, the working leg is brought from sur le cou-de-pied to retiré, then opens in the desired direction as the supporting knee straightens. The leg moves evenly until reaching the angle of 45 or 90 degrees and is sustained momentarily in the extended position before slowly returning to sur le cou-de-pied as the supporting leg executes a demi-plié.

**Battement fondu développé relevé** [*bat-M$\overline{AHN}$ fawn-DEW dayv-law-PAY ruhl-VAY*]. Battement fondu developed and raised. This is performed in the same manner as battement fondu développé. As the supporting leg straightens, the dancer rises to the demi-pointe and performs a développé at 45 or 90 degrees.

**Battement fondu simple** [*bat-M$\overline{AHN}$ fawn-DEW S$\overline{EN}$-pluh*]. Simple battement fondu. From the fifth position the R foot moves to sur le cou-de-pied devant while the L leg does a demi-plié, then the R leg opens forward with a small développé to the fourth position front, pointing the toe on the ground as the L leg straightens. The R foot returns to sur le cou-de-pied and the movement is repeated to the second position and to the fourth position back. In the latter case, the foot passes sur le cou-de-pied derrière. The knee is not raised and the leg is not lifted in battement fondu simple.

**Battement fouetté** [*bat-M$\overline{AHN}$ fweh-TAY*]. Whipped battement. From the second position en l'air, the working foot is swept across the floor so that the pointed toes strike the floor, finishing in a pointed position in front or back of the ankle of the supporting leg. *See* Flic-flac; Fouetté, petit; Fouetté à terre.

**Battement frappé** [*bat-M$\overline{AHN}$ fra-PAY*]. Struck battement. An exercise in which the dancer forcefully extends the working leg from a cou-de-pied position to the front, side or back. This exercise strengthens the toes and insteps and develops the power of elevation. It is the basis of the allégro step, the jeté.

**Battement frappé (Cecchetti method)** [*bat-M$\overline{AHN}$ fra-PAY*]. The working foot is placed sur le cou-de-pied devant with the knee bent, all five toes resting on the floor sur la demi-pointe, and the face of the heel touching the supporting leg just above the ankle joint. With a strong movement from the knee, the foot is thrust out to the second position, striking the ball of the foot on the floor and rising several inches off the floor in a strong point. The foot is then returned to the original position sur le cou-de-pied, sliding behind the supporting leg without striking the ground. The movement is repeated alternately devant and derrière with the strong accent in the second position. Battement frappé may also be executed to the fourth position devant or derrière. It is also performed with the supporting leg sur la demi-pointe.

**Battement frappé (French School)** [*bat-M$\overline{AHN}$ fra-PAY*]. From the second position pointe tendue, the working foot beats the supporting leg sur le cou-de-pied devant or derrière in the wrapped position.

**Battement frappé (Russian School)** [*bat-M$\overline{AHN}$ fra-PAY*]. The movement starts with the working foot pointed in the second position. The working foot beats the supporting leg sur le cou-de-pied devant in either the wrapped or pointed position. Then, with a strong movement from the knee, the foot is thrust out to the second position, with the toe pointed. The foot then returns sur le cou-de-pied derrière. The movement is repeated alternately with the strong accent in the second position. Battement frappé may also be executed en croix. It is also performed with the supporting leg sur la demi-pointe.

**Battement frappé double** [*bat-MAHN fra-PAY DOO-bluh*]. Double battement struck. This is similar to the battement frappé, except that the foot beats sur le cou-de-pied devant and then passes sur le cou-de-pied derrière before being extended in the first battement frappé. The next beating will be sur le cou-de-pied derrière and then sur le cou-de-pied devant before the extension in the second position. Battements frappés doubles are usually done immediately after a series of battements frappés.

**Battement frappé pointé** [*bat-MAHN fra-PAY pwen-TAY*]. Battement struck and pointed. The movement starts in the second position with the working foot pointe tendue. The working foot beats the supporting leg sur le cou-de-pied devant, then is extended to the second position pointe tendu à terre. The foot returns sur le cou-de-pied derrière and the movement is repeated alternately with the strong accent in the pointed position. Battements frappés pointés may also be executed en croix. They may also be done with a relevé on the supporting leg. In this case, the supporting heel is lowered into a demi-plié as the working foot points in the open position and is raised as the working foot beats sur le cou-de-pied. *See* Battement frappé.

**Battement frappé pointé double** [*bat-MAHN fra-PAY pwen-TAY DOO-bluh*]. Double battement struck and pointed. The working foot beats sur le cou-de-pied devant and derrière, or vice versa, before being extended in the open position pointe tendue à terre.

**Battement glissé** [*bat-MAHN glee-SAY*]. Battement glided or slipped. A term of the French School. Same as battement dégagé, battement tendu jeté.

**Battement jeté, grand** [*grahn bat-MAHN zhuh-TAY*]. Large battement thrown. A term of the Russian School for a grand battement.

**Battement jeté balancé, grand** [*grahn bat-MAHN zhuh-TAY ba-lahn-SAY*]. Large battement thrown and rocked. A term of the Russian School. Grands battements jetés balancés are a series of grands battements executed with a continuous swinging movement through the first position to the fourth position front and back (or vice versa) to an angle of 90 degrees or more. As the leg is thrown forcefully forward, the body leans backward; then, as the leg is thrown backward, the body leans forward.

**Battement jeté balançoire, grand** [*grahn bat-MAHN zhuh-TAY ba-lahn-SWAHR*]. Large battement thrown and like a seesaw. A term of the Russian School. Same as battement jeté balancé, grand.

**Battement jeté passé, grand** [*grahn bat-MAHN zhuh-TAY pa-SAY*]. Large battement thrown and passed. A term of the Russian School. The working leg is thrown forward at 90 degrees or higher with the body inclining slightly backward. The leg then bends with the thigh well turned out to the side. The pointed toe, with heel well forward, passes the supporting knee and the body comes erect. The leg then extends backward at 90 degrees or higher with the body inclining forward; the leg is then lowered and the body straightens before the movement is repeated. The movement may also be reversed. This battement may be combined with other grands battements jetés or combined with ronds de jambe par terre.

**Battement jeté piqué, grand** [*grahn bat-MAHN zhuh-TAY pee-KAY*]. Large battement thrown and pricked. A term of the Russian School. Same as grand battement fini piqué.

**Battement jeté pointé, grand** [*grahn bat-MAHN zhuh-TAY pwen-TAY*]. Large battement thrown and pointed. A term of the Russian School. Same as grand battement fini piqué.

**Battement piqué, petit** [*puh-TEE bat-MAHN pee-KAY*]. Little pricked battement. Dégagé the working foot to the second or fourth position à terre, then lift the toe slightly. Lower the foot, striking the pointed toes on the floor, then immediately raise the foot and close to the fifth position. *See* Battement tendu jeté pointé.

**Battement pointé à terre, grand** [*grahn bat-MAHN pwen-TAY a tehr*]. Large battement pointed on the ground. A term of the French School. Same as grand battement fini piqué.

**Battement raccourci** [*bat-MAHN ra-koor-SEE*]. Battement shortened. A term of the French School. Same as battement retiré.

**Battement raccourci or retiré, grand** [*grahn bat-MAHN ra-koor-SEE* (or) *ruh-tee-RAY*]. Large battement shortened or withdrawn. The working leg executes a grand battement, then is immediately withdrawn to the knee with a sharp movement and lowered to the first or fifth position. This battement may be executed devant, à la seconde or derrière.

**Battement relevé lent** [*bat-MAHN ruhl-VAY lahn*]. Battement raised slowly. A term of the Russian School. From the fifth position slide the foot to pointe tendue to either the fourth or second position and slowly raise the outstretched leg with strongly pointed toes to 45 or 90 degrees or higher. Slowly lower the leg to pointe tendue and close it to the fifth position. Battement relevé lent may be done in all directions.

**Battement retiré** [*bat-MAHN ruh-tee-RAY*]. Battement withdrawn or shortened. A term of the French School and the Cecchetti method. From the fifth position the working foot is lifted so that the toe is touching the hollow at the back of the knee of the supporting leg, and the thigh raised to the second position en l'air. With a staccato movement the foot is raised and lowered, alternating in the fifth position front and back, the accent being on the downward movement. This is a very useful exercise for warming up and is especially useful as a preparation for développés, helping to lift the thigh well up and to turn out.

**Battement serré** [*bat-MAHN seh-RAY*]. Battement tightened continuously. A term of the French School. Same as battement battu.

**Battement soutenu** [*bat-MAHN soot-NEW*]. Battement sustained. Fifth position R foot front. Fondu on the L leg, sliding the R foot (with straight knee) to the fourth position front, to the second position or to the fourth position back, pointe tendue. Straighten the L knee, closing the R foot in the fifth position. This exercise is usually executed en croix at the barre and may also be performed with a petit développé before the R foot points on the floor. The L leg then straightens and rises on the demi-pointe as the R leg is drawn to it and both legs join in the fifth position on the demi-pointes.

**Battement soutenu, grand** [*grahn bat-MAHN soot-NEW*]. Large battement sustained. From the fifth position the dancer does a grand battement forward, to the side or backward, simultaneously executing a demi-plié on the supporting leg. The supporting leg then straightens and the dancer rises on the demi-pointe as the working leg closes in the fifth position on demi-pointe. The movement is then repeated.

**Battement sur le cou-de-pied, petit** [*puh-TEE bat-MAHN sewr luh koo-duh-PYAY*]. Small battement on the ankle. This is an exercise at the bar in which the working foot is held sur le cou-de-pied and the lower part of the leg moves out and in, changing the foot from sur le cou-de-pied devant to sur le cou-de-pied derrière and vice versa. Petits battements are executed with the supporting foot à terre, sur la demi-pointe or sur la pointe.

**Battement sur le cou-de-pied, petit (Cecchetti method)** [*puh-TEE bat-MAHN sewr luh koo-duh-PYAY*]. The foot is held so that the side of the heel is just above the ankle bone of the supporting leg with all five toes on the floor as in the position sur la demi-pointe. In this position the foot is passed from sur le cou-de-pied devant to sur le cou-de-pied derrière with an action of the lower leg working from the knee as a stationary pivot. When the supporting foot is raised sur la demi-pointe, the toes of the working foot are forced downward. *See* Cou-de-pied, sur le (Cecchetti method).

**Battement sur le cou-de-pied, petit (Russian School)** [*puh-TEE bat-MAHN sewr luh koo-duh-PYAY*]. The working foot is wrapped around the ankle of the supporting leg with the heel well forward and the toes pressed down and back. *See* Cou-de-pied, sur le (Russian School).

**Battement sur le talon, petit** [*puh-TEE bat-MAHN sewr luh ta-LAWN*]. Small battement on the heel. Same as battement battu.

**Battement tendu** [*bat-MAHN tahn-DEW*]. Battement stretched. A battement tendu is the commencing portion and ending portion of a grand battement and is an exercise to force the insteps well outward. The working foot slides from the first or fifth position to the second or fourth position without lifting the toe from the ground. Both knees must be kept straight. When the foot reaches the position pointe tendue, it then returns to the first or fifth position. Battements tendus may also be done with a demi-plié in the first or fifth position. They should be practiced en croix.

**Battement tendu, double** [*DOO-bluh bat-MAHN tahn-DEW*]. Double battement stretched. A term of the Russian School. Same as battement tendu relevé.

**Battement tendu jeté** [*bat-M̄ĀHN* *t̄ahn-D̄EW* *zhuh-TAY*]. Battement stretched and thrown. A term of the Russian School. Same as battement dégagé.

**Battement tendu jeté balancé** [*bat-M̄ĀHN* *t̄ahn-D̄EW* *zhuh-TAY* *ba-l̄ahn-SAY*]. Battement stretched, thrown and rocked. A term of the Russian School. Battements tendus jetés balancés are a series of battements jetés in which the working leg sweeps forward and backward with a continuous movement through the first position at 25 degrees.

**Battement tendu jeté balançoire** [*bat-M̄ĀHN* *t̄ahn-D̄EW* *zhuh-TAY* *ba-l̄ahn-SWAHR*]. Battement stretched and thrown like a seesaw. Same as battement tendu jeté balancé.

**Battement tendu jeté en cloche** [*bat-M̄ĀHN* *t̄ahn-D̄EW* *zhuh-TAY* *āhn klawsh*]. Battement stretched and thrown like a bell. Same as battement tendu jeté balancé.

**Battement tendu jeté pointé** [*bat-M̄ĀHN* *t̄ahn-D̄EW* *zhuh-TAY* *pwēn-TAY*]. Battement stretched, thrown and pointed. A term of the Russian School. Dégagé the working foot to the second or fourth position à terre, then lift the toe slightly and lower to the floor one or more times. The foot is then closed to the fifth position. *See* Battement piqué, petit.

**Battement tendu pour batterie** [*bat-M̄ĀHN* *t̄ahn-D̄EW* *poor bat-REE*]. Battement stretched for beaten steps. This type of battement tendu is an exercise done at the bar in preparation for the study of beats. The dancer transfers the working leg in front and in back of the supporting leg to a height of 45 degrees to the second position. Fifth position R foot front. Open the R leg to the second position with strongly pointed toes and stretched instep; immediately lower the R leg to the fifth position front, striking the calves and allowing the foot to flex with the R heel well forward. The leg rebounds slightly to the side with flexed foot, then beats the left calf in the back before being thrown to the second position with pointed toes and stretched instep. The movement is then reversed. The accent of the movement is in the strong rebound of the leg to second position at 45 degrees. The number of transfers depends on the step for which this exercise serves as a preparation. For assemblé battu, one transfer is made; for entrechat, two or more are necessary.

**Battement tendu relevé** [*bat-M̄ĀHN* *t̄ahn-D̄EW* *ruhl-VAY*]. Battement stretched and raised. A term of the Cecchetti method. An exercise to develop the insteps. It is usually taken in the second position but may also be done to the fourth position. Fifth position R foot front. Dégagé the R foot to the second position, lower the R heel to the ground, re-arch the R foot to the pointe tendue position, close the R foot to the fifth position back. After the next dégagé the working foot will close in the front. Same as battement tendu, double (Russian School).

**Batterie** [*bat-REE*]. The French technical term for beaten steps. A collective term meaning the entire vocabulary of beats. Any movement in which the legs beat together or one leg beats against the other, the actual beating being done with the calves. Both legs must be equally well extended during a beat. Never beat with one leg while the other is in a passive state. Batterie is divided into grande batterie and petite batterie, according as the elevation is large or small.

**Batterie, grande** [*grahnd bat-REE*]. Large beating steps. Comprises all the beaten steps requiring elevation, cabriole, grand jeté dessus en tournant battu, entrechat de volée, and so on.

**Batterie, petite** [*puh-TEET bat-REE*]. Small beating steps. Comprises all the small beaten steps which do not require much elevation but must be performed with rapidity and brilliance of execution. Much of the work is done by the insteps and the beats should be clean and well crossed. All brisés, jetés battus, entrechats trois, quatre and cinq, changements, and so on, are examples of petite batterie.

**Battu** [*ba-TEW*]. Beaten. Any step embellished with a beat is called a pas battu. As, for example, in assemblé battu. *See* Pas battu.

**Beats.** The dancer executes a beat during a jump by striking the calves sharply together. There are three classifications of beats: pas battus, entrechats and brisés.

**Body alignment.** *See* Directions or body alignment.

**Bras** [*brah*]. Arms.

**Bras, à deux** [*a duh brah*]. With two arms. This is an extended position of the arms with the palms down. Both arms are extended forward with the back arm held higher than the front arm. *See* Arabesque à deux bras *and* Third arabesque *in the section* "The Cecchetti method" *under* Arabesque.

**Bras, demi-** [*duh-mee-BRAH*]. Half arms. A halfway position of the arms. The arms are extended forward at half the height and half the width of the second position, with the hands open and palms slightly forward as if asking for something.

**Bras, port de** [*pawr duh brah*]. *See* Port de bras.

**Bras, positions des** [*paw-zee-SYAWN day brah*]. Positions of the arms. Although the positions of the feet are standard in all methods, the positions of the arms are not, each method having its own set of arm positions. The Cecchetti method has five standard positions with a derivative of the fourth position and two derivatives of the fifth position. The French School has a preparatory position and five standard positions. These positions are used in some Russian schools. The Russian School (Vaganova) has a preparatory position and three standard positions of the arms.

CECCHETTI METHOD (see illustrations, pp. 130 & 131)

*First position:* The arms are curved and held at the sides with the fingertips just touching the thighs.

*Second position:* The arms are held out to the sides in a sweeping line so that the elbow is slightly lower than the shoulder and the wrist slightly lower than the elbow. The palms of the hands face the audience. There is also a demi-seconde position of the arms. This is a position in which the arms are held out to the sides in a position halfway between the first position and the second position. The palms of the hands are turned inward as in the first position. This position is used in steps of allégro, such as temps de cuisse, contretemps and glissade, in which the arms open from the fifth position en bas to the demi-seconde position and close again in the fifth position en bas.

*Third position:* The arms are held with one arm curved in front of the body as in the fifth position en bas and the other arm slightly rounded and opened to the side as in the demi-seconde position.

*Fourth position:* There are two fourth positions of the arms, the fourth position en avant and the fourth position en haut. *Fourth position en avant:* One arm is opened to the second position and the other is rounded and raised in front of the body opposite the lower ribs, forming half of the fifth position en avant. *Fourth position en haut:* One arm is opened to the second position while the other is raised above the head, forming half of the fifth position en haut.

When the arms are en arabesque, the forward arm is said to be extended in the fourth position front and the backward arm is said to be extended in the fourth position back.

*Fifth position:* Whenever the arms form a circle they are said to be in the fifth position. There are three fifth positions of the arms: (1) Fifth position en bas (or low), in which the rounded arms rest on the thighs. (2) Fifth position en avant (or forward), in which the rounded arms are raised in front of the body. (3) Fifth position en haut (or high), in which the rounded arms are raised above the head. *Fifth position en bas:* The arms form a circle, with the fingertips a few inches apart and the back edge of the hands touching the thighs. *Fifth position en avant:* The arms form a circle in front of the body opposite the lower ribs with the palms of the hands facing the body. *Fifth position en haut:* The arms form a circle above and in front of the head so that the fingertips are just within the line of vision.

The fifth position en avant is familiarly termed the gate or door, because in passing from a low position to a high one the arms generally pass through this position. In passing from a high position to a low one the arms are generally lowered in a line with the sides.

FRENCH SCHOOL (see illustration, p. 132)

*Preparatory position, or bras au repos:* The arms are slightly rounded and held at the sides with the fingertips just touching the thighs. Corresponds to Cecchetti first position.

*First position:* The arms form a circle in front of the body in line with the fork of the ribs. Corresponds to Cecchetti fifth position en avant.

*Second position:* The arms are held out to the sides as in the Cecchetti second position.

*Third position:* One arm is curved above the head while the other is held out to the side. Also termed "bras en attitude." Corresponds to the Cecchetti fourth position en haut.

*Fourth position:* One arm is curved above the head while the other is curved in front of the body in line with the fork of the ribs.

*Fifth position:* Both arms are curved above the head as in the Cecchetti fifth position en haut. This position is also termed "bras en couronne."

RUSSIAN SCHOOL (VAGANOVA) (see illustration, p. 133)

*Preparatory position:* Arms curved and held low in front of the body. Corresponds to the Cecchetti fifth position en bas.

*First position:* Arms form a circle in front of the body on a level with the stomach. Corresponds to the Cecchetti fifth position en avant.

*Second position:* Arms drawn to the sides, elbows slightly rounded, with the lower part of the arm from the elbow to the wrist on a level with the elbow.

*Third position:* Arms circled above the head. Corresponds to the Cecchetti fifth position en haut.

**Bras au repos** [*brah zoh ruh-POH*]. Arms at ease. A preparatory position of the arms used in the French School. The arms are slightly rounded and held at the sides with the fingertips just touching the thighs. Corresponds to the first position, Cecchetti method.

**Bras bas** [*brah bah*]. Arms low or down. This is the dancer's "attention." The arms form a circle with the palms facing each other and the back edge of the hands resting on the thighs. The arms should hang quite loosely but not allowing the elbows to touch the sides. This position corresponds to the fifth position en bas, Cecchetti method.

**Bras croisé** [*brah krwah-ZAY*]. This position of the arms corresponds to the fourth position en avant, Cecchetti method. One arm is brought up to the gateway, while the other is taken out to the side. The head is turned so that the dancer looks over the shoulder of the croisé arm.

**Bras en attitude** [*brah zah na-tee-TEWD*]. Arms held as in attitude. *See* Bras, positions des (French School).

**Bras en couronne** [*brah zahn koo-RAWN*]. Arms in the shape of a crown. A position in which the arms are rounded above the head. A term of the French School. Corresponds to the fifth position en haut, Cecchetti method.

**Bras en lyre** [*brah zahn leer*]. Arms in the shape of a lyre. A term of the French School. In this modification of the fifth arm position, one hand is held above the other so that the arms resemble the shape of a lyre.

**Brisé** [*bree-ZAY*]. Broken, breaking. A small beating step in which the movement is broken. Brisés are commenced on one or two feet and end on one or two feet. They are done dessus, dessous, en avant and en arrière. Fundamentally a brisé is an assemblé beaten and traveled. The working leg brushes from the fifth position to the second position so that the point of the foot is a few inches off the ground, and beats in front of or behind the other leg, which has come to meet it; then both feet return to the ground simultaneously in demi-plié in the fifth position.

**Brisé dessous** [*bree-ZAY duh-SOO*]. Brisé under. Fifth position R foot front. Demi-plié and slide the R foot with a sweeping movement a little farther back than the second position so that the point is a few inches off the ground. Spring upward and sideways off the L foot, throwing it toward the R and beating the calves together with the R leg in back. The landing is made in demi-plié in the fifth position R foot in front. Brisé dessous can best be described as an assemblé devant traveled to the side and beaten.

**Brisé dessus** [*bree-ZAY duh-SEW*]. Brisé over. Fifth position R foot back. Demi-plié and slide the R foot with a sweeping movement a little farther forward than the second position so that the point is a few inches off the ground. Spring upward and sideways off the L foot, throwing it toward the R and beating the calves together with the R leg in the front. The landing is made in demi-plié in the fifth position R foot back. Brisé dessus can best be described as an assemblé derrière traveled to the side and beaten.

**Brisé dessus-dessous** [*bree-ZAY duh-SEW-duh-SOO*]. Brisé over-under. In the Russian and French Schools, brisé dessus is a brisé forward that finishes on one leg; brisé dessous is a brisé backward that finishes on one leg. Same as brisé volé en avant and brisé volé en arrière.

**Brisé en arrière** [*bree-ZAY ah na-RYEHR*]. Brisé backward. This brisé is commenced with the back foot, which beats in the back and closes in the front. Brisé en arrière can best be described as an assemblé dessus traveled backward and beaten.

**Brisé en avant** [*bree-ZAY ah na-VAHN*]. Brisé forward. This brisé is commenced with the front foot, which beats in the front and closes in the back. Brisé en avant can best be described as an assemblé dessous traveled forward and beaten.

**Brisé en tournant** [*bree-ZAY ahn toor-NAHN*]. Brisé, turning. This is a series of four brisés done with a quarter-turn on each brisé. If the turn is made turning to the side of the front foot, the turn is en dedans; if the turn is made turning to the side of the rear foot, the turn is en dehors.

*En dedans:* Fifth position croisé R foot back. Execute four brisés dessus with the R foot, making a quarter-turn on each brisé and turning to the left (en dedans).

*En dehors:* Fifth position croisé R foot front. Execute four brisés dessous with the R foot, making a quarter-turn on each brisé and turning to the right (en dehors).

**Brisé télémaque** [*bree-ZAY tay-lay-MAK*]. This is an enchaînement of petite batterie of the French School composed by a dancer named Télémaque. It was originally done in 3/4 (mazurka) time, but another variation exists in 4/4 time. Many versions of brisé télémaque exist today.

**Brisé télémaque in 3/4 (mazurka) time** [*bree-ZAY tay-lay-MAK*]. Traveling diagonally to the right (toward corner 1; see illustration, p. 138), brisé dessus R, changement battu (royale), entrechat trois derrière R; traveling straight back, brisé en arrière R, changement battu (royale), entrechat trois derrière L. The enchaînement is then repeated to the other side.

**Brisé télémaque in 4/4 time** [*bree-ZAY tay-lay-MAK*]. Traveling diagonally forward toward corner 1, brisé dessus R, two changements battus (royale), entrechat cinq derrière R; traveling straight back, brisé en arrière R, two changements battus (royale), entrechat cinq derrière L. The enchaînement is then repeated to the other side.

**Brisé volé** [*bree-ZAY vaw-LAY*]. Flying brisé. In this brisé the dancer finishes on one foot after the beat, the other leg crossed either front or back. The foundation of this step is a fouetté movement with a jeté battu. In the Russian and French Schools the raised leg finishes sur le cou-de-pied devant or derrière and the brisé volé is done like a jeté battu. In the Cecchetti method, the working foot passes through the first position to the fourth position, the calves are beaten together and on alighting the free leg is extended forward or back with a straight knee.

**Brisé volé en arrière** [*bree-ZAY vaw-LAY ah na-RYEHR*]. Brisé flying backward. A term of the Cecchetti method. After executing brisé volé en avant, sweep the L foot backward through the first position to the fourth position back (effacé) so that the pointed toe is raised a few inches off the floor. Spring upward and slightly backward, beating the calves together, R leg front. Land on the L foot in demi-plié with the R leg extended to the fourth position (croisé) back, the R toe pointed about a foot off the floor.

**Brisé volé en avant** [*bree-ZAY vaw-LAY ah na-VAHN*]. Brisé flying forward. A term of the Cecchetti method. Fifth position croisé, R foot back. Demi-plié and slide the R foot to the fourth position (effacé) front so that the pointed toe is raised a few inches off the floor. Spring upward and slightly forward, beating the calves together, R leg front. Land on the R foot in demi-plié with the L leg extended to the fourth position (croisé) front, the pointed L toe about a foot off the floor.

**Cabriole** [*ka-bree-AWL*]. Caper. An allegro step in which the extended legs are beaten in the air. Cabrioles are divided into two categories: petite, which are executed at 45 degrees, and grande, which are executed at 90 degrees. The working leg is thrust into the air, the underneath leg follows and beats against the first leg, sending it higher. The landing is then made on the underneath leg. Cabriole may be done devant, derrière and à la seconde in any given position of the body such as croisé, effacé, écarté, etc.

**Cabriole, double** [*DOO-bluh ka-bree-AWL*]. Double cabriole. This is a cabriole in which one leg strikes the other in the air two or more times before landing.

**Cabriole, grande** [*grahnd ka-bree-AWL*]. Big cabriole. A step of elevation with the leg thrust high into the air at 90 degrees.

**Cabriole, petite** [*puh-TEET ka-bree-AWL*]. Little cabriole. A small cabriole executed at 45 degrees with little elevation.

**Cabriole à la seconde** [*ka-bree-AWL ah la suh-GAWND*]. Cabriole to the second position. Cabriole à la seconde follows the same principle as for devant and derrière. The leg which opens to the side may be either the backward or forward one according to the preceding step.

**Cabriole derrière** [*ka-bree-AWL deh-RYEHR*]. Cabriole behind. This cabriole is done in either croisé or effacé, and follows the same technique as cabriole devant, but the back leg opens to the desired position and is therefore on top and is beaten from below by the supporting leg. The position of the body is en arabesque.

**Cabriole devant** [*ka-bree-AWL duh-VAHN*]. Cabriole in front. This cabriole may be done facing either croisé or effacé. The most widely used cabriole is the cabriole devant in effacé. Fifth position R foot front. Demi-plié and open the R leg forward in effacé. Leap upward off the L foot. While the body is in the air the L leg is drawn to the R and beats it with the calf, sending the R leg higher. The legs must be fully extended with the knees taut and the toes well pointed. The landing is made on the L foot in demi-plié. If the cabriole is ouverte the R leg remains in the air in effacé, but if the cabriole is fermée the R leg closes in demi-plié in the fifth position front. The leg may be raised à la hauteur or à la demi-hauteur according as the cabriole is grande or petite.

**Cabriole fermée** [*ka-bree-AWL fehr-MAY*]. Closed cabriole. In the cabriole fermée the working leg is closed to the fifth position.

**Cabriole fouettée, grande** [*grahnd ka-bree-AWL fweh-TAY*]. Big cabriole whipped. This is a cabriole devant in effacé finishing en arabesque.

**Cabriole italienne** [*ka-bree-AWL ee-ta-LYEN*]. Italian cabriole. This is a variation of the cabriole fouettée in which the beat occurs after the body has turned into the arabesque position.

**Cabriole ouverte** [*ka-bree-AWL oo-VEHRT*]. Open cabriole. If the cabriole is ouverte, the working leg is held in the air in the desired pose, such as arabesque, effacé devant, croisé devant and so on.

**Cadre** [*KA-druh*]. Framework or division. A term of the French School. Refers to the divisions in the Paris Opéra ballet. *See* Défilé.

**Cambré** [*kahn-BRAY*]. Arched. The body is bent from the waist, backward or sideways, the head following the movement of the body.

**Cambré renversé** [*kahn-BRAY rahn-vehr-SAY*]. Renversé arched or tilted. A term of the French School. Same as pas de bourrée renversé.

**Carré, en** [*ahn ka-RAY*]. *See* Quarré, en.

**Cavalier.** The male partner of the ballerina.

**Cecchetti, Enrico** [*en-REE-koh cheh-KET-tee*]. This Italian dancer and ballet master (1850–1928) was born in Rome, son of Cesare Cecchetti and Serafina Casagli. He studied with Giovanni Lepri, who was a pupil of the great Carlo Blasis, and made his debut at La Scala, Milan, in

1870. He toured Europe as a premier danseur and made his debut at the Maryinski Theatre, St. Petersburg, in 1887. He accepted the position of second ballet master at the Maryinski Theatre in 1890 and two years later became instructor at the Imperial School. His pupils included Pavlova, Nijinsky, Karsavina, Fokine, Preobrajenska, Kchessinska and Egorova. In 1902 he left for Warsaw, where he became director of the Imperial School, and in 1905 returned to Italy. Returning to Russia, he opened a private school and later became the private tutor of Anna Pavlova, touring the world with her. From 1909 to 1918 he was the official instructor to the Diaghilev Ballet Company. From 1918 until 1923 he had a private school in London. He then returned to Italy and became ballet master at La Scala in 1925. He devoted the rest of his life to teaching and perfecting his teaching methods.

**Cecchetti method.** Enrico Cecchetti, one of the world's outstanding teachers of ballet, established a system of passing on the tradition of ballet to future generations of dancers. This system, the Cecchetti method, was codified and recorded by Cyril Beaumont, Stanislas Idzikowski, Margaret Craske and Derra de Moroda. The method has a definite program of strict routine and includes a table of principal set daily exercises for each day of the week. The Cecchetti Society was formed in London in 1922 to perpetuate his method of teaching. In 1924 the Society was incorporated into the Imperial Society of Teachers of Dancing. Entrance to the Society is by examination and students must pass through a carefully graded system which has done much to raise the standard of dancing and teaching throughout the British Empire.

**Centre practice.** Centre practice, or exercices au milieu, is the name given to a group of exercises similar to those à la barre but performed in the centre of the room without the support of the bar. These exercises are usually performed with alternate feet and are invaluable for obtaining good balance and control.

**Chaînés** [*sheh-NAY*]. Chains, links. This is an abbreviation of the term "tours chaînés déboulés": a series of rapid turns on the points or demi-pointes done in a straight line or in a circle. *See* Déboulés; Tour, petit.

**Chaînés papillon** [*sheh-NAY pa-pee-YAWN*]. Chaînés like a butterfly. This is a series of chaînés with the arms held out to the side in the second position. As the R foot steps forward, the R arm is lowered and the L raised; then, as the second half of the turn is done on the L foot, the L arm is lowered and the R raised.

**Changé, changée** [*shahn-ZHAY*]. Changed. If the term changé is added to the name of a step, the feet have changed places during the step and the foot originally in front will have finished in the back or vice versa. *See* Changer, sans.

**Changement battu** [*shahnzh-MAHN ba-TEW*]. Changement beaten. Same as royale.

**Changement de pieds** [*shahnzh-MAHN duh pyay*]. Change of feet. The term is usually abbreviated to changement. Changements are springing steps in the fifth position, the dancer changing feet in the air and alighting in the fifth position with the opposite foot in the front. They are done petit and grand.

**Changement de pieds, grand** [*grahn shahnzh-MAHN duh pyay*]. Large change of feet. This changement requires a deeper demi-plié and a much stronger push from the floor in order to rise higher. The dancer should aim at remaining the shortest length of time on the ground and as long as possible in the air. In the Cecchetti method and the French School the knees are bent in the air and the feet drawn up so that the flat of the toes of both feet meet.

**Changement de pieds, petit** [*puh-TEE shahnzh-MAHN duh pyay*]. Little change of feet. Fifth position R foot front. Demi-plié and push from the floor, extending the toes and arching the feet in the air. On coming down, change the feet so that the L foot will be in the front. Land in the fifth position, first toes, then heels, and finish in demi-plié in the fifth position. For more advanced students there is another variation of petit changement. It is similar to the above but the feet do not leave the floor; the toes are touching the floor all the time as if the dancer were only rising on the toes. The movement is done very rapidly in a series without any pause or plié. This is an excellent exercise for the ankles and insteps and gives brilliancy and rapidity to the petite batterie.

**Changement de pieds en tournant** [*shahnzh-MAHN duh pyay ahn toor-NAHN*]. Change of feet, turning. This step is done petit and grand with a quarter-turn on each changement. The turn is done at the moment of the jump and is always begun in the direction of the front foot. If the R foot is in front, the turn is to the right; if the L foot is in front, the turn is to the left. Grand changement en tournant may also be done with half-turns and full turns.

**Changement de pieds sur les pointes** [*shahnzh-MAHN duh pyay sewr lay pwent*]. Change of feet on the points. Changements are done on the points with a moderate jump, contracting the insteps slightly and with the muscles of the foot held taut. The jump is small but must be high enough to allow the knees, insteps and toes to be quickly stretched in the air. The step may be done in a series, in place, traveling in a diagonal or turning in place.

**Changer, sans** [*sahn shahn-ZHAY*]. Without change. Indicates that a step or series of steps is to be done with the feet remaining in the same relative position. As, for example, in échappés à la seconde sans changer. If the feet are in the fifth position R foot front, the R foot will close in the front on each échappé.

**Changer de pied** [*shahn-ZHAY duh pyay*]. To change feet. Indicates that the feet at the end of a step will have reversed their position.

**Character dancing.** *See* Danse de caractère.

**Chassé** [*sha-SAY*]. Chased. A step in which one foot literally chases the other foot out of its position; done in a series. See following two entries.

**Chassé (Cecchetti method)** [*sha-SAY*]. In the Cecchetti method a chassé is a glide into an open position and is finished in demi-plié. This movement can be executed in all the directions, making seven chassés: (1) Fourth effacé en avant. (2) Fourth croisé en avant. (3) Seconde. (4) Fourth effacé en arrière. (5) Fourth croisé en arrière. (6) Passé en avant. (7) Passé en arrière. Fifth position R foot front. Demi-plié on both feet and, keeping the weight equally distributed, slide the R foot, keeping the knee bent, to the second or fourth position. Straighten the knees with the L foot pointe tendue. The step may be finished by holding the open position or closing the extended foot to the fifth position. In the execution of a chassé passé, the heel of the working foot must be fully raised until the foot is arched. A chassé passé en avant is a forward movement starting with the back foot and finishing in the fourth position front, while a chassé passé en arrière starts with the front foot and travels back into the fourth position.

**Chassé (French and Russian Schools)** [*sha-SAY*]. This may be performed en avant, en arrière and de côté, in the directions croisé, effacé and ecarté.

**Chassé en avant (French and Russian Schools)** [*sha-SAY ah na-VAHN*]. Fifth position R foot front. Demi-plié, spring into the air and alight in fondu with the R foot sur le cou-de-pied devant. Slide the R foot to the fourth position with the weight on the R foot. Draw the L foot to the R, springing into the air with the feet in the fifth position, toes extended. The L foot then lands in fondu, the R foot immediately slides out again and the movement is continued. For chassé en arrière, reverse the movement. Chassé de côté is done in the same manner, cutting under (behind) each time. Called "temps levé chassé" in the Cecchetti method.

**Chassé en tournant** [*sha-SAY ahn toor-NAHN*]. Chassé, turning. Execute a tour en l'air, land on the back foot and chassé en avant.

**Cheville** [*shuh-VEE-yuh*]. The ankle joint.

**Choreographer, choregrapher.** This is the term applied to one who composes or invents ballets or dances.

**Choreography, choregraphy.** This is a term used to describe the actual steps, groupings and patterns of a ballet or dance composition.

**Cinq** [*senk*]. Five. As, for example, in entrechat cinq.

**Cinquième** [*sen-KYEM*]. Fifth. As in cinquième arabesque.

**Ciseaux** [*see-ZOH*]. Scissors. This is a scissor-like movement made by opening the feet to a wide second position sur les pointes, or by jumping into the air and opening both legs to the second position en l'air. *See* Écarté en l'air.

**Class.** The daily lesson taken by dancers throughout their career. *See* Leçon.

**Classical ballet.** (1) The traditional style of ballet, which stresses the academic technique developed through the centuries of the existence of ballet. (2) A ballet in which the style and structure adhere to the definite framework established in the nineteenth century. Examples of classical ballets are *Coppélia, The Sleeping Beauty, The Nutcracker* and *Swan Lake.*

**Classical walk.** This is a slow, dignified walk done by the ballerina and danseur noble at their entrance and during the adage of a grand pas de deux. As the pointed toe stretches forward it reaches the ground first, then the heel is lowered so that the foot is slightly turned out in the fourth position. The moment the heel touches the ground, the weight is transferred forward, then the back knee bends and with a small développé the back foot steps forward to repeat the step. *See* Pas marché.

**Cloche, en** [*ahn klawsh*]. Like a bell. Refers to grands battements executed continuously devant and derrière through the first position. *See* Battement en cloche, grand.

**Coda.** (1) The finale of a classical ballet in which all the principal dancers appear separately or with their partners. (2) The final dance of the classic pas de deux, pas de trois or pas de quatre.

**Collé** [*kaw-LAY*]. Adhering, glued. Both legs are kept tightly together in mid-air in a jump. *See* Temps de poisson.

**Composé, composée** [*kawn-poh-ZAY*]. Composite or compound. As, for example, in ballonné composé.

**Compound step.** A step made up of two or more steps or portions of steps under one name. Examples are ballonné composé (made up of ballonné simple, chassé movement and fermé); sissonne doublée (made up of sissonne ouverte, coupé and assemblé).

**Conditional position.** A term of the Russian School. It refers to a position sur le cou-de-pied in which the foot is pointed on the ankle. *See* Cou-de-pied, sur le (Russian School).

**Contretemps** [*kawn-truh-TAHN*]. Beating against time. A term of the Cecchetti method and the French School. This is a compound step consisting of a coupé dessous, chassé effacé en avant, fermé, temps levé and chassé passé croisé en avant. It is executed quickly and prior to the beat of the music. It is a very useful step for traveling to the side. Fourth position L foot back and pointe tendue. Raise the L foot slightly off the ground, spring off the R foot and jump forward on the L foot—bending the knee—so that the L foot falls in a short fourth position front. Bring the R foot sur le cou-de-pied devant and immediately slide it—bending the knee—to the second or fourth position, transferring the weight to it. Close the L foot to the fifth position back, keeping the knees bent. Finish with a demi-contretemps.

**Contretemps, demi-** [*duh-MEE-kawn-truh-TAHN*]. Half-beating against time. A term of the Cecchetti method and the French School. Demi-contretemps is the second half of the full contretemps and is used mostly as a preparatory step. It is composed of a temps levé and a chassé passé croisé en avant. Fifth position R foot front. Spring upward off the R foot and bring the L foot sur le cou-de-pied derrière. Come to the ground on the R foot in demi-plié and slide the L foot forward with a chassé passé croisé en avant. Demi-contretemps may also be executed from the fourth position, L foot back, pointe tendue.

**Corps** [*kawr*]. Body.

**Corps de ballet** [*kawr duh ba-LAY*]. The dancers in a ballet who do not appear as soloists.

**Corps de face** [*kawr duh fahss*]. Body facing front.

**Corps penché de côté** [*kawr p͞ahn-SHAY duh koh-TAY*]. Body bending to the side.

**Corps penché en arrière** [*kawr p͞ahn-SHAY ah na-RYEHR*]. Body bending backward. *See* Cambré.

**Corps penché en avant** [*kawr p͞ahn-SHAY ah na-V͞AHN*]. Body bending forward.

**Coryphée** [*kaw-ree-FAY*]. Leader. A leading member of the corps de ballet. One of the grades in the cadre of the Paris Opéra.

**Côté, de** [*duh koh-TAY*]. Sideways. Used to indicate that a step is to be made to the side, either to the right or to the left. See floor plan, p. 125.

**Côté cour** [*koh-TAY koor*]. "Court side," a stage direction. In French theaters this is the dancer's left-hand side of the stage or the public's right.

**Côté jardin** [*koh-TAY zhar-D͞EN*]. "Garden side," a stage direction. In French theaters this is the dancer's right-hand side of the stage or the public's left.

**Cou-de-pied** [*koo-duh-PYAY*]. "Neck" of the foot. The part of the foot between the ankle and the base of the calf is termed the cou-de-pied.

**Cou-de-pied, sur le** [*sewr luh koo-duh-PYAY*]. On the cou-de-pied. The working foot is placed on the part of the leg between the base of the calf and the beginning of the ankle.

**Cou-de-pied, sur le (Cecchetti method)** [*sewr luh koo-duh-PYAY*]. In the Cecchetti method, sur le cou-de-pied devant is the position of the working foot placed with the outside face of the heel in front of the supporting foot just above the ankle bone with all five toes resting on the floor sur la demi-pointe. Sur le cou-de-pied derrière is the same position with the inside face of the heel placed behind the supporting foot just above the ankle joint.

**Cou-de-pied, sur le (Russian School)** [*sewr luh koo-duh-PYAY*]. In the Russian School there are two positions sur le cou-de-pied devant: the wrapped or basic position and the pointed or conditional position. There is one basic position sur le cou-de-pied derrière. The foot is completely stretched in all positions.

1. Sur le cou-de-pied devant in the wrapped or basic position is the

position of one foot placed between the ankle and base of the supporting leg just under the calf muscle. The sole, with instep stretched and toes pointed, encircles the ankle so that the pointed toes are behind the heel of the supporting foot. This position is used for petits battements sur le cou-de-pied and battements frappés.

2. In sur le cou-de-pied devant in the pointed or conditional position, the pointed foot is placed so that the side of the small toe touches the supporting leg above the ankle joint. This position is used for battements fondus, battements soutenus, sissonne simple, développés, etc. There is also a high conditional position in which the pointed toe is placed halfway up the shin bone (this is used for pirouettes) and a low conditional position with the small toe of the working foot touching the edge of the slipper of the supporting foot. The low conditional position is always done on point or demi-pointe and is used for battements battus.

3. In the basic position sur le cou-de-pied derrière, the inside face of the heel is pressed against the supporting leg just below the base of the calf muscle with the foot completely stretched and the toes pointing downward.

**Coupé** [*koo-PAY*]. Cut, cutting. A small intermediary step done as a preparation or impetus for some other step. It takes its name from the fact that one foot cuts the other away and takes its place. Coupé may also be done in a series from one foot to the other. It may be performed sauté or as a terre à terre step, croisé or effacé.

**Coupé ballonné** [*koo-PAY ba-law-NAY*]. *See* Ballonné, coupé.

**Coupé brisé** [*koo-PAY bree-ZAY*]. Also termed coupé jeté. A compound step consisting of coupé dessous and jeté battu dessus. After the coupé dessous the working leg is taken around to the back for the jeté battu dessus. The beat should be done with both legs behind, not under the body.

**Coupé-chassé-coupé-jeté en tournant** [*koo-PAY-sha-SAY-koo-PAY-zhuh-TAY ahn toor-NAHN*]. A compound step consisting of a coupé dessous with about three-quarters of a turn en dehors, chassé en avant completing the turn, coupé dessous making a half-turn, and a grand jeté en avant completing the turn. This step is usually executed in a series en manège. *See* Coupé-chassé en tournant; Coupé jeté en tournant; Tour de reins.

**Coupé-chassé en tournant** [*koo-PAY-sha-SAY ahn toor-NAHN*]. A compound step consisting of a coupé dessous with a half-turn and a chassé en avant with a half-turn. A favorite finishing step from the Cecchetti method. This step should be done at a fast speed and with the body leaning at an angle.

**Coupé dessous** [*koo-PAY duh-SOO*]. Coupé under. A coupé is said to be dessous or under when one foot cuts under the heel of the supporting foot. Fourth position R foot back, pointe tendue. Demi-plié on the L foot, then with a spring draw the R foot toward the L foot and finish in fondu on the R foot in the place vacated by the L foot and with the L foot extended à la quatrième devant à terre or demi-hauteur, depending on the movement to follow. Coupé dessous may also be done beginning with the R foot sur le cou-de-pied derrière. Demi-plié on the L foot; spring into the air, extending the toes, and land on the R foot with the L foot sur le cou-de-pied devant. If the coupé is taken as a terre à terre step the dancer draws the R foot behind the L foot into the fifth position on the demi-pointes. Fondu on the R leg, raising the L foot sharply in front of the R ankle.

**Coupé dessous en tournant** [*koo-PAY duh-SOO ahn toor-NAHN*]. Coupé under, turning. Fourth position L foot back, pointe tendue à terre. Execute a demi-rond de jambe en dedans with the L foot, à la demi-hauteur. Spring onto the L foot, making a complete turn to the right. Land in demi-plié on the L foot with the R foot sur le cou-de-pied devant.

**Coupé dessus** [*koo-PAY duh-SEW*]. Coupé over. A coupé is said to be dessus or over when one foot cuts over the toe of the supporting foot. This is the reverse of the coupé dessous.

**Coupé-fouetté raccourci** [*koo-PAY-fweh-TAY ra-koor-SEE*]. This compound step consists of a coupé dessous, the foot that is cut away being whipped out to seconde en l'air, then whipped to the back of the supporting leg with a petit fouetté followed by a temps levé. The step can be done in two ways: low, with the toe brushing the ground and a small temps levé; or high, with the extension at hip level and a well-lifted temps levé.

**Coupé jeté** [*koo-PAY zhuh-TAY*]. *See* Coupé brisé.

**Coupé jeté en tournant** [*koo-PAY zhuh-TAY ahn toor-NAHN*]. A compound step consisting of a coupé dessous making a three-quarter turn and a grand jeté en avant to complete the turn. The step is usually done in a series either en manège or en diagonale. *See* Tour de reins.

**Couronne, en** [*ahn koo-RAWN*]. In the shape of a crown. A term of the French School for a position of the arms rounded above the head. As, for example, in the fifth position of the arms.

**Couru** [*koo-REW*]. Running. As, for example, in pas de bourrée couru.

**Croisé, croisée** [*krwah-ZAY*]. Crossed. One of the directions of épaulement. The crossing of the legs with the body placed at an oblique angle to the audience. The disengaged leg may be crossed in the front or in the back.

**Croisé derrière (Cecchetti method)** [*krwah-ZAY deh-RYEHR*]. Crossed in back. Croisé derrière is one of the eight directions of the body, Cecchetti method. In this position the dancer stands at an oblique angle to the audience, facing either one of the two front corners of the room. The leg farther from the audience is pointed in the fourth position back à terre or raised to the fourth position en l'air. The arms are placed en attitude, with the arm that is low being on the same side as the leg that is extended. The body and head incline toward the low arm, so that the dancer seems to be looking out toward the audience under the high arm. See illustration, p. 135.

**Croisé derrière (Russian School)** [*krwah-ZAY deh-RYEHR*]. In the Russian School, croisé derrière is done with the same leg position as in the Cecchetti method. The torso is held erect and the arms are reversed so that the high arm is on the same side as the extended leg. The head is turned and inclined toward the low arm. See illustration, p. 136.

**Croisé devant** [*krwah-ZAY duh-VAHN*]. Crossed in front. Croisé devant is one of the eight directions of the body, Cecchetti method. In this position the dancer stands at an oblique angle to the audience, facing either one of the two front corners of the room. The leg nearer the audience is pointed in the fourth position front à terre or raised to the fourth position en l'air. The arms are placed en attitude, with the arm that is low being on the same side as the leg that is extended. The body and head are slightly inclined toward the low arm. See illustration, p. 134.

**Croisé en arrière** [*krwah-ZAY ah na-RYEHR*]. Crossed backward. A direction for the execution of a step. Used to indicate that a step beginning with the R foot is executed in a diagonal direction toward the left back corner of the stage or room. Similarly a step beginning with the L foot will be executed toward the right back corner of the room. See floor plan, p. 125.

**Croisé en avant** [*krwah-ZAY ah na-VAHN*]. Crossed forward. A direction for the execution of a step. Used to indicate that a step beginning with the R foot is executed in a diagonal direction toward the left front corner of the stage or room. Similarly a step beginning with the L foot will be executed toward the right front corner of the room. See floor plan, p. 125.

**Croix, en** [*ahn krwah*]. In the shape of a cross. Indicates that an exercise is to be executed to the fourth position front, to the second position and to the fourth position back, or vice versa. As, for example, in battements tendus en croix (*see* Battement tendu).

**Csárdás** [*CHAHR-dahsh*]. The national dance of Hungary. It consists of two movements, *lassú* (slow) and *friska* (fast). It was first introduced in ballet as a character dance in the first act of Saint-Léon's *Coppélia* in 1870.

**Cuisse** [*kweess*]. Thigh.

**Danse** [*dahnss*]. Dance.

**Danse de caractère** [*dahnss duh ka-rak-TEHR*]. Dance of character, character dance. Any national or folk dance, or a dance based on movements associated with a particular profession, trade, personality or mode of living.

**Danse d'école** [*dahnss day-KAWL*]. Dance of the school. The classical style. *See* Ballet d'école.

**Danseur** [$\overline{dahn}$-S*UHR*]. Male dancer.

**Danseur, premier** [*pruh-MYAY* $\overline{dahn}$-S*UHR*]. First dancer. A leading male dancer of a company.

**Danseur étoile, premier** [*pruh-MYAY dahn-S*UHR* ay-TWAHL*]. First star dancer. The highest rank in the cadre of the Paris Opéra for a male dancer.

**Danseur noble** [$\overline{dahn}$-S*UHR* NAW-*bluh*]. Noble dancer. A premier danseur excelling in the classical style.

**Danseuse** [$\overline{dahn}$-S*UHZ*]. Female dancer.

**Danseuse, première** [*pruh-MYEHR* $\overline{dahn}$-S*UHZ*]. First dancer. A leading female dancer in a company. The French term for a ballerina next in rank below première danseuse étoile.

**Danseuse étoile, première** [*pruh-MYEHR dahn-S*UHZ* ay-TWAHL*]. First star dancer. The highest rank in the cadre of the Paris Opéra for a female dancer.

**Danseuse travestie** [$\overline{dahn}$-S*UHZ* tra-ves-TEE*]. Disguised dancer. A female dancer dressed as a male and taking a male part. Except in Russia, this was a common practice from the 1840s until the beginning of the twentieth century. The custom in Western Europe was killed by the virile dancing of Nijinsky and other male dancers of the Diaghilev company.

**Déboîté** [*day-bwah-TAY*]. Disjointed. A term applied to an emboîté sur les pointes executed en arrière. Déboîtés travel backward, the front foot swishing out and closing at the back. *See* Emboîté en reculant.

**Déboulés** [*day-boo-LAY*]. Rollings like a ball. A term of the French School for a series of demi-tours executed alternately on each foot, moving forward in a single direction. When turning to the right the first half-turn will be on the R foot; then the L foot steps forward and completes the turn. The feet are held very close together in the first position and the turns are done as quickly as possible. Déboulés are done on the points or demi-pointes. *See also* Chaînés; Tour, petit.

**Décor** [*day-KAWR*]. Decoration. The scenery and properties used in a ballet.

**De côté** [*duh koh-TAY*]. *See* Côté, de.

**Dedans, en** [$\overline{ahn}$ duh-D*AHN*]. Inward. In steps and exercises the term en dedans indicates that the leg, in a position à terre or en l'air, moves in a circular direction, counterclockwise from back to front. As, for example, in rond de jambe à terre en dedans. In pirouettes the term indicates that a pirouette is made inward toward the supporting leg.

**Défilé** [*day-fee-LAY*]. This is a term used at the Paris Opéra for the appearance of the entire ballet company on the stage. On rare occasions the partition dividing the famous "Foyer de la Danse" from the back of the stage is removed for the défilé of dancers. The entire company, from the élèves to the étoiles, appears on the stage. The défilé of dancers is as follows: (1) Élèves (apprentice dancers; also known as "les petits rats"). (2) Premiers quadrilles, seconds quadrilles (corps de ballet). (3) Coryphées (leaders of the corps de ballet). (4) Grands sujets, petits sujets (soloists). (5) Premières danseuses (ballerinas). (6) Premières danseuses étoiles (prima ballerinas). Each "cadre" (framework or division) has its corresponding number of male dancers also.

**Dégagé, or pas dégagé** [*day-ga-ZHAY* (or) *pah day-ga-ZHAY*]. Disengaged or disengaging step. A dégagé is the pointing of the foot in an open position with a fully arched instep. It is not a transfer of weight. Dégagé is performed devant, à la seconde and derrière in all the directions of the body. *See* Piqué à terre; Pointe tendue.

**Dégagé à la quatrième devant en l'air (croisée) en tournant en dehors** [*day-ga-ZHAY a lah ka-tree-EM duh-VAHN ahn lehr (krwah-ZAY) ahn toor-NAHN ahn duh-AWR*]. Dégagé to the fourth position front in the air (crossed), turning outward. A term of the Cecchetti method. From the position croisé derrière en l'air, the dancer turns slowly en dehors on the flat of the foot, rotating the raised leg in the hip socket to the second position en l'air, then turns the body from the waist to finish in the position croisé devant en l'air. *See* Detourné en l'air.

**Dégagé à l'arabesque en tournant en dedans** [*day-ga-ZHAY a la-ra-BESK ahn toor-NAHN ahn duh-DAHN*]. Dégagé with arabesque turning inward. A term of the Cecchetti method. The dancer stands in the position croisé devant en l'air and slowly turns en dedans on the flat of the foot, passing the raised leg to the second position en l'air, then turning the body from the waist and rotating the raised leg in the hip socket. The dancer finishes in the position croisé derrière en l'air. *See* Détourné en l'air.

**Dégagé en l'air** [*day-ga-ZHAY ahn lehr*]. Dégagé in the air. The raising of a leg à la demi-hauteur, devant, à la seconde or derrière.

**Dégagé en tournant** [*day-ga-ZHAY ahn toor-NAHN*]. Dégagé, turning. A term of the Cecchetti method for a rotation of the working leg on the axis of the hip joint, performed à terre or en l'air, en dedans or en dehors. *See* Détourné en l'air.

**Dehors, en** [*ahn duh-AWR*]. Outward. In steps and exercises the term en dehors indicates that the leg, in a position à terre or en l'air, moves in a circular direction, clockwise. As, for example, in rond de jambe à terre en dehors. In pirouettes the term indicates that a pirouette is made outward toward the working leg.

**Demi** [*duh-MEE*]. Half.

**Demi-arabesque** [*duh-MEE-a-ra-BESK*]. Half-arabesque. A term of the French School for an arabesque in which the free leg is raised at half-height. *See* Arabesque à la demi-hauteur.

**Demi-attitude** [*duh-MEE-a-tee-TEWD*]. *See* Attitude, demi-.

**Demi-bras** [*duh-mee-BRAH*]. Half-arms. A halfway position of the arms. *See* Bras, demi-.

**Demi-caractère** [*duh-MEE-ka-rak-TEHR*]. Semi-character. A demi-caractère dance is one having the form of character dancing but executed with steps based on the technique of classical ballet. A demi-caractère dancer is one suited to character or mime roles, not a strictly classical dancer.

**Demi-contretemps** [*duh-MEE-kawn-truh-TAHN*]. Half-counterbeating. *See* Contretemps, demi-.

**Demi-détourné** [*duh-MEE-day-toor-NAY*]. Half-détourné. *See* Détourné, demi-.

**Demi-hauteur** [*duh-MEE-oh-TUHR*]. Half-height. A term of the French School for a position of the extended leg raised to a point midway between a position of the foot à terre and its equivalent en l'air. In other words, about knee height. *See* Demi-position.

**Demi-plié** [*duh-MEE-plee-AY*]. Half-bend of the knees. All steps of elevation begin and end with a demi-plié. *See* Plié.

**Demi-pointes, sur les** [*sewr lay duh-mee-PWENT*]. On the half-points. Indicates that the dancer is to stand high on the balls of the feet and under part of the toes. Also used in the singular, "sur la demi-pointe."

**Demi-position** [*duh-MEE-paw-zee-SYAWN*]. Half-position. A term of the Cecchetti method for a position of the foot at a point midway between a position of the foot à terre and its equivalent en l'air. *See* Demi-hauteur.

**Demi-seconde position** [*duh-MEE-suh-GAWND paw-zee-SYAWN*]. Half-second position. A term of the Cecchetti method to indicate a position of the arms midway between the first and second positions. The hands are turned inward so that the thumbnails face the audience. This position is used in steps such as glissade devant, temps de cuisse and so on. In these steps the arms open from the fifth position en bas to the demi-seconde position and close again in the fifth position en bas. The demi-seconde position is also used in certain of the eight directions of the body, in which case the palm of the hand always faces front. As, for example, in croisé devant.

**Demi-tour** [*duh-mee-TOOR*]. Half-turn.

**Derrière** [*deh-RYEHR*]. Behind, back. This term may refer to a movement, step or placing of a limb in back of the body. In reference to a particular step (for example, glissade derrière), the addition of derrière implies that the working foot is closed at the back.

**Descendant, en** [*ahn day-sahn-DAHN*]. Coming down. A term of the French School to imply that the working leg passes from back to front so that the dancer moves downstage, or that a step travels in a forward direction.

**Dessous** [*duh-SOO*]. Under. Indicates that the working foot passes behind the supporting foot. As, for example, in assemblé dessous.

**Dessus** [*duh-SEW*]. Over. Indicates that the working foot passes in front of the supporting foot. As, for example, in assemblé dessus.

**Détiré** [*day-tee-RAY*]. Drawn out. A term of the French School for a drawing out or stretching of the leg at the bar. Fifth position R foot front. Raise the R leg in a high retiré devant and take the inward side of the heel of the R foot with the R hand. Demi-plié on the L leg and stretch the R leg and arm forward. Carry the stretched R leg to the second position as high as possible while straightening the L knee and still holding the heel. The exercise may also be done with the hand crossed under the raised leg so that the heel is held on the outward side. *See* Pied dans la main.

**Détourné** [*day-toor-NAY*]. Turned aside. A détourné is a pivot turn on both points or demi-pointes. It is a complete turn toward the back foot and reverses the position of the feet. *See* Piqué détourné; Temps de pointe détourné.

**Détourné, demi-** [*duh-MEE-day-toor-NAY*]. Half-détourné. This is a half-turn in which the dancer turns toward the back foot, bringing the back foot in the front, and lowering the heels on completing the half turn.

**Détourné à terre** [*day-toor-NAY a tehr*]. Turned aside on the ground. A term of the French School. From the fourth position croisé, L foot back and pointe tendue, the dancer turns to the left by little shifts of the R heel, making a demi-tour and finishing with the L leg pointe tendue, croisé devant.

**Détourné en l'air** [*day-toor-NAY ahn lehr*]. Turned aside in the air. A term of the French School. This is a movement of adagio. From a pose in arabesque croisée, the dancer turns en dehors by small shifts of the heel while rotating the raised leg in the hip socket and finishing in the pose croisé devant. *See* Dégagé en tournant.

**Deux** [*duh*]. Two.

**Deuxième** [*duh-ZYEM*]. Second.

**Devant** [*duh-VAHN*]. In front. This term may refer to a step, movement or the placing of a limb in front of the body. In reference to a particular step (for example, jeté devant), the addition of the word "devant" implies that the working foot is closed in the front.

**Développé, temps** [*tahn dayv-law-PAY*]. Time developed, developing movement. Through common usage the term has become abridged to développé. A développé is a movement in which the working leg is drawn up to the knee of the supporting leg and slowly extended to an open position en l'air and held there with perfect control. The hips are kept level and square to the direction in which the dancer is facing. Développés are performed à la quatrième devant, à la seconde and à la quatrième derrière and may be executed in all directions of the body. They are done with the supporting foot flat on the ground, on the demi-pointe, full point or en fondu. In the Cecchetti method, the working foot is brought up to the retiré position with the toe pointed at the side of the knee (retiré de côté) before extending the leg in the required direction. In the Russian and French Schools, the pointed toe is brought to retiré devant before extending the leg forward or to retiré derrière before extending the leg backward. When performing a développé to second position, the front foot is brought to retiré devant and then extended, or the back foot is brought to retiré derrière and then extended.

**Développé à la quatrième derrière** [*dayv-law-PAY a lah ka-tree-EM deh-RYEHR*]. Développé to the fourth position back. Fifth position R foot back. Raise the R foot sur le cou-de-pied derrière and slowly draw the pointed foot up the back of the leg to retiré derrière. With the knee pressed well outward, slowly extend the pointed toe backward to the fourth position en l'air. The pointed foot is then lowered to the floor and closed in the fifth position. In développé à la quatrième derrière the body inclines slightly forward.

**Développé à la quatrième devant** [*dayv-law-PAY a lah ka-tree-EM duh-VAHN*]. Développé to the fourth position front. Fifth position R foot front. Raise the R foot sur le cou-de-pied devant in either the pointed or wrapped position, then slowly draw the pointed foot up the front of the leg to retiré devant. With the knee pressed well outward, slowly extend the pointed toe forward to the fourth position en l'air. The pointed foot is slowly lowered to the floor and closed in the fifth position.

**Développé à la seconde** [*dayv-law-PAY a lah suh-GAWND*]. Développé to the second position en l'air. The foot is drawn up to the retiré position front or back before extending the leg to the second position en l'air.

**Développé en fondu** [*dayv-law-PAY ahn fawn-DEW*]. Développé, sinking. The working leg executes a développé while the supporting knee bends in fondu.

**Développé passé** [*dayv-law-PAY pa-SAY*]. Développé, passing. The working foot passes the supporting knee from front to back and extends in développé (développé passé en arrière), or the working foot passes the supporting knee from back to front and extends in développé (développé passé en avant). This développé may be executed with a relevé, a piqué or a temps levé.

**Diagonale, en** [*ahn dya-gaw-NAL*]. In a diagonal. Indicates that a step is to be done traveling in a diagonal direction.

**Directions of movements.** *See* Côté, de; Descendant, en; Diagonale, en; Manège, en; Reculant, en; Salle, autour de la; and so on.

**Directions or body alignment.** The direction in which the dancer stands in relation to the audience is very important. If all the steps and poses were taken en face, the dance would be very monotonous. The diagrammatic floor plan (p. 125) shows the feet in the fifth position facing the various directions, using the R foot and starting a step forward, backward or to the side, the top of the page being the audience. For instance, a chassé when taken with the R foot toward the right front corner of the room (corner 1; diagram, p. 138) is a chassé effacé en avant but if the chassé is taken toward the left front corner of the room (corner 2) with the R foot it becomes a chassé croisé en avant.

**Directions or positions of the body.** *See* Positions of the body, basic, Cecchetti method; Positions of the body, basic, Russian and French Schools.

**Divertissement** [*dee-vehr-tees-MAHN*]. Diversion, enjoyment. A suite of numbers called "entrées," inserted into a classic ballet. These short dances are calculated to display the talents of individuals or groups of dancers.

**Dos à dos** [*doh za doh*]. Back to back.

**Dos au public** [*doh oh pew-BLEEK*]. Back to the audience.

**Double** [*DOO-bluh*]. Double. As, for example, in pirouette double (a double pirouette).

**Doublé, doublée** [*doo-BLAY*]. Doubled. As, for example, in sissonne doublée.

**Double work.** All movements in which one dancer is partnered or supported by another. *See* Adage; Enlèvement; Pas de deux.

**Droite, à** [*a drwaht*]. To the right.

**Écart, grand** [*grahn tay-KAR*]. Large écarté. The split.

**Écarté** [*ay-kar-TAY*]. Separated, thrown wide apart. Écarté is one of the eight directions of the body, Cecchetti method. In this position the dancer faces either one of the two front corners of the room. The leg nearer the audience is pointed in the second position à terre or raised to the second position en l'air. The torso is held perpendicular. The arms are held en attitude with the raised arm being on the same side as the extended leg. The head is raised slightly and turned toward the raised arm so that the eyes look into the palm of the hand. See illustration, p. 134.

**Écarté derrière (Russian School)** [*ay-kar-TAY deh-RYEHR*]. Écarté back. The dancer faces either one of the two front corners of the room (corners 2 or 8; see diagram p. 138) with the leg that is farther from the audience pointed in the second position à terre or raised to the second position en l'air. When the position is taken with the L leg extended, the dancer stands at an oblique angle to the audience, facing corner 8 with the L in second position pointe tendue à terre or raised to the second position en l'air pointing toward corner 6. The arms are held with the L arm curved over the head in the line of vision and the R arm held in demi-seconde position. The body leans to the right with the head turned to the right and the eyes looking down at the extended R arm. See illustration, p. 137.

**Écarté devant (Russian School)** [*ay-kar-TAY duh-VAHN*]. Écarté front. The dancer faces either one of the two front corners of the room (corners 2 or 8; see diagram, p. 138) with the leg that is closer to the audience pointed in the second position à terre or raised to the second position en l'air. When this position is taken with the R leg extended, the dancer stands at an oblique angle to the audience, facing corner 8 with the R leg in the second position pointe tendue à terre or raised to the second position en l'air pointing toward corner 2. The arms are held with the R arm curved over the head in the line of vision and the L arm held in demi-seconde position. The body leans to the left with the head turned to the right and the eyes looking up at the R hand. See illustration, p. 137.

**Écarté en l'air** [*ay-kar-TAY ahn lehr*]. Separated, thrown wide apart in the air. The dancer springs into the air, throwing both legs to a wide second position, then lands with the feet closed. The jump may also be done throwing one leg forward and one back. *See* Ciseaux.

**Échappé** [*ay-sha-PAY*]. Escaping or slipping movement. An échappé is a level opening of both feet from a closed to an open position. There are two kinds of échappés: échappé sauté, which is done with a spring from the fifth position and finishes in a demi-plié in the open position, and échappé sur les pointes, or demi-pointes, which is done with a relevé and has straight knees when in the open position. In each case échappés are done to the second or fourth position, both feet traveling an equal distance from the original center of gravity.

**Échappé, double** [*doob lay-sha-PAY*]. Double échappé. A term of the Russian School. This is an échappé on the points with a relevé in the open position before closing the feet in the fifth position. It is done to the second position or to the fourth position, either croisé or effacé.

**Échappé battu** [*ay-sha-PAY ba-TEW*]. Échappé beaten. Demi-plié in the fifth position R foot front; spring into the air and open the legs to the second position. Come to the floor in the second position in demi-plié. Again spring into the air and beat the R leg in front of the L leg. Finish in demi-plié, fifth position R foot back. The actual beat is performed on the calves and both legs beat. Échappé battu may also be finished on one leg, with the other leg sur le cou-de-pied either devant or derrière.

**Échappé changé** [*ay-sha-PAY shahn-ZHAY*]. Échappé changing. This is an échappé to the second position, either sauté or relevé, in which the position of the feet changes on the closing in the fifth position.

**Échappé royale** [*ay-sha-PAY rwah-YAL*]. Échappé with royale. Performed the same as échappé battu except that before the legs open into the second position they are beaten together.

**Échappé sans changer** [*ay-sha-PAY sahn shahn-ZHAY*]. Échappé without change. This is an échappé to the second position, either sauté or relevé, with no change of feet on the closing in the fifth position.

**Échappé sauté** [*ay-sha-PAY soh-TAY*]. Échappé, jumping or springing. This échappé is done to either the second or fourth position. The direction of the body can be en face or facing any of the directions. Échappé sauté is done either grand or petit.

**Échappé sauté, grand** [*grahn tay-sha-PAY soh-TAY*]. Big échappé, jumping. After a deep demi-plié in the fifth position the dancer springs into the air as high as possible, extending the legs in the fifth position. This closed position is maintained until the height of the jump is reached, then the legs are thrown apart into second position in the air and the dancer alights in demi-plié in the second position. On the return jump to fifth position, the dancer springs into the air with the legs extended in the second position until the top of the spring, then the feet are closed in the fifth position in the air and the dancer alights in demi-plié in the fifth position. This échappé may also be finished landing on one foot in a big pose such as attitude, arabesque, etc.

**Échappé sauté, petit** [*puh-TEE tay-sha-PAY soh-TAY*]. Little échappé, jumping. Fifth position R foot front. Demi-plié, push off the floor with extended toes and straightened knees and immediately open the legs to the second position in the air, then land in demi-plié in the second position. Again spring into the air in the same manner and return to the fifth position in demi-plié. The step may be repeated with the same foot in front or executed alternately front and back. In the Cecchetti method, the knees are bent and the feet drawn up on the return jump from the second position. Échappé sauté may also be done to the fourth position croisé or effacé. Échappé may also be done finishing on one foot on the return from the second or fourth position with the other foot held sur le cou-de-pied either devant or derrière.

**Échappé sauté en tournant** [*ay-sha-PAY soh-TAY ahn toor-NAHN*]. Échappé, jumping and turning. Petit échappé and grand échappé sauté are done with quarter or half-turns. The jump from the fifth position to the second position is done turning, then the jump returning to the fifth position is done in place.

**Échappé sur les pointes** [*ay-sha-PAY sewr lay pwent*]. Échappé on the points or toes. Fifth position R foot front. Demi-plié and, with a little spring, open the feet to the second or fourth position sur les pointes. The feet should glide rapidly to the open position and both feet must move evenly. On reaching the open position both knees must be held taut. With a little spring return to the fifth position in demi-plié. If the échappé is done in the second position the R foot may be closed either front or back. In échappé to the fourth position facing en face, croisé or effacé, the movement is done from the fifth position to the fourth position without change. Échappés may also be done en croix.

**Échappé to second position finishing on on leg.** A term of the Russian School. Fifth position R foot front. Demi-plié and échappé sur les pointes to the second position; demi-plié in the second position, then spring on the L pointe, taking the R foot sur le cou-de-pied derrière; demi-plié in the fifth position, R foot back. The step may also be done finishing on one leg with the free foot sur le cou-de-pied devant.

**École** [*ay-KAWL*]. School. As in école française, école russe.

**Effacé, effacée** [*eh-fa-SAY*]. Shaded. One of the directions of épaulement, in which the dancer stands at an oblique angle to the audience so that a part of the body is taken back and almost hidden from view. This direction is termed "ouvert" in the French method. Effacé is also used to qualify a pose in which the legs are open (not crossed). This pose may be taken devant or derrière, either à terre or en l'air.

**Effacé derrière (Russian School)** [*eh-fa-SAY deh-RYEHR*]. Effacé in back. This position is the exact opposite of effacé devant. The dancer stands at an oblique angle to the audience, facing either one of the two front corners of the room. The leg closer to the audience is pointed in the fourth position back à terre or raised to the fourth position en l'air. The arms are placed en attitude, the arm that is high being on the same side as the leg that is extended. The body leans slightly forward over the supporting leg. The head is turned toward the high arm with the eyes looking into the palm of the hand. In the French School this pose is termed "quatrième ouverte derrière." See illustration, p. 137.

**Effacé devant** [*eh-fa-SAY duh-VAHN*]. Effacé in front. Effacé devant is one of the eight directions of the body, Cecchetti method. In this position the dancer stands at an oblique angle to the audience, facing either one of the two front corners of the room. The leg farther from the audience is pointed in the fourth position front à terre or raised to the fourth position en l'air. The arms are placed en attitude, the arm that is low being on the same side as the leg that is extended. The body leans slightly back from the waist. The head is inclined toward the high arm with the eyes looking out to the audience. In the French School this pose is termed "quatrième ouverte devant." See illustration, p. 134.

**Effacé en arrière** [*eh-fa-SAY ah na-RYEHR*]. Effacé moving backward. A direction in which a given step is executed. The French School term is "ouvert en arrière." See floor plan, p. 125.

**Effacé en avant** [*eh-fa-SAY ah na-VAHN*]. Effacé moving forward. A direction in which a given step is executed. The French School term is "ouvert en avant." See floor plan, p. 125.

**Élan** [*ay-LAHN*]. Attack. Pertains to the manner in which a dancer attacks a step, both emotionally and physically.

**Élancé, élancée** [*ay-lahn-SAY*]. Darting. When this term is used with a step it indicates that the step is to be done in a darting manner. Any jump performed élancé is done just above the surface of the floor with one or both legs strongly stretched and toes well pointed. For example, an assemblé dessus traveled to the side would be an assemblé élancé.

**Élancer** [*ay-lahn-SAY*]. To dart. One of the seven movements in dancing.

**Élévation** [*ay-lay-va-SYAWN*]. Élévation is the ability of a dancer to attain height in dancing. It is a term used to describe the height attained in springing steps such as entrechats, grands jetés and so on, combined with ballon, so that the dancer jumps with a graceful elasticity like the bouncing movement of a rubber ball which touches the ground a moment and then rebounds into the air. The elevation is reckoned by the distance between the pointed toes of the dancer in the air and the ground. In alighting after a pas d'élévation the tips of the toes should reach the ground first, quickly followed by the sole and then the heel. All steps of elevation begin and end with a demi-plié.

**Élévation, pas d'** [*pah day-lay-va-SYAWN*]. Step of elevation. Any movement which involves a jump or spring.

**Élève** [*ay-LEV*]. Pupil, student. The apprentice dancers at the Paris Opéra are known as "les élèves" or "les petits rats."

**Emboîté** [*ahn-bwah-TAY*]. Fitted together, "boxed." The name is derived from the close fitting of the feet like a lid upon a box. It is a type of jeté done without a brush of the working foot. Fifth position R foot back. Demi-plié, spring into the air, bringing the R foot forward with knee slightly bent; land in demi-plié on the L foot with the R foot in front of the L ankle. The step is then done to the other side by springing on the R foot and landing with the L foot in front of the R ankle. The step travels en avant and alternates from one leg to the other. The bent leg must move beyond the supporting leg during each change. The movement may also be executed en arrière by bringing the free leg from front to back on each change. The term emboîté as described above is used in the Russian School and the Cecchetti method. The French School terms this step "petit jeté." The French emboîté is done only sur les pointes or demi-pointes. *See* Emboîté sur les pointes.

**Emboîté, grand** [*grahn tahn-bwah-TAY*]. Large or big emboîté. Executed the same as emboîté except that the leg is thrown up higher and is less bent at the knee.

**Emboîté en descendant** [*ahn-bwah-TAY ahn day-sahn-DAHN*]. A term of the French School. Emboîtés en descendant are a series of emboîtés done moving downstage toward the audience. *See* Emboîté sur les pointes.

**Emboîté en reculant** [*ahn-bwah-TAY ahn ruh-kew-LAHN*]. A term of the French School for a series of emboîtés done moving upstage away from the audience. *See* Déboîté.

**Emboîté en tournant** [*ahn-bwah-TAY ahn toor-NAHN*]. Emboîté, turning. These are quick jumping turns done either in a straight line or in a circle. The jumps are not high but should have a light elastic quality. Emboîté en tournant is done the same as simple emboîté but a complete turn is done with each two emboîtés. Fifth position R foot front. Demi-plié and spring into the air toward the right, bringing the L leg forward in a bent position, crossing the foot close to the supporting ankle and turning so that the landing is made in demi-plié on the R foot with the back to the audience. Spring off the R foot, still traveling to the right and completing the turn so that the landing is made en face with a demi-plié on the L foot, R foot forward in a bent position crossing close to the L ankle.

**Emboîté en tournant en dedans (Cecchetti method)** [*ahn-bwah-TAY ahn toor-NAHN ahn duh-DAHN*]. *See* Emboîté en tournant.

**Emboîté en tournant en dehors (Cecchetti method)** [*ahn-bwah-TAY ahn toor-NAHN ahn duh-AWR*]. Emboîté, turning outward. Fifth position R foot front. Demi-plié and spring upward into the air with the R foot sur le cou-de-pied devant or retiré devant, making a complete turn to the right (en dehors). The landing is made on the L foot in demi-plié, then the R foot is closed in demi-plié in the fifth position front.

**Emboîté en tournant sur les pointes** [*ahn-bwah-TAY ahn toor-NAHN sewr lay pwent*]. Emboîté, turning on the points. These turns are done traveling in a diagonal or in a circle. Fifth position croisé R foot front. Demi-plié and dégagé the R foot to the second position at 45 degrees; piqué on the R foot, turning one half-turn en dedans with the L foot sur le cou-de-pied devant; step on the L point in fifth position, turning one half-turn en dehors with the R foot sur le cou-de-pied devant. To continue the series of turns, step on the R point to the second position.

**Emboîté sur les pointes** [*ahn-bwah-TAY sewr lay pwent*]. Emboîté on the points. In the French School emboîté is done only on the points or demi-pointes. It is done with a movement forward on the points or demi-pointes moving from fifth to fifth. The back foot swishes out to the side in a small seconde en l'air with the toe pointed, then is brought in and closed in the fifth position front. Both knees are kept taut. The movement is then repeated with the other foot. The movement is also done moving backward, closing the front foot to the back on each step. It is then termed "déboîté."

**En** [*ahn*]. In; while. For all expressions beginning with "en," see the following word. For instance, for the definition of "En arrière" see "Arrière, en."

**Enchaînement** [*ahn-shen-MAHN*]. Linking. A combination of two or more steps arranged to fit a phrase of music.

**En-dehors** [*ahn duh-AWR*]. A term of the French School for turn-out (*q.v*).

**Enlèvement** [*ahn-lev-MAHN*]. Carrying off. The male dancer lifts his partner in the air in a step or pose.

**Entrechat** [*ahn-truh-SHAH*]. Interweaving or braiding. A step of beating in which the dancer jumps into the air and rapidly crosses the legs before and behind each other. Entrechats are counted from two to ten according to the number of crossings required and counting each crossing as two movements, one by each leg; that is, in an entrechat quatre each leg makes two distinct movements.

Entrechats are divided into two general classes: the even-numbered entrechats, or those which land on two feet—deux, quatre, six, huit and dix—and the odd-numbered entrechats, or those which land on one foot—trois, cinq, sept and neuf. In all entrechats both legs beat equally. Even-numbered entrechats are done en face or en tournant, while odd-numbered entrechats are done devant, derrière, en tournant, de côté or de volée. In the Cecchetti method, entrechats are done with the knees bent and the feet drawn up so that one foot beats against the other from the base of the calf downward.

**Entrechat cinq** [*ahn-truh-SHAH senk*]. Five crossings. Entrechat cinq is similar to entrechat quatre (*q.v*), except that the landing is made on one foot, the other being placed sur le cou-de-pied either devant or derrière.

*Entrechat cinq devant:* Fifth position R foot front. Demi-plié and with a small jump open the legs slightly, beat the calves together with the R leg in the back, open the legs and land on the L foot with the R foot sur le cou-de-pied devant.

*Entrechat cinq derrière*: Fifth position R foot back. Demi-plié and with a small jump open the legs slightly, beat the calves together with the R leg in the front, open the legs and land on the L foot with the R foot sur le cou-de-pied derrière.

**Entrechat cinq de volée** [*ahn-truh-SHAH senk duh vaw-LAY*]. Fifth position R foot back. Glissade derrière, thrust the R leg out to the second position en l'air, pushing from the ground with the L foot. The L leg meets the R leg, beating it in the back, then the legs open, R leg beats in back of L, legs open, and the landing is made in demi-plié in the fifth position R foot front. The Russian School (Vaganova) terms this "entrechat six de volée." The French School terms this "entrechat cinq de volée." The Cecchetti method term is "entrechat six de côté."

**Entrechat cinq fermé** [*ahn-truh-SHAH senk fehr-MAY*]. This is a term of the French School. It is composed of an entrechat quatre commenced from the second position and finished in the fifth position. *See* Royale fermée.

**Entrechat cinq ouvert** [*ahn-truh-SHAH senk oo-VEHR*]. This is a term of the French School. It is composed of an entrechat quatre completed in the air, with the landing then made in the second position. *See* Royale ouverte.

**Entrechat cinq ramassé** [*ahn-truh-SHAH senk ra-ma-SAY*]. This step is also known as "sissonne fermée battue," as it is really a sissonne fermée with the beat of an entrechat quatre. It is usually done in a series, en avant, en arrière or de côté. *See* Sissonne fermée battue.

**Entrechat deux** [*ahn-truh-SHAH duh*]. Two crossings. An entrechat deux is a changement de pieds. *See* Changement. To execute changement battu, *see* Royale.

**Entrechat de volée** [*ahn-truh-SHAH duh vaw-LAY*]. Flying entrechat. Entrechat de volée is done in flight in any direction and is usually preceded by a demi-contretemps or a glissade. The landing is made in the fifth position.

**Entrechat dix** [*ahn-truh-SHAH deess*]. Ten crossings.

**Entrechat huit** [*ahn-truh-SHAH weet*]. Eight crossings. Same as entrechat six (*q.v*), except that another crossing is added. If the R foot starts in the fifth position front it will finish in the fifth position front.

**Entrechat neuf** [*ahn-truh-SHAH nuhf*]. Nine crossings. The same as an entrechat huit (*q.v*), except that the landing is made on one foot with the other foot sur le cou-de-pied either devant or derrière.

**Entrechat quatre** [$\overline{ahn}$-truh-SHAH KA-truh]. Four crossings. Fifth position R foot front. Demi-plié and with a small jump slightly open the legs and beat the calves together R leg in back. Slightly open the legs and finish in demi-plié in the fifth position R foot front.

**Entrechat royale** [$\overline{ahn}$-truh-SHAH rwah-YAL]. See Royale.

**Entrechat sept** [ahn-truh-SHAH set]. Seven crossings. Entrechat sept is similar to entrechat six (q.v), except that the landing is made on one foot with the other foot sur le cou-de-pied either devant or derrière.

*Entrechat sept devant:* Fifth position R foot back. Demi-plié and with a jump open the legs; R leg beats in front of L leg; open legs; R leg beats in back of L leg; open legs and finish in demi-plié on the L foot with the R foot sur le cou-de-pied devant.

*Entrechat sept derrière:* Fifth position R foot front. Demi-plié and with a strong jump open the legs; R leg beats in back of L leg; open legs; R leg beats in front of L leg; open legs and finish in demi-plié on the L foot with the R foot sur le cou-de-pied derrière.

**Entrechat six** [$\overline{ahn}$-truh-SHAH seess]. Six crossings. Demi-plié in the fifth position R foot front. With a strong jump open the legs, beat the R leg behind the L, open the legs, beat the R leg in front of the L, open the legs and finish in demi-plié in the fifth position, R foot back.

**Entrechat six de côté** [$\overline{ahn}$-truh-SHAH seess duh koh-TAY]. A term of the Cecchetti method. See Entrechat cinq de volée.

**Entrechat six de volée** [$\overline{ahn}$-truh-SHAH seess duh vaw-LAY]. A term of the Russian School. See Entrechat cinq de volée.

**Entrechat trois** [$\overline{ahn}$-truh-SHAH trwah]. Three crossings. Entrechat trois is finished on one foot with the other sur le cou-de-pied either devant or derrière.

*Entrechat trois derrière:* Fifth position R foot front. Demi-plié and with a small jump open the legs into a narrow second position in the air. Beat the R leg in front of the L, slightly open the legs and land on the L foot in demi-plié with the R foot sur le cou-de-pied derrière.

*Entrechat tròis devant:* Fifth position R foot back. Demi-plié and with a small jump open the legs in a narrow second position in the air. Beat the R leg behind the L, slightly open the legs and land on the L foot in demi-plié with the R foot sur le cou-de-pied devant.

**Entrée** [$\overline{ahn}$-TRAY]. Entrance. The term is given to the arrival of a dancer or group of dancers who perform a number in a divertissement. The term also applies to the beginning of a grand pas de deux in which the danseuse and danseur make their entrance. See Pas de deux, grand.

**Entrelacé, entrelacée** [$\overline{ahn}$-truh-la-SAY]. Interlaced. For example, jeté entrelacé.

**Enveloppé** [$\overline{ahn}$-vuh-law-PAY]. Enveloped. A term of the French School. Enveloppé is a rotation of the body turning en dedans on the supporting leg (either relevé or sauté) while the other leg envelops or encircles it. Enveloppé is used to give momentum to inward turns. Fifth position

R foot front. Raise the L leg in back à la demi-hauteur and execute a grand rond de jambe en dedans, closing the L foot on the R shinbone and turning one complete turn to the right. The L foot may finish retiré devant or may be brought back into attitude or arabesque.

**Épaulé, épaulée** [*ay-poh-LAY*]. Shouldered. A term of the Cecchetti method to indicate a pose in which the dancer stands at an oblique angle to the audience in an arabesque position (the second arabesque, Cecchetti method) with the body facing one or other of the two front corners of the stage. The shoulders are held square to the line of direction, the arm nearer the audience extended forward and the corresponding leg extended to the fourth position back à terre or en l'air. The head is inclined and turned toward the audience. Épaulé is one of the eight directions of the body, Cecchetti method. See illustration, p. 135.

**Épaulé derrière (Russian School)** [*ay-poh-LAY deh-RYEHR*]. Épaulé back. This position is exactly the same as the Cecchetti épaulé, but is taken facing either one of the two upper corners of the room (corners 6 or 4; see diagram, p. 138) with the extended leg nearer the audience. See illustration, p. 137.

**Épaulement** [*ay-pohl-MAHN*]. Shouldering. The placing of the shoulders. A term used to indicate a movement of the torso from the waist upward, bringing one shoulder forward and the other back with the head turned or inclined over the forward shoulder. The two fundamental positions of épaulement are croisé and effacé. When épaulement is used the position of the head depends upon the position of the shoulders and the shoulder position depends upon the position of the legs. Épaulement gives the finishing artistic touch to every movement and is a characteristic feature of the modern classical style compared to the old French style, which has little épaulement.

**Épaulement croisé** [*ay-pohl-MAHN krwah-ZAY*]. Shouldering croisé. The dancer stands in the fifth position R foot front, facing the left front corner of the room with the head turned to the right shoulder. If the dancer faces the right front corner of the room, the L foot will be in front and the head will turn over the left shoulder.

**Épaulement effacé** [*ay-pohl-MAHN eh-fa-SAY*]. Shouldering effacé. The dancer stands in the fifth position L foot front, facing the left front corner of the room with the head turned to the right shoulder. If the dancer faces the right front corner of the room, the R foot will be in front and the head will turn over the left shoulder.

**Équilibre** [*ay-kee-LEE-bruh*]. Equilibrium; aplomb. (1) The ability of the dancer to balance and hold a pose. (2) The balancing of the body on demi-pointe or full point in any required position.

**Étendre** [*ay-TAHN-druh*]. To stretch. One of the seven movements in dancing.

**Étendu** [*ay-tahn-DEW*]. Outstretched, extended. The second half of a plié when the legs straighten.

**Étoile** [*ay-TWAHL*]. Star. A title given to certain premières danseuses and premiers danseurs of the Paris Opéra (première danseuse étoile or premier danseur étoile) to indicate that they are the leading dancers. *See* Défilé.

**Exercices à la barre** [*eg-zehr-SEESS a lah bar*]. Exercises at the bar (or barre). A group of exercises performed by the dancer while clasping a bar with one hand. This bar, generally a cylindrical piece of wood, is fastened horizontally to the walls of the practice room at a height of about three feet six inches from the floor. Bar exercises, or side practice, are the foundation of classical ballet and are to the dancer what scales are to the pianist. Every ballet lesson begins with these exercises. It is at the bar that the dancer acquires the fundamental training for the attributes he must possess. These exercises are essential for developing the muscles correctly, turning the legs out from the hips and gaining control and flexibility of the joints and muscles. The exercises at the bar can be simple or varied but in general they include the following movements:

(1) Pliés in the first, second, fourth and fifth positions.
(2) Battements tendus.
(3) Battements tendus jetés.
(4) Battements fondus.
(5) Ronds de jambe à terre.
(6) Battements frappés.
(7) Adagio.
(8) Petits battements sur le cou-de-pied.
(9) Ronds de jambe en l'air.
(10) Grands battements.

**Exercices au milieu** [*eg-zehr-SEESS oh mee-LYUH*]. Exercises in the centre, that is, centre practice. A group of exercises similar to those at the bar but performed without the support of the bar in the centre of the practice room. Exercices au milieu help the dancer to acquire uprightness and balance. A more popular term for these exercises is centre practice.

**Extended positions of the arms.** When the arms and hands are held straight in any position, the position is said to be extended or ouverte. For example, the fifth position en haut, taken with the hands turned out so that the arms form a V, is called cinquième position ouverte.

**Extension** [*eks-tahn-SYAWN*]. Term used to describe the ability of a dancer to raise and hold her extended leg en l'air. A dancer is said to have a good extension if, when doing a développé à la seconde, she is able to hold and sustain the raised leg above shoulder level.

**Face, de** [*duh fahss*]. In front, full face. A position or step executed facing the audience. See floor plan, p. 125.

**Face, en** [*ahn fahss*]. Opposite (the audience); facing the audience.

**Failli** [*fah-YEE*]. Giving way. A fleeting movement done on one count.

Fifth position croisé, R foot front. Demi-plié, spring into the air with the feet held close together and, while in the air, turn the body effacé so that the L shoulder comes forward and the head turns toward the L shoulder. Land on the R foot in demi-plié with the L leg opened in effacé derrière at 45 degrees; immediately slide the L foot through the first position to the fourth position croisé in demi-plié with the weight on the L foot, L knee bent and body inclined to the left.

**Faux, fausse** [*foh, fohss*]. False.

**Faux entrechat cinq ramassé** [*foh zahn-truh-SHAH senk ra-ma-SAY*]. False entrechat cinq picked up. Same as sissonne fermée.

**Fermé, fermée** [*fehr-MAY*]. Closed. Indicates that both feet are in a closed position or that the feet at the end of a step are brought to a closed position. As, for example, in position fermée, sissonne fermée.

**Finale.** The final section of a classic ballet. *See* Coda.

**Finger turns.** These are turns in which the girl partner is supported by the boy. The boy stands in back of the girl, his R hand raised above the girl's head with the index finger pointed downward. The girl grasps his finger with her R hand. The boy's L hand is held forward to the left side of the girl with her L hand resting on it. The girl does a sous-sus to the fifth position on point, takes her R foot to retiré and executes a développé croisé devant. From this position she pushes from the boy's L hand, executes a fouetté rond de jambe en tournant and continues turning with a series of pirouettes, still holding the boy's index finger. At the completion of the pirouettes she stops herself by quickly grasping the boy's L hand. *See* Fouetté rond de jambe en tournant en dehors (supported).

**Fish dive.** This is a term used in double (supported) work for various lifts in which the danseuse is supported by the danseur in a poisson position. He may hold her above his head in a horizontal fish dive or she may fall from a sitting position on his shoulder and be caught in a fish dive, and so on.

**Fixed points of the practice room or stage (Cecchetti method).** See illustration, p. 138. In the Cecchetti method the corners and centre of each side of the practice room are numbered to help the dancer develop a sense of direction. The dancer stands in the centre of the room, facing side 5, which is the front of the room or audience. The numbers are used to indicate the direction to be taken by the dancer in a given step or pose.

**Fixed points of the practice room or stage (Russian School [Vaganova]).** See illustration, p. 138. To determine the direction for a movement or a pose or to indicate the degree of the turn of the body, the corners and the sides of the practice room are numbered in the Russian School as well. The dancer stands in the centre of the room facing side 1, which is the front of the room or audience.

**Fléchir** [*flay-SHEER*]. To bend. As, for example, in fléchir les genoux (bend the knees).

**Flic-flac** [*fleek-FLAK*]. A crack, as of a whip. A term of the Russian School. A flicking or lashing movement done in exercises at the bar and in the centre of the room. It is composed of whipping movements from second position at 45 degrees through the fifth position front and back (or back and front) close to the supporting leg; then the leg is opened again to the second position at 45 degrees. Flic-flac is performed en dedans, en dehors and en tournant. It may also be performed with a rise to the demi-pointe on the final extension to second position. *En dedans:* From the second position en l'air at 45 degrees, whip the foot downward, bending the knee and brushing the ball of the foot along the floor passing through fifth position front and finishing with the pointed toe crossed in front, beyond sur le cou-de-pied; throw the pointed foot outward toward second position without brushing the floor; fling the foot downward through fifth position, brushing the floor and finishing with the pointed toe crossed behind, beyond sur le cou-de-pied. The foot is then opened to the second position en l'air at 45 degrees. *En dehors:* Reverse the movement, crossing behind, then in front of, the supporting ankle.

**Flic-flac en tournant** [*fleek-FLAK ahn toor-NAHN*]. Flic-flac, turning. The turn may be en dedans or en dehors. The "flic" is done on the whole foot and the "flac" on demi-pointe. *En dehors:* From the second position en l'air at 45 degrees, the leg is whipped downward, bending the knee and brushing the ball of the foot through the fifth position so that the pointed foot is crossed in back, beyond sur le cou-de-pied. The dancer then rises on the demi-pointe of the supporting leg and makes a full turn en dehors while the working foot opens slightly and brushes along the floor to cross in front of the supporting leg. The working leg is then immediately thrown out to the second position at 45 degrees. *En dedans:* This is done in the same manner, crossing the working foot in front of, then in back of, the supporting leg and turning en dedans on demi-pointe. During the turn, either en dehors or en dedans, the arms provide the force. They are lowered from the second position to the preparatory position, then raised to the first position and opened to the second position.

**Fondu, fondue** [*fawn-DEW*]. Sinking down. A term used to describe a lowering of the body made by bending the knee of the supporting leg. Saint-Léon wrote, "Fondu is on one leg what a plié is on two." In some instances the term fondu is also used to describe the ending of a step when the working leg is placed on the ground with a soft and gradual movement. An example of this is jeté fondu.

**Fouetté** [*fweh-TAY*]. Whipped. A term applied to a whipping movement. The movement may be a short whipped movement of the raised foot as it passes rapidly in front of or behind the supporting foot (*see* Flic-flac) or the sharp whipping around of the body from one direction to another. There is a great variety of fouettés: petit fouetté, which may be devant, à la seconde or derrière and executed à terre, sur la demi-pointe or sauté; and grand fouetté, which may be sauté, relevé and en tournant.

**Fouetté, demi-** [*duh-MEE-fweh-TAY*]. Half-fouetté. This is a fouetté en l'air in which the dancer makes a quarter-turn. The dancer, facing the audience, raises either leg to the second position en l'air, then with a sharp movement turns into an arabeque in profile to the audience while rotating the raised leg in the hip socket. The step may be done sauté or with a relevé on the supporting leg. *See* Fouetté en face, grand (Cecchetti method).

**Fouetté, petit** [*puh-TEE fweh-TAY*]. Little fouetté. Stand with the R foot opened to the second position so that the pointed toe is a few inches off the ground. With a sharp movement sweep the pointed toe of the R foot along the ground so that the foot crosses the ankle a little beyond sur le cou-de-pied, either devant or derrière.

**Fouetté à terre** [*fweh-TAY a tehr*]. Fouetté on the ground. A term of the Cecchetti method for a petit fouetté.

**Fouetté à terre en dedans (Ceccehetti method)** [*fweh-TAY a tehr a̅h̅n duh-DAH̅N̅*]. Fouetté on the ground inward. From the second position in the air, the foot is swept across the floor and brought to sur le cou-de-pied devant, then quickly passed to sur le cou-de-pied derrière. The movement is similar to a petit battement sur le cou-de-pied. *See* Flic-flac (en dedans).

**Fouetté à terre en dehors (Ceccehetti method)** [*fweh-TAY a tehr a̅h̅n duh-AWR*]. Fouetté on the ground outward. From the second position in the air, the foot is swept across the floor and brought to sur le cou-de-pied derrière then quickly passed to sur le cou-de-pied devant. *See* Flic-flac (en dehors).

**Fouetté à terre en tournant (Cecchetti method)** [*fweh-TAY a tehr a̅h̅n toor-NAH̅N̅*]. Fouetté on the ground, turning. *En dedans:* Execute a fouetté à terre en dedans with the R foot and at the same time execute a pirouette en dedans on the L foot. At the end of the pirouette, lower the L heel. *See* Flic-flac en tournant (en dedans). *En dehors:* Execute a fouetté à terre en dehors with the R foot and at the same time execute a pirouette en dehors on the L foot. At the finish of the turn, lower the L heel to the ground. *See* Flic-flac en tournant (en dehors).

**Fouetté battu** [*fweh-TAY ba-TEW*]. Fouetté beaten. This is a petit fouetté executed with a beat. Stand on the R foot with the L foot sur le cou-de-pied devant. Spring off the R foot, opening the L foot to the second position so that the toe is a few inches off the ground. Beat the R behind the L and land on the R foot in demi-plié with the L foot sur le cou-de-pied derrière. *See* Ballonné battu.

**Fouetté effacé, grand (Russian School)** [*gra̅h̅n fweh-TAY eh-fa-SAY*]. Large fouetté shaded. In this fouetté the dancer makes a half-turn from the pose effacé devant en l'air to the pose effacé derrière en l'air (or vice versa). It may be performed with a relevé or a jump on the supporting leg.

*En dehors:* Fourth position croisé L foot pointed back. On the upbeat, demi-plié on the R leg with the L foot sur le cou-de-pied derrière. Step on the L demi-pointe with the R foot sur le cou-de-pied devant and turn to face corner 2; fondu on the L leg with the R leg half-bent in effacé devant; at the same time bend the body to the right with the R arm in the second position and the L arm in the first position; straighten the body and relevé on the L leg, carrying the stretched R leg in grand rond de jambe en dehors at 90 degrees, turning the body to effacé derrière; simultaneously the L arm rises to the third position and opens to the second position as the R arm is raised to the third position. Lower the L heel in demi-plié in the pose attitude effacée derrière.

*En dedans:* The movement is reversed. The R leg is half-bent in effacé derrière at 45 degrees with the body bent back; perform a grand rond de jambe en dedans and finish with the R leg stretched at 90 degrees in the pose effacé devant.

**Fouetté en face, grand (Cecchetti method)** [*grahn fweh-TAY ahn fahss*]. Large fouetté facing the audience. This fouetté is executed on pointe, on demi-pointe or with a jump.

*En dehors:* Fourth position croisé L foot pointed back and the arms in the fifth position en bas. On the upbeat, demi-plié on the R leg, raising the L foot sur le cou-de-pied derrière; step on the L demi-pointe and raise the R foot sur le cou-de-pied devant. Demi-plié on the L foot and développé the R leg à la quatrième devant en face, raising the arms to the fourth position en avant (L arm crossed in front of the body); relevé on the L foot and in one sweeping movement execute a grand rond de jambe en dehors, ending in the fourth Cecchetti arabesque facing the audience. At the same time, move the L arm in a semicircle so that it rises above the head and opens to the second position; as the L arm is lowered, the R arm is raised above the head, then lowered and extended forward.

*En dedans:* Fourth position croisé L foot pointed forward and the arms in the fifth position en bas. On the upbeat, demi-plié on the R leg, raising the L foot sur le cou-de-pied devant; step on the L demi-pointe and raise the R foot sur le cou-de-pied derrière. Demi-plié on the L foot and développé the R leg à la quatrième derrière en face, raising the arms to the fourth position en avant (L arm across the body); relevé on the L foot and in one sweeping movement execute a grand rond de jambe en dedans and lower the L heel in demi-plié with the R leg extended to the fourth position front en l'air. At the same time, raise the L arm above the head and open it to the second position, and raise the R arm from the second position to above the head. The head is turned toward the R arm.

**Fouetté en tournant, grand (Russian School)** [*grahn fweh-TAY ahn toor-NAHN*]. Large fouetté, turning. This fouetté may be done on demi-pointe, on point or with a jump. It is usually done en dedans and may be finished in attitude croisée, attitude effacée or any of the arabesques.

*En dedans:* Fourth position croisé L foot pointed forward with the arms in the preparatory position. On the upbeat, step on the L foot in demi-plié; relevé on the L foot, throwing the R leg to the second position at 90 degrees, turning the body en face and opening the arms to the second position; demi-plié on the L leg, turning en dedans to face corner 6, sweeping the R leg down through the first position and forward at 90 degrees (as the leg sweeps forward, the arms lower to the first position and rise with a strong movement to the third position on the battement); simultaneously, relevé on the L demi-pointe, bending the body back, then quickly turn to face corner 2 and demi-plié in the third arabesque.

*En dehors:* Fourth position croisé L foot pointed back. On the upbeat, step on the L foot in demi-plié; relevé on the L foot and execute a grand battement to the second position at 90 degrees, opening the arms to the second position. Demi-plié on the L foot, sweeping the R leg through the first position to third arabesque and relevé in third arabesque (the arms rise to third arabesque through the preparatory position). Turn en dehors on demi-pointe to the pose croisé devant at 90 degrees. Lower the L heel in demi-plié.

**Fouetté en tournant à la seconde, grand (Russian School)** [*grahn fweh-TAY a lah suh-GAWND*]. Large fouetté, turning in the second position. This fouetté is done on point or demi-pointe. It is a variety of the popular fouetté rond de jambe en tournant.

*En dehors:* Fifth position R foot front. Demi-plié on the L leg with the R foot retiré devant; relevé on the L foot and throw the R leg to the second position at 90 degrees; demi-plié on the L foot and relevé, turning en dehors while bending the R knee and passing the R foot behind, then in front of, the L knee. Demi-plié on the L foot and continue the series of turns, taking two counts for each fouetté. The arms open to the second position with the leg, then are brought into first position on the turn.

*En dedans:* The working leg is thrown to the second position at 90 degrees, then the knee bends and the foot is passed in front of, then behind, the supporting knee while turning en dedans.

**Fouetté en tournant en dedans, grand (Cecchetti method)** [*grahn fweh-TAY ahn toor-NAHN ahn duh-DAHN*]. Large fouetté, turning inward. Stand on the L foot in the first arabesque facing side 6. Demi-plié and sweep the R leg to the fourth position front en l'air toward side 6, lowering the arms to the fifth position en bas, and raise them to the fifth position en avant; rise on the L demi-pointe and turn to the left until the body faces side 8. Leave the R arm and the R leg pointing to side 8 and sharply turn the body to the left to face side 6, raising the L arm to the fourth position en haut. When the body faces side 6, extend the L arm forward and lower the L heel in demi-plié in the first arabesque. This fouetté may also be done with a jump.

**Fouetté en tournant en diagonale, grand (Russian School)** [*grahn fweh-TAY ahn toor-NAHN ahn dya-gaw-NAL*]. Large fouetté, turning and traveling in a diagonal. This fouetté is taken traveling in a diagonal from corner 2 to corner 6 or from corner 8 to corner 4. Stand on the R leg in arabesque effacée à terre at corner 2 with the arms in either the first or second arabesque. On the upbeat, demi-plié on the R leg, opening the arms to the second position and do a chassé en avant toward corner 6, bringing the legs together in the fifth position with a sliding jump close to the floor; step on the L foot in demi-plié toward corner 6 and jump, throwing the R leg forward at 90 degrees; simultaneously the body faces corner 6 and the arms are raised from a low first position to the third position, while the body turns en dedans in the air to face corner 2 and lands in demi-plié on the L leg in the fourth arabesque. The step is then repeated toward corner 6, throwing the L leg forward and turning en dedans to land in demi-plié in the first arabesque facing corner 2.

**Fouetté raccourci** [*fweh-TAY ra-koor-SEE*]. Fouetté shortened. This movement is similar to a petit fouetté. From the second position en l'air, the working foot is cut sharply behind the supporting leg by bending the knee of the working leg without lowering the thigh.

**Fouetté rond de jambe en tournant** [*fweh-TAY rawn duh zhahnb ahn toor-NAHN*]. Whipped circle of the leg turning. This is the popular turn in which the dancer executes a series of turns on the supporting leg while being propelled by a whipping movement of the working leg. The whipping leg should be at hip level, with the foot closing in to the knee of the supporting leg. Fouettés are usually done in a series. They may be executed en dehors or en dedans.

*En dehors (Russian School):* Fourth position R foot back. Execute a pirouette en dehors on the L leg. Fondu on the L leg, at the same time opening the R leg to the second position en l'air. Relevé on the L point or demi-pointe, executing a tour en dehors and whipping the R foot in back of, then quickly in front of, the L knee. Fondu on the L leg, opening the R leg to the second position en l'air.

*En dehors (Cecchetti method):* Fourth position R foot back. Execute a pirouette en dehors on the L leg. Fondu on the L leg, at the same time extending the R leg to quatrième position devant en l'air (croisé devant). Relevé on the L point or demi-pointe, sweeping the R leg to the second position en l'air, and execute a tour en dehors, bringing the R foot to side and front of L knee. Fondu on the L foot, extending the R leg forward again. Three-quarters of the turn should be made with the R foot in position on the supporting knee. This fouetté may also be executed from a preparation starting with a pas de bourrée en dedans and finishing with a coupé dessous, opening the working leg to quatrième devant croisé.

*En dedans (Russian School):* Fouetté en dedans is done in the same manner as en dehors. After a pirouette en dedans the extension is made to the second position en l'air; next the foot is brought in front of, then in back of, the supporting knee.

*En dedans (Cecchetti method):* After a pirouette en dedans the working leg is extended to the fourth position derrière en l'air; then with a demi-rond de jambe en l'air en dedans the foot is brought to the front of the supporting knee.

**Fouetté rond de jambe en tournant en dehors (supported)** [*fweh-TAY rawn duh zhahnb ahn toor-NAHN ahn duh-AWR*]. Whipped circle of the leg turning outward (supported). This is a fouetté in which the girl, supported by the boy, holds one hand above her head, grasping the boy's index finger. After a sous-sus the girl does a développé croisé devant and executes one, two or more fouettés ronds de jambe en tournant, stopping herself by quickly grasping the boy's free hand with her free hand. *See* Finger turns.

**Fouetté sauté, grand** [$\overline{grahn}$ *fweh-TAY soh-TAY*]. Large fouetté, jumping. This fouetté is performed with a temps levé on the supporting foot instead of a relevé. There are numerous kinds of grands fouettés sautés. The step is preceded by a glissade, sissonne simple, failli, etc. *See* Fouetté effacé, grand (Russian School) *and* Fouetté en tournant, grand (Russian School).

**Fouetté sauté en face, grand (Russian School)** [$\overline{grahn}$ *fweh-TAY soh-TAY ahn fahss*]. Large fouetté, jumping, facing front. Fourth position croisé L foot pointed forward with the arms in a low first position. Step on the L foot in demi-plié and push off the floor, throwing the R leg to the second position at 90 degrees; simultaneously raise the arms to the third position. With a sharp movement turn into the first arabesque in profile and land on the L leg in demi-plié. To repeat the movement with the other leg, do a small temps levé on the L foot and step croisé en avant on the R leg, lowering the arms; then immediately push off from the floor in the second grand fouetté.

**Frappé, frappée** [*fra-PAY*]. Struck. *See* Battement frappé.

**French School.** The French School of ballet began in the court ceremonies of the French monarchs. Louis XIV studied with the famous ballet master Pierre Beauchamp and established the first academy of dancing, known as the Académie Royale de Musique and de Danse, in Paris in 1661. The École de Danse de l'Opéra was founded in 1713 and is now known as the École de Danse du Théâtre National de l'Opéra. Among its most famous ballet masters were Beauchamp, Pécour, Lany, Noverre, G. and A. Vestris, M. and P. Gardel, F. Taglioni, Mazilier, Saint-Léon, Mérante, Staats, Aveline and Lifar. The French School was known for its elegance and soft, graceful movements rather than technical virtuosity. Its influence spread throughout Europe and is the basis of all ballet training.

**Friska** [*FRISH-kah*]. The fast movement of the csárdás (*q.v*).

**Galop** [*ga-LOH*]. A gay early nineteenth-century dance in 2/4 time. A galop is often used as a finale to a series of ballet divertissements.

**Gargouillade** [*gar-goo-YAD*]. Gurgling or rumbling. In the Cecchetti method and the French School the step resembles a pas de chat with a double rond de jambe, actually a rond de jambe and a half with the commencing leg. A brilliant executant will also do a double rond de jambe with the closing leg. The step may be done either en dehors or en dedans.

**Gargouillade (Russian School)** [*gar-goo-YAD*]. *See* Rond de jambe double.

**Gargouillade en dedans (Cecchetti method)** [*gar-goo-YAD* $\overline{ahn}$ *duh-*

*DAHN*]. Gargouillade inward. Fifth position R foot back. Execute a double rond de jambe en l'air en dedans à la demi-hauteur with the R leg and finish with the R foot at the side of the L knee. Spring upward and to the right off the L foot, landing in demi-plié on the R foot and bringing the L foot to the side of the R knee. (A double rond de jambe en l'air en dehors without the final extension à la seconde may be executed with the L foot before bringing it to the side of the knee.) Close the L foot in demi-plié in the fifth position front.

**Gargouillade en dehors (Cecchetti method)** [*gar-goo-YAD ahn duh-AWR*]. Gargouillade outward. Fifth position R foot front. Execute a double rond de jambe en l'air en dehors à la demi-hauteur with the R leg and finish with the R foot at the L knee. Spring upward and to the right off the L foot, landing in a demi-plié on the R foot and bringing the pointed L foot to the side of the R knee. (A double rond de jambe en l'air en dedans without the final extension à la seconde may be executed with the L foot before bringing it to the R knee.) Close the L foot to the fifth position front in demi-plié. This step is often preceded by a coupé dessous.

**Gargouillade volé (Cecchetti method)** [*gar-goo-YAD vaw-LAY*]. Gargouillade flown. Fifth position R foot back. Execute a double rond de jambe en l'air en dedans à la demi-hauteur with the R leg and finish with the R foot in retiré at the side of the L knee. Spring off the L foot onto the R and land in demi-plié sur place, turning the body effacé. As the R foot comes to the ground, draw the L point upward to the side of the R knee and open it to the fourth position en l'air, pointing to the left front corner of the room. Immediately lower the L foot to the fourth position, pointe tendue, body remaining effacé.

**Gateway, the.** This is a position of the arms in which the arms are held rounded in front of the body with the fingertips on a level with the bottom of the breastbone. The backs of the hands face outward with the arms rounded so that the elbows are a little below the shoulders and the wrists a little below the elbows with the point of the elbows imperceptible. This position corresponds to the fifth position en avant of the Cecchetti method and the first position of the Russian and French Schools. When the arms are raised from a low position to a high one, the arms generally pass through the gateway. *See* Port de bras.

**Gauche, à** [*a gohsh*]. To the left.

**Gavotte** [*ga-VAWT*]. This was originally a peasant dance but became a fashionable court dance during the reigns of Louis XIV and XV. It was later revived by Gardel at the Paris Opéra, where it became the basis for brilliant solos.

**Genou** [*zhuh-NOO*]. Knee.

**Gigue** [*zheeg*]. Jig. An early eighteenth-century dance in 2/4 time.

**Glissade** [*glee-SAD*]. Glide. A traveling step executed by gliding the working foot from the fifth position in the required direction, the other foot closing to it. Glissade is a terre à terre step and is used to link other steps. After a demi-plié in the fifth position the working foot glides along the floor to a strong point a few inches from the floor. The other foot then pushes away from the floor so that both knees are straight and both feet strongly pointed for a moment; then the weight is shifted to the working foot with a fondu. The other foot, which is pointed a few inches from the floor, slides into the fifth position in demi-plié. When a glissade is used as an auxiliary step for small or big jumps, it is done with a quick movement on the upbeat. Glissades are done with or without change of feet, and all begin and end with a demi-plié. There are six glissades: devant, derrière, dessous, dessus, en avant, en arrière, the difference between them depending on the starting and finishing positions as well as the direction. Glissade may also be done sur les pointes.

**Glissade changée** [*glee-SAD sh$\overline{ahn}$-ZHAY*]. Glissade, changing. In this glissade the feet alternate each time in the fifth position; that is, if the R foot is in back in the fifth position and the glissade is done to the right, the R foot will finish in the fifth position front, and vice versa. *See* Glissade dessous; Glissade dessus.

**Glissade derrière** [*glee-SAD deh-RYEHR*]. Glissade in back. This glissade travels to the side and is commenced with the back foot, which remains in the back at the finish. Fifth position R foot back; demi-plié and slide the pointed toe of the R foot to the second position. With a slight spring from the L foot, shift the weight to the R foot, bending the knee, and slide the pointed L foot to the fifth position front, lowering the heel and bending the knee.

**Glissade dessous** [*glee-SAD duh-SOO*]. Glissade under. This glissade travels to the side and is commenced with the front foot, which finishes at the back. Fifth position R foot front; demi-plié and slide the pointed toe of the R foot to the second position. With a slight spring from the L foot, shift the weight to the R foot, bending the knee, and slide the pointed L foot to the fifth position front, lowering the heel and bending the knee.

**Glissade dessus** [*glee-SAD duh-S$\underline{EW}$*]. Glissade over. This glissade travels to the side and is commenced with the back foot, which finishes in the front. Fifth position R foot back; demi-plié and slide the pointed toe of the R foot to the second position. With a slight spring from the L foot, shift the weight to the R foot, bending the knee, and slide the pointed L foot to the fifth position back, lowering the heel and bending the knee.

**Glissade devant** [*glee-SAD duh-V$\overline{AHN}$*]. Glissade in front. This glissade travels to the side and is commenced with the front foot, which remains in front at the finish. Fifth position R foot front; demi-plié and slide the pointed toe of the R foot to the second position. With a slight spring from the L foot, shift the weight to the R foot, bending the knee, and slide the pointed L foot to the fifth position back, lowering the heel and bending the knee.

**Glissade en arrière** [*glee-SAD ah na-RYEHR*]. Glissade backward. This glissade commences with the back foot and finishes with it in the back, traveling en arrière, croisé en arrière or effacé en arrière. Fifth position R foot back; demi-plié and slide the pointed toe of the R foot to the fourth position back. With a slight spring from the L foot, shift the weight to the R foot, bending the knee, and slide the pointed L foot to the fifth position front, lowering the heel and bending the knee. Note: In all glissades the heel of the commencing foot must be lowered to the floor before the heel of the closing foot.

**Glissade en avant** [*glee-SAD ah na-VAHN*]. Glissade forward. This glissade commences with the front foot and finishes with it in the front, traveling en avant, croisé en avant or effacé en avant. Fifth position R foot front; demi-plié and slide the pointed toe of the R foot to the fourth position front. With a slight spring from the L foot, shift the weight to the R foot, bending the knee, and slide the pointed L foot to the fifth position back, lowering the heel and bending the knee.

**Glissade piquée** [*glee-SAD pee-KAY*]. Glissade pricked. Same as glissade précipitée.

**Glissade précipitée** [*glee-SAD pray-see-pee-TAY*]. Glissade hurried. This is a quick glissade, about half the size of an ordinary glissade. It is always followed by a posé and the two steps together take the same amount of time as an ordinary glissade. Glissade précipitée is usually done devant or dessus but it may also be taken derrière, dessous, en avant and en arrière.

**Glissade pressée** [*glee-SAD preh-SAY*]. Glissade pressed, hurried. Same as glissade précipitée.

**Glissade sur les pointes** [*glee-SAD sewr lay pwent*]. Glissade on the toes. Fifth position R foot back. Demi-plié and slide the pointed R foot to the second position; step directly onto the point with straight knee and quickly close the L foot on point to the fifth position front. Demi-plié, lowering the heels to the floor. The glissade may be done dessous, dessus, devant, derrière, en avant and en arrière, in all directions of the body.

**Glissé** [*glee-SAY*]. Glided, gliding. As, for example, in battement glissé.

**Glisser** [*glee-SAY*]. To glide. One of the seven movements in dancing.

**Grand, grande** [*grahn, grahnd*]. Big, large. As, for example, in grand battement. (To find terms starting with "grand," look up the second word of the term.)

**Hands.** *See* Positions of the hand (Cecchetti method).

**Haut, en** [*ahn oh*]. High. Used to indicate a high position of the arms. As, for example, in cinquième position en haut.

**Hauteur, à la** [*a lah oh-TUHR*]. To the height. A term of the French School. A position in which the working leg is raised at right angles to the hip. As, for example, in quatrième devant à la hauteur, which is the same as à la quatrième devant en l'air or grande quatrième devant.

**Head movements (Cecchetti method).** (1) When traveling forward on alternate feet the dancer inclines his head slightly toward the shoulder corresponding to the foot that is advanced. When traveling backward on alternate feet the dancer inclines his head slightly toward the shoulder opposite to the foot that makes the step backward. In some steps traveled forward, when épaulement is used, the head is not inclined, but instead is slightly turned toward the forward shoulder.

(2) When the dancer faces front and executes a rond de jambe à terre en dehors, the head is inclined to the side opposite to the foot that makes the movement. When the dancer faces front and executes a rond de jambe à terre en dedans, the head is inclined to the same side as the foot that makes the movement.

(3) When the dancer faces front and turns his body away from the audience to the right or left, the head inclines toward the side to which he turns, as in a series of échappés to the second position.

(4) In turning movements such as pirouettes, the head is the last part to leave the front of the room as the body turns and the first to arrive as the body completes the turn (*see* Spotting).

**Head movements (Russian School).** In the Russian School there is an unwritten rule, with a few exceptions, never to dance with the body en face. Épaulement is used and the head is always turned in the direction of the forward shoulder.

**Head positions.** *See* Positions of the head.

**Hortensia** [*awr-tahn-SYAH*]. A male dancer's step in which the dancer jumps into the air with the legs drawn up, one in front of the other, then reverses their position in the air several times before landing with the feet apart again. The legs do not beat.

**Incliné, inclinée** [*en-klee-NAY*]. Inclined. For example, arabesque inclinée.

**Italian School.** The Imperial Dancing Academy connected with La Scala in Milan was opened in 1812. Its greatest period began when Carlo Blasis, Italian dancer and teacher, became its director in 1837. Blasis published two textbooks, *Treatise on the Art of Dancing* and *Code of Terpsichore*, in which he codified his teaching methods and all that was known of ballet technique. These books form the basis of our modern classical training. Blasis trained most of the famous Italian dancers of the era, and his pupil Giovanni Lepri was the teacher of Enrico Cecchetti, one of the greatest teachers in the history of ballet. It was Cecchetti who brought the Italian School to its peak. The Italian School was known for its strong, brilliant technique and the virtuosity of its dancers, who astonished the audience with their difficult steps and brilliant turns.

**Jambe** [*zhahnb*]. Leg.

**Jarret** [*zha-REH*]. Ham (bend of the knee).

**Jarreté** [*zhar-TAY*]. Close-legged, knock-kneed. The opposite of arqué, or bowlegged (*q.v*). When the jarreté dancer stands in the first position the knee joints touch or nearly touch, the calves touch but the heels are separated. This type of dancer is usually slightly built, extremely loose-limbed and supple and has high, beautiful insteps which are often weak.

**Jeté, grand** [*grahn zhuh-TAY*]. Large jeté. In this step the legs are thrown to 90 degrees with a corresponding high jump. It is done forward to attitude croisée or effacée, and to all the arabesques. It may also be done backward with the leg raised either croisé or effacé devant. Grand jeté is always preceded by a preliminary movement such as a glissade, pas couru or coupé.

**Jeté, pas** [*pah zhuh-TAY*]. Throwing step. A jump from one foot to the other in which the working leg is brushed into the air and appears to have been thrown. There is a wide variety of pas jetés (usually called merely jetés) and they may be performed in all directions.

**Jeté, petit** [*puh-TEE zhuh-TAY*]. Small jeté. From a demi-plié in the fifth position the working foot glides along the floor until it reaches a position à la demi-hauteur. The supporting foot springs from the floor and the landing is made in fondu on the working leg with the other foot extended in the air or sur le cou-de-pied. Petit jeté is done dessus, dessous, en avant, en arrière and en tournant.

**Jeté bateau** [*zhugh-TAY ba-TOH*]. Boat-like jeté. This is a term of the French School. The step consists of a ballotté executed en avant and en arrière. *See* Ballotté.

**Jeté-battement** [*zhuh-TAY-bat-MAHN*]. This is a petit battement executed during a jeté. It is an exercise of the centre practice and is excellent for foot and instep work and the gaining of brilliancy in batterie. The movement is terre à terre and is done dessus or dessous.

**Jeté-battement dessous** [*zhuh-TAY-bat-MAHN duh-SOO*]. Jeté-battement under. This is the reverse of jeté-battement dessus (see below), consisting of a jeté dessous and a double battement frappé, passing the foot sur le cou-de-pied devant, then derrière, and following with a dégagé to the second position.

**Jeté-battement dessus** [*zhuh-TAY-bat-MAHN duh-SEW*]. Jeté-battement over. Fifth position R foot back. Demi-plié and slide the R foot to a short second position, pointe tendue; spring on the R foot, terre à terre, coming to the ground sur la demi-pointe on the same spot the R foot held at the beginning of the step. Immediately lower the R heel to the ground with a fondu and execute a double battement frappé with the L foot bringing the L foot sur le cou-de-pied derrière, then sur le cou-de-pied devant, and follow immediately with a battement frappé to the second position. To repeat to the other side, spring on the L foot in the same manner and execute a double battement frappé with the R foot. Épaulement should be used with this exercise. Either the same shoulder can be brought forward or the shoulder opposite to the foot executing the battement sur le cou-de-pied. This exercise is usually performed 16 times traveling straight forward (en avant) and is then followed by a series of 16 jetés-battements dessous.

**Jeté battu** [*zhuh-TAY ba-TEW*]. Jeté beaten. Both jeté dessus and jeté dessous may be beaten.

**Jeté battu dessous** [*zhuh-TAY ba-TEW duh-SOO*]. Jeté beaten (and closed) under. Fifth position R foot front. Demi-plié and brush the R foot to the second position at 45 degrees; spring off the L foot, pointing the toes well, and with both knees straight beat the calves together, R leg front. Open legs slightly and land in demi-plié on the R foot with the L foot sur le cou-de-pied devant.

**Jeté battu dessus** [*zhuh-TAY ba-TEW duh-SEW*]. Jeté beaten (and closed) over. Fifth position R foot back. Demi-plié and brush the R foot to the second position at 45 degrees; spring off the L foot, pointing the toes well, and with both knees straight beat the calves of the legs together, R leg in back. Open legs slightly and land in demi-plié on the R foot with the L foot sur le cou-de-pied derrière.

**Jeté derrière** [*zhuh-TAY deh-RYEHR*]. Jeté in back. This is a term of the Cecchetti method. The adverb "derrière" implies that the working foot is closed in the back. *See* Jeté dessous.

**Jeté dessous** [*zhuh-TAY duh-SOO*]. Jeté under. Fifth position R foot front. Demi-plié and brush the R foot to the second position (battement frappé); spring off the L foot, pointing the toes well, and land on the R foot in demi-plié with the L foot sur le cou-de-pied devant. After the spring the R foot should return to the ground a little in back of the position vacated by the L foot. The step does not travel from side to side. When done in a series the demi-plié on the supporting leg will be omitted after the first jeté, since the leg will already be bent.

**Jeté dessus** [*zhuh-TAY duh-SEW*]. Jeté over. Fifth position R foot back. Demi-plié and brush the R foot to the second position at 45 degrees; spring off the L foot, pointing the toes well, and land on the R foot in demi-plié with the L foot sur le cou-de-pied derrière. After the spring the R foot should return to the ground a little in front of the position vacated by the L foot. The step does not travel from side to side. When done in a series the demi-plié on the supporting leg will be omitted after the first jeté since the leg will already be bent.

**Jeté dessus en tournant, grand** [*grahn zhuh-TAY duh-SEW ahn toor-NAHN*]. Large jeté over and turning. A term of the French School. Same as jeté entrelacè.

**Jeté dessus en tournant battu, grand** [*grahn zhuh-TAY duh-SEW ahn toor-NAHN ba-TEW*]. Large jeté over, turning and beaten. This is a grand jeté dessus en tournant performed with a beat. The leg which is thrust forward in grand battement beats behind or on top of the other leg after the body has turned one half-turn in the air; the legs then pass each other in the air and the dancer lands again on the leg that made the grand battement. *See* Jeté dessus en tournant, grand.

**Jeté devant** [*zhuh-TAY duh-VAHN*]. Jeté in front. This is a term of the Cecchetti method. The adverb "devant" implies that the working foot is closed in the front. *See* Jeté dessus.

**Jeté en arrière, grand** [*grahn zhuh-TAY ah na-RYEHR*]. Large jeté moving backward. This jeté is seldom used, as no impetus can be gained from the preparatory pas couru. After the pas couru, step back on the L foot in the direction effacé en arrière with a good plié and push off from this foot, at the same time thrusting the R leg back in a grand battement at 90 degrees. The landing is made on the R leg in demi-plié with the L leg extended in croisé devant en l'air.

**Jeté en arrière, petit** [*puh-TEE zhuh-TAY ah na-RYEHR*]. Little jeté traveling backward. Fifth position, R foot back. Demi-plié and glide the R foot along the floor and into the air at 45 degrees; spring off the supporting foot and land in fondu on the R foot with the L foot sur le cou-de-pied devant or extended to the fourth position devant at 45 degrees. This jeté may also be taken croisé en arrière or effacé en arrière.

**Jeté en avant** [*zhuh-TAY ah na-VAHN*]. Jeté forward. This jeté is done either petit or grand.

**Jeté en avant, grand** [*grahn zhuh-TAY ah na-VAHN*]. Large jeté forward. A big leap forward preceded by a preliminary movement such as a pas couru or a glissade, which gives the necessary push-off. The jump is done on the foot which is thrown forward as in grand battement at 90 degrees, the height of the jump depending on the strength of the thrust and the length of the jump depending on the strong push-off of the other leg which is thrust up and back. The dancer tries to remain in the air in a definitely expressed attitude or arabesque and descends to the ground in the same pose. It is important to start the jump with a springy plié and finish it with a soft and controlled plié.

**Jeté en avant, petit** [*puh-TEE zhuh-TAY ah na-VAHN*]. Little jeté traveling forward. Fifth position R foot front. Demi-plié and glide the R foot along the floor and into the air at 45 degrees; spring off the supporting foot and land in fondu on the R foot with the L foot sur le cou-de-pied derrière or extended to the fourth position derrière at 45 degrees. This jeté may also be taken croisé en avant or effacé en avant.

**Jeté en descendant, petit** [*puh-TEE zhuh-TAY ahn day-sahn-DAHN*]. Little jeté coming down (moving downstage). A term of the French School. Same as jeté dessus.

**Jeté en remontant, petit** [*puh-TEE zhuh-TAY ahn ruh-mawn-TAHN*]. Little jeté going up (moving upstage). A term of the French School. Same as jeté dessous.

**Jeté en tournant, grand** [*grahn zhuh-TAY ahn toor-NAHN*]. Large jeté, turning. A term of the French and Russian Schools. Fifth position R foot front. Execute a sissonne tombée to the fourth position croisé into a demi-plié on the R foot, bending the body forward; coupé dessous L, throwing the R leg forward to 90 degrees, making a quarter-turn en dehors; immediately spring into the air, continuing the turn to the right, and land on the R foot in demi-plié in attitude croisée derrière. The whole movement is executed without a pause. *See* Tour de reins.

**Jeté en tournant en arrière, grand (Cecchetti method)** [*grahn zhuh-TAY ahn toor-NAHN ah na-RYEHR*]. Large jeté, turning and moving backward. Same as jeté entrelacé (Russian School); jeté dessus en tournant, grand (French School).

**Jeté en tournant en avant, grand (Cecchetti method)** [*grahn zhuh-TAY ahn toor-NAHN ah na-VAHN*]. Large jeté, turning and moving forward. Fourth position R foot front, pointe tendue. Step to the right on the R foot. Spring into the air, executing a grand rond de jambe en dedans with the L leg and turning in the air to the right. During the turn, bring the L foot to retiré devant, then quickly pass the R foot to retiré devant (both knees are bent as the feet pass each other in the air). Come to the ground in demi-plié on the L foot with the R foot in retiré devant. *See* Saut de basque.

**Jeté en tournant par demi-tours** [*zhuh-TAY ahn toor-NAHN par duh-mee-TOOR*]. Jeté, turning by half-turns. These jetés are like the jetés dessus or dessous done traveling to the side and making a half-turn with each jeté. The first half-turn will be en dedans and the next en dehors.

**Jeté en tournant par terre** [*zhuh-TAY ahn toor-NAHN par tehr*]. Jeté, turning close to the floor. Fifth position R foot front. Demi-plié, throw the R foot with a gliding movement on the floor, in the direction effacé en avant, into a jeté en avant, keeping the jeté close to the floor; land on the R foot in demi-plié in arabesque with the L leg à la demi-hauteur; jump into the air, joining the L leg behind the R in the fifth position, making a complete turn to the right. Land on the L foot in demi-plié with the R foot sur le cou-de-pied devant. This jeté is performed consecutively, en diagonale or en manège.

**Jeté entrelacé** [*zhuh-TAY ahn-truh-la-SAY*]. Jeté interlaced. A term of the Russian School. This jeté is done in all directions and in a circle. It is usually preceded by a chassé or a pas couru to give impetus to the jump. Stand on the R leg facing corner 2 in the second arabesque à terre. On the upbeat, demi-plié and raise the L leg to 45 degrees, inclining the body slightly forward; step on the L foot in demi-plié toward corner 6, opening the arms to the second position; throw the R leg forward to 90 degrees (passing through the first position) toward corner 6 and push off the floor with the L leg. At the same time, lower the arms, then quickly raise them through the first position to the third position to help provide force for the jump. During the jump the body turns in the air to the left and the L leg is thrown out (the legs almost come together and appear to interlace), passes the R in the air and finishes in the back at 90 degrees. The landing is made on the R leg in demi-plié in the first arabesque facing corner 2, on the spot from which the jump began. In the French School this is called "grand jeté dessus en tournant"; in the Cecchetti method, "grand jeté en tournant en arrière."

**Jeté entrelacé, double** [*DOO-bluh zhuh-TAY ahn-truh-la-SAY*]. Double jeté entrelacé. A term of the Russian School. This step is performed only by male dancers with a strong technique. After the working leg has been thrown forward at 90 degrees, the other leg comes to meet it and the body leans back so that it forms a horizontal position in the air and does a double turn in the air before landing in arabesque.

**Jeté entrelacé battu** [*zhuh-TAY ahn-truh-la-SAY ba-TEW*]. Jeté entrelacé with a beat. After the R leg is thrown forward at 90 degrees, the L leg beats beneath the R, then the legs change so that the L leg beats in front and again in back; the body turns in the air and the L leg is thrown backward to land on the R leg in arabesque.

**Jeté enveloppé** [*zhuh-TAY ahn-vuh-law-PAY*]. Jeté enveloped. This is a term of the French School. The jeté enveloppé is a jeté dessus done en tournant en dedans, making a complete turn or a half-turn. Fifth position R foot front. Brush the L leg to the second position à la demi-hauteur and execute a demi-grand rond de jambe en dedans, making a complete turn to the right in the air. Land on the L foot in demi-plié, facing the audience, with the R leg raised en raccourci derrière or en attitude.

**Jeté fermé** [*zhuh-TAY fehr-MAY*]. Jeté closed. This is a jeté in which the feet close to the fifth position. It is performed in two counts. The demi-plié is done on the upbeat, the transfer of weight on the first count and the close to the fifth position on the second count. It may be performed derrière, devant and changé in the directions croisé, effacé and écarté. For jeté fermé derrière, demi-plié in the fifth position R foot back; throw the R foot to the second position at 90 degrees; and spring off the L foot, traveling to the right and opening the L leg to the second position at 90 degrees. Land on the R foot in fondu and lower the L foot pointe tendue, then slide the L foot into the fifth position front in demi-plié, inclining the torso and head to the right.

**Jeté fondu de côté** [*zhuh-TAY fawn-DEW duh koh-TAY*]. Jeté melting or sinking, to the side. Jeté fondu is technically the same as jeté fermé, the only difference being in the ending. The closing leg is put down softly and gradually into the fifth position.

**Jeté fondu sur la pointe (Russian School)** [*zhuh-TAY fawn-DEW sewr lah pwent*]. This is a soft, flowing step performed in a series en diagonale, either forward or backward. *En avant:* Fifth position croisé L foot front. Traveling toward corner 2, demi-plié on the upbeat and execute a petit développé effacé devant with the R leg; piqué forward on the R foot and développé L croisé devant at 45 degrees. As the L leg straightens, a soft fondu is made on the R foot. The step is then continued with a jeté fondu on the L leg while doing a petit développé effacé devant with the R leg. *En arrière:* This is done in the same manner, reversing the direction and stepping backward onto point.

**Jeté fouetté, grand** [*grahn zhuh-TAY fweh-TAY*]. Large jeté whipped. This is a grand jeté en avant ending with a rotation of the back leg in the hip socket so that the dancer lands facing the opposite direction from which he began the step, with his back leg extended in quatrième devant en l'air.

**Jeté pas de chat, grand** [*grahn zhuh-TAY pah duh shah*]. Big pas de chat thrown. A term of the Russian School. This step may be done in a series or combined with other jumps, in a straight line, in a diagonal or in a circle. It is always preceded by a glissade or a coupé. Fifth position croisé L foot front. Traveling from corner 6 toward corner 2, execute a glissade derrière with the R foot; push off from both legs, raising the R foot to the left knee, and fling it forward in a quick développé in an unturned-out position to 90 degrees; simultaneously, open the L leg backward at 90 degrees so that the legs form a split. The jump finishes in demi-plié on the R leg and then the L foot does a passé par terre to the fourth position croisé and pushes off again in the next grand jeté pas de chat. The arms are held as in first arabesque or à deux bras.

**Jeté passé** [*zhuh-TAY pa-SAY*]. Jeté passed. There are three kinds of jeté passé, forward, backward and to the side. All forms are preceded by a step into a demi-plié or a pas couru of three or five steps with an emphasis on the demi-plié at the end of the pas couru.

**Jeté passé en avant** [*zhuh-TAY pa-SAY ah na-VAHN*]. Jeté passed forward. The legs are thrown forward at 45 or 90 degrees (petit jeté passé or grand jeté passé). Stand in the pose croisé devant with the L foot front and pointe tendue. Step on the L foot in demi-plié in the direction effacé en arrière, raising the R leg forward. Spring from the L foot, throwing the L leg forward into the air and bending the torso back. There should be a moment in the air when both legs pass each other, then the landing is made on the R foot with the L leg croisé devant en l'air. The L leg may also pass by means of a développé into the pose croisé devant.

**Jeté passé en arrière** [*zhuh-TAY pa-SAY ah na-RYEHR*]. Jeté passed backward. The legs are thrown backward at 45 or 90 degrees (petit jeté passé or grand jeté passé). Stand in the pose croisé derrière with the R foot back and pointe tendue. Step on the R foot in demi-plié in the direction effacé en avant, raising the L leg in back. Spring upward from the R foot, throwing the R leg backward into the air and bending the torso back. There should be a moment in the air when both legs pass each other, then the landing is made on the L foot in attitude croisée derrière. Also called "pas de papillon."

**Jeté passé de côté in second position** [*zhuh-TAY pa-SAY duh koh-TAY*]. Jeté passed to the side in second position. This jeté passé is done at 90 degrees and the landing is made in third (Russian) arabesque, attitude croisée derrière or to the pose effacé devant. The leg may do the passé through first position with a stretched knee or by means of a développé.

**Jeté piqué sur la pointe** [*zhuh-TAY pee-KAY sewr lah pwent*]. Jeté pricked on the point. A term of the Cecchetti method. This is a small step on the points transferring the weight from one point to the other with the free foot raised sur le cou-de-pied devant or derrière.

**Jeté renversé, grand** [*grahn* zhuh-TAY *rahn*-vehr-SAY]. Large jeté, upset. Fifth position R foot back. Demi-plié and throw the R leg to grande seconde. Spring off the L foot and land on the R foot in attitude croisée. Execute a pas de bourrée en tournant en dehors with the L foot, bending the body to the right and then backward.

**Jeté-rotation** [zhuh-TAY-raw-ta-SYAWN]. Jeté rotation. Fifth position R foot front. Jeté dessus on the L foot, making a half-turn en dehors. Relevé on the L foot, completing the turn, and développé the R leg to quatrième devant croisé. Tombé croisé en avant on the R foot. This step is usually done in a series.

**Jeté sur la pointe (Cecchetti method)** [zhuh-TAY *sewr* lah *pwent*]. Jeté on the point. In the Cecchetti method a jeté sur la pointe is similar to a posé, but whereas a posé is a quick movement used in allégro, a jeté sur la pointe is a slow movement used in adage.

**Jeté sur la pointe (Russian School)** [zhuh-TAY *sewr* lah *pwent*]. Jeté on the point. In the Russian School this term is used like the French School term "piqué." It is a step onto the point of one foot from a demi-plié. It is done either petit or grand in all directions and poses. In a petit jeté, after stepping on point, the other foot is immediately placed sur le cou-de-pied, either devant or derrière. In a grand jeté, the working leg is raised to 45 degrees, then a wide step is taken on point and the other leg raised at 90 degrees in attitude or arabesque. In the poses croisé and effacé devant and écarté devant and derrière, the working leg steps onto point and the other leg is raised to the pose with a quick développé.

**Jeté sur les pointes (French School)** [zhuh-TAY *sewr* lay *pwent*]. Jeté on the points. These jetés are petits jetés dessus or dessous taken on the full point. There is no extension to the side.

**Jeté volé de côté** [zhuh-TAY vaw-LAY duh koh-TAY]. Jeté, flying to the side. This is a grand jeté to the second position finishing in attitude croisée or arabesque croisée derrière. *See* Jeté passé de côté in second position.

**Labanotation.** This is a system of dance notation invented by the Hungarian-born teacher Rudolf von Laban. This system has been developed and perfected by the Dance Notation Bureau, which was founded in New York in 1940 and introduced the term in 1953. Many ballets have been notated by the Bureau, which has compiled a library of works in Labanotation, including the previous edition of the present book (notated by Allan Miles).

**Lassú** [LAH-shoo]. The slow movement of the csárdás (*q.v*).

**Leçon** [luh-SAWN]. Lesson. The daily class taken by dancers throughout their career to continue learning and to maintain technical proficiency.

It consists of exercices à la barre (side practice) followed by exercices au milieu (centre practice), port de bras, pirouette practice and petit and grand allégro. See these terms.

**Leotard.** A tightly fitting practice or stage costume for dancers, covering the body from neck to thighs or to the ankles. There are many varieties, such as short-sleeve and sleeveless versions. The version worn by its inventor, the French acrobat Jules Léotard, in the middle of the nineteenth century had long sleeves and covered the body from neck to ankles.

**Levé, temps** [$\overline{tahn}$ *luh-VAY*]. Time raised or raising movement. *See* Temps levé.

**Lié, temps** [$\overline{tahn}$ *lyay*]. Time linked or linking movement. *See* Temps lié.

**Lift.** The lifting of the danseuse by her male partner. *See* Enlèvement; Porté.

**Ligne** [*LEEN-yuh*]. Line. The outline presented by a dancer while executing steps and poses. A dancer is said to have a good or bad sense of line according to the arrangement of head, body, legs and arms in a pose or movement. A good line is absolutely indispensable to the classical dancer.

**Limbering.** Before leaving the bar, dancers often do stretching exercises, of which there is a great variety, to further loosen and extend their muscles.

**Lyre, en** [$\overline{ahn}$ *leer*]. Like a lyre. A term of the French School. *See* Bras en lyre.

**Lyrical dancing.** A poetic style of dancing with a lovely, flowing quality.

**Maillot** [*mah-YOH*]. The French term for tights. A tightly fitting garment covering the dancer's body up to the waist or armpits.

**Mains** [$\overline{men}$]. Hands. *See* Positions of the hand (Cecchetti method).

**Maître or maîtresse de ballet** [*MEH-truh* (or) *meh-TRESS duh ba-LAY*]. Ballet master or mistress. The person responsible for the training of the dancers in a company. The maître or maîtresse de ballet also conducts company rehearsals.

**Manège, en** [$\overline{ahn}$ *ma-NEZH*]. As at a riding school or in a circus ring. A term of the French School. Indicates that the dancer is to travel around the room in a circle while performing a combination of steps or turns. *See* Salle, autour de la.

**Manèges** [*ma-NEZH*]. Circular. A term applied to steps or enchaînements executed in a circle.

**Marquer** [*mar-KAY*]. To stamp, to mark the accents in a step. Also to mark or "walk through" the steps of an enchaînement or variation.

**Mazurka or mazurek.** A Polish folk dance in 3/4 time which has been introduced into a number of ballets as a character dance.

**Methods** (French: **Méthodes** [*may-TAWD*]). Academic ballet as we know it today came into being in the year 1661, when King Louis XIV of France founded the Académie Royale de Musique et de Danse. Although individual Milanese dancing-masters had been renowned since the fifteenth century, the permanent Imperial Dancing Academy connected with La Scala Theatre was not opened until 1812. The Academy at Milan influenced Paris and especially Russia through the rules of education drawn up by Carlo Blasis, who became director of the Academy in 1837 and rapidly made it the centre of ballet activity.

By the middle of the nineteenth century the ballet centres of the world had shifted from Paris and Milan to St. Petersburg and Moscow. The Russian School first derived its technique from France but by the middle of the nineteenth century it had acquired an international aspect through the influence of international artists. From the beginning of the second half of the nineteenth century Russian ballet was dominated by Marius Petipa, a Frenchman, and Christian Johannsen, a Swede. Then in 1874 Enrico Cecchetti, the last great exponent of the Italian School, arrived in Russia. These three men working on generations of Russian dancers developed Russian ballet, making it as much a system as Italian or French ballet. Actually the French method is in the greatest proportion in the Russian School.

**Milieu, au** [*oh mee-LYUH*]. In the middle or centre. *See* Centre practice; Exercices au milieu.

**Mime.** The art of using the face and body to express emotion and dramatic action.

**Mimer** [*mee-MAY*]. To mime or mimic. To express dramatic action or emotion or to convey a story by means of gesture and facial expression.

**Minuet.** A dignified dance in 3/4 time introduced during the reign of Louis XIV.

**Modifications.** All the steps, poses and movements are subject to certain terms which indicate to the dancer in what direction or in what manner any given step or position is to be executed. These terms are known as modifications. Examples are: devant, en l'air, battu, en croix, fermé, and so on. See the illustrations on pages 125, 129, 134 and 136, and the articles to which they refer.

**Monter** [*mawn-TAY*]. To rise, to mount. To rise on the points or demi-pointes. A term of the French School.

**Movements in dancing.** There are seven movements in dancing: élancer, to dart; étendre, to stretch; glisser, to glide or slide; plier, to bend; relever, to raise; sauter, to jump; tourner, to turn round.

**Neuf** [*nuhf*]. Nine.

**Notation.** There is no universally accepted system of recording the choreography of ballets although many systems of dance notation have been devised by dancers and choreographers. At present, there are two systems of notation in general use, Labanotation (*q.v*) and Benesh notation.

**Opposition.** The term refers to the "law" by which the arm position is in opposition to the leg that is in front, whether that leg is the supporting or the working leg. For example, if the dancer's R leg is in the front, the arms are placed in opposition by raising the L arm in the front, either curved or extended, and extending the R arm to the side or back.

**Ouvert, ouverte** [*oo-VEHR, oo-VEHRT*]. Open, opened. This may refer to positions (the second and fourth positions of the feet are positions ouvertes), limbs, directions, or certain exercises or steps. In the French School the term is used to indicate a position or direction of the body similar to effacé, that is, à la quatrième devant ouvert or effacé devant en l'air.

**Ouvert en arrière** [*oo-VEHR ah na-RYEHR*]. Open backward. A term of the French School. Used to indicate that a step beginning with the R foot is executed in a diagonal direction backward toward the right back corner of the room. Similarly, a step beginning with the L foot will be executed toward the left back corner of the room. Example, chassé ouvert en arrière. See floor plan diagram, p. 125. Same as effacé en arrière.

**Ouvert en avant** [*oo-VEHR ah na-VAHN*]. Open forward. A term of the French School. Used to indicate that a step beginning with the R foot is executed in a diagonal direction forward toward the right front corner of the room. Similarly, a step beginning with the L foot will be executed toward the left front corner of the room. Example: Chassé ouvert en avant. See floor plan diagram, p. 125. Same as effacé en avant.

**Ouverture de jambe** [*oo-vehr-TEWR duh zhahnb*]. Opening of the leg. The ouverture de jambe is a term of the French School; the step resembles the grand rond de jambe en l'air, but whereas the latter is taken slowly and preceded by a développé, the ouverture de jambe is taken from grande quatrième devant or derrière and is done in one quick movement or stroke, either en dedans or en dehors.

**Pas** [*pah*]. Step. A simple step or a compound movement which involves a transfer of weight. Example: pas de bourrée. "Pas" also refers to a dance executed by a soloist (pas seul), a duet (pas de deux), and so on.

**Pas allé** [*pah a-LAY*]. Walking step. This is a simple walking step in which the whole foot is placed on the floor, not the toe first as in pas marché.

**Pas assemblé** [*pah a-sahn-BLAY*]. Assembled step. A basic step of allégro. *See* Assemblé.

**Pas ballotté** [*pah ba-law-TAY*]. Tossed step. *See* Ballotté.

**Pas battus** [*pah ba-TEW*]. Beaten steps. Any step done with a beat is called a pas battu. The pas battus include such steps as assemblé, jeté, ballonné, sissonne, échappé, saut de basque, jeté entrelacé, etc.

**Pas brisé** [*pah bree-ZAY*]. Breaking step. *See* Brisé.

**Pas composé** [*pah kawn-poh-ZAY*]. Compound step. A term of the French School for any of various combinations of steps. *See* Compound step; Enchaînement.

**Pas coupé** [*pah koo-PAY*]. Cutting step. *See* Coupé.

**Pas couru** [*pah koo-REW*]. Running step. Pas couru is a run in any direction and is composed of three or five running steps on the demi-pointes to gain momentum for such steps as grand jeté en avant, grand jeté pas de chat, etc. The demi-plié at the end of the pas couru is emphasized, followed by the step for which it serves as a springboard. The term is also used for a run on point in an unturned-out first position.

**Pas d'action** [*pah dak-SYAWN*]. Dance action. A scene in a ballet that expresses emotion or tells a story by means of mime and dance. Examples of pas d'action are to be found in *Giselle*, Act I, in *Coppélia* and in *The Sleeping Beauty*.

**Pas de basque** [*pah duh bask*]. Basque step. A characteristic step of the national dances of the Basques that has been adapted to ballet use. There are two types of pas de basque; pas de basque glissé, which is done close to the floor, and pas de basque sauté, which is jumped. The step is performed en avant, en arrière and en tournant.

**Pas de basque battu (Cecchetti method)** [*pah duh bask ba-TEW*]. Pas de basque, beaten. Fifth position R foot front. Demi-plié and spring off the L foot, raising the R foot a few inches off the floor, toward corner 1. While the body is in the air, beat the feet (from the base of the calves down) together, R foot front, and simultaneously interchange them. Land on the R foot in demi-plié and immediately close the L foot in demi-plié in the fifth position front.

**Pas de basque en arrière, grand** [*grahn pah duh bask ah na-RYEHR*]. Large pas de basque, traveling backward. To perform this, reverse the movements of grand pas de basque en avant (*q.v.*). It may also be performed eliminating the demi-grand rond de jambe en dedans, in which case the step begins with a jeté de côté at 90 degrees.

**Pas de basque en avant, grand** [*grahn pah duh bask ah na-VAHN*]. Large pas de basque, traveling forward. Fifth position croisé, R foot front. Demi-plié and execute a demi-grand rond de jambe en dehors to the second position at 90 degrees; spring to the right on the R foot, landing in demi-plié, and simultaneously execute a développé croisé devant with the L toe passing the R knee before extending forward at 90 degrees; step on the L demi-pointe croisé en avant and quickly bring the R foot to the fifth position back on demi-pointe, then demi-plié in fifth position croisé.

**Pas de basque en descendant** [*pah duh bask ahn day-sahn-DAHN*]. Pas de basque, coming down (stage). A term of the French School. Same as pas de basque en avant.

**Pas de basque en détournant, grand** [*grahn pah duh bask ahn day-toor-NAHN*]. A term of the French School. Same as grand pas de basque en tournant.

**Pas de basque en remontant** [*pah duh bask ahn ruh-mawn-TAHN*]. Pas de basque, going up (stage). A term of the French School. Same as pas de basque en arrière.

**Pas de basque en tournant** [*pah duh bask ahn toor-NAHN*]. Pas de basque, turning. This is a compound step consisting of a pas de basque en avant turning a half-turn en dedans, followed by a pas de basque en arrière turning a half-turn en dehors, to make one complete turn.

**Pas de basque en tournant, grand** [*grahn pah duh bask ahn toor-NAHN*]. Large pas de basque, turning. This is done like the grand pas de basque (en avant) but the first two movements are done with straight legs. Demi-plié in the fifth position. Execute a demi-grand rond de jambe en dehors at 90 degrees with the R leg, spring upward and execute a demi-grand rond de jambe en dedans at 90 degrees with the L leg. Alight in fondu on the R leg and close the L leg to the fifth position front, turning quickly en dedans on the balls of the feet. Finish in demi-plié in the fifth position R foot front.

**Pas de basque glissé en arrière** [*pah duh bask glee-SAY ah na-RYEHR*]. Pas de basque, gliding backward. To perform this, reverse the movements of pas de basque glissé en avant (*q.v.*). It may also be performed eliminating the demi-rond de jambe en dedans, in which case the step begins with a battement soutenu to the second position.

**Pas de basque glissé en avant** [*pah duh bask glee-SAY ah na-VAHN*]. Pas de basque, gliding forward. Fifth position croisé, R foot front. Demi-plié and slide the R foot croisé devant, pointe tendue, and immediately execute a demi-rond de jambe à terre en dehors; jump on the R foot in demi-plié without getting off the floor and extend the L foot pointe tendue to the second position; glide the L foot through the first position (the Cecchetti method glides through the fifth), allowing the knee to bend, to the fourth position front (croisé); the weight is then taken on the L foot and both knees straighten as the R foot is pointed in croisé derrière; the R foot then executes a coupé dessous or is closed to the fifth position croisé derrière in demi-plié.

**Pas de basque par terre** [*pah duh bask par tehr*]. Pas de basque on the ground. A term of the Russian School. Same as pas de basque glissé (en avant or en arrière).

**Pas de basque sauté en avant** [*pah duh bask soh-TAY ah na-VAHN*]. Pas de basque, jumping forward. This is done in the same manner as the pas de basque glissé en avant, but the legs are raised off the floor and the step is jumped. Execute the demi-rond de jambe en dehors slightly off the floor, then spring to the working foot and step forward to the fourth position croisé. Finish with a coupé dessous or close in the fifth position in demi-plié. *Pas de basque sauté en arrière* is done in the same manner, reversing the directions.

**Pas de basque sur les pointes** [*pah duh bask sewr lay pwent*]. Pas de basque on the points. A term of the Cecchetti method. Stand in the fourth position croisé R foot front, pointe tendue. Execute a demi-rond de jambe en l'air en dehors (demi-hauteur), springing onto the R point. Immediately bring the L foot to the fifth position front sur la pointe. Remaining on the points, turn the body to the right until it returns to the starting position, changing the feet so that the R foot is in front. Lower the heels and demi-plié in the fifth position, or fondu on the L leg, extending the R leg to the fourth position en l'air croisé (demi-hauteur). *See* Tour de basque.

**Pas de batterie** [*pah duh bat-REE*]. Beating steps. A term of the French School. *See* Battu.

**Pas déboîté** [*pah day-bwah-TAY*]. Disjointed step. *See* Déboîté.

**Pas de bourrée** [*pah duh boo-RAY*]. Bourrée step. Pas de bourrée is done dessous, dessus, devant, derrière, en avant, en arrière and en tournant en dedans and en dehors, on the point or demi-pointe.

**Pas de bourrée bateau** [*pah duh boo-RAY ba-TOH*]. Boat-like pas de bourrée. A term of the French School. This is a pas de bourrée en avant taken in an effacé direction and ending with the free foot extended à la demi-hauteur. This is immediately followed by a pas de bourrée en arrière taken in an effacé direction and ending with the free foot extended à la demi-hauteur. *See* Pas de bourrée en arrière; Pas de bourrée en avant.

**Pas de bourrée changé sur les pointes** [*pah duh boo-RAY shahn-ZHAY sewr lay pwent*]. Pas de bourrée, changing, on the toes. A series of quick little steps in place on the points or demi-pointes. Fifth position R foot front. Step on the L point crossed behind the R, take a tiny step on the R point to the right, then step on the L point crossed in front of the R. Repeat starting with the R foot. The step is done alternating sides as rapidly as possible and remaining sur place.

**Pas de bourrée couru** [*pah duh boo-RAY koo-REW*]. Pas de bourrée, running. A term of the French School. This is a progression on the points or demi-pointes by a series of small, even steps with the feet close together. It may be done in all directions or in a circle. Same as pas de bourrée suivi.

**Pas de bourrée couru en cinquième** [*pah duh boo-RAY koo-REW ahn sen-KYEM*]. Pas de bourrée, running, in the fifth position. A term of the French School. This pas de bourrée is done on the points or demi-pointes. The back foot should start the action and remain the leader throughout the duration of the step. Fifth position, R foot front. Take a tiny step to the right on the L point, then close the R point to the fifth position front; step to the right again with the L foot, and so on. When traveling to the left the L foot will be in front and the R foot will lead. This pas de bourrée may be taken in all directions and in a circle. *See* Pas de bourrée suivi.

**Pas de bourrée couru en première** [*pah duh boo-RAY koo-REW ahn pruh-MYEHR*]. Pas de bourrée, running, in the first position. This step travels en avant, en arrière and so on. The feet are in the first position on the points or demi-pointes, without a turn-out, and the step is done traveling with a series of tiny steps closing in the first position.

**Pas de bourrée derrière** [*pah duh boo-RAY deh-RYEHR*]. Pas de bourrée in back. Fifth position R foot front. Demi-plié and dégagé the R foot to the second position en l'air à la demi-hauteur. Bring the R foot to the fifth position back, rising on the demi-pointes, and immediately open the L foot to the second position, stepping on the demi-pointe. Bring the R foot in back of the L and lower both heels to the ground in the fifth position, demi-plié. The dégagé movement of this step may be started from the fifth position front or back.

The following will be an aid in remembering the four common pas de bourrée:

Pas de bourrée dessous: step behind, side, front.
Pas de bourrée dessus: step front, side, behind.
Pas de bourrée devant: step front, side, front.
Pas de bourrée derrière: step behind, side, behind.

All can be commenced with either the front or back foot.

**Pas de bourrée dessous** [*pah duh boo-RAY duh-SOO*]. Pas de bourrée under. Fifth position R foot back. Demi-plié and dégagé the R foot to the second position en l'air à la demi-hauteur. Bring the R foot to the fifth position back, rising on the demi-pointes, and immediately open the L foot to the second position, stepping on the demi-pointe. Bring the R foot in front of the L and lower both heels to the ground, demi-plié. This step may also be done bringing the free foot sur le cou-de-pied or to the knee on each step and finishing with the back foot sur le cou-de-pied. In this case the dégagé to the second position may be omitted. This step may also be done commencing with the R foot in the front. For a memory aid, *see* Pas de bourrée derrière.

**Pas de bourrée dessous en tournant** [*pah duh boo-RAY duh-SOO ahn toor-NAHN*]. Pas de bourrée under, turning. This pas de bourrée is done turning en dehors. Fifth position R foot front or back. Demi-plié and dégagé the R foot to the second position so that the point is a little off the ground. Step on the R demi-pointe in the fifth position back, rising on the L demi-pointe and making a half-turn en dehors to the right. Step on the demi-pointe of the L foot, completing the turn to face front, and demi-plié in the fifth position R foot front. The turn may also be done lifting the free foot sur le cou-de-pied on each step, as: L foot sur le cou-de-pied devant, R foot sur le cou-de-pied devant and finishing with the L foot sur le cou-de-pied derrière. The French School terms this step "pas de bourrée détourné." *See* Pas de bourrée en tournant en dehors.

**Pas de bourrée dessus** [*pah duh boo-RAY duh-SEW*]. Pas de bourrée over. Fifth position R foot front. Demi-plié and dégagé the R foot to the second position en l'air à la demi-hauteur. Bring the R foot to the fifth position front, rising on the demi-pointes, and immediately open the L foot to the second position, stepping on the demi-pointe. Bring the R foot in back of the L in the fifth position and lower both heels to the ground and demi-plié. This step may also be done bringing the free foot sur le cou-de-pied or to the knee on each step and finishing with the front foot sur le cou-de-pied. In this case the dégagé to the second position may be omitted. The step may also be done commencing with the R foot in the back. For a memory aid, *see* Pas de bourrée derrière.

**Pas de bourrée dessus en tournant** [*pah duh boo-RAY duh-SEW ahn toor-NAHN*]. Pas de bourrée over, turning. This pas de bourrée is done turning en dedans. Fifth position R foot back. Demi-plié and dégagé the R foot to the second position so that the point is a little off the ground. Step on the R demi-pointe in the fifth position front, rising on the L demi-pointe and making a half-turn en dedans to the left. Step on the demi-pointe of the L foot, completing the turn to face front, and demi-plié in the fifth position R foot back. The turn may also be done lifting the free foot sur le cou-de-pied on each step, as: L foot sur le cou-de-pied derrière, R foot sur le cou-de-pied derrière and finishing L foot sur le cou-de-pied devant. The French School terms this step "pas de bourrée enveloppé en tournant." *See* Pas de bourrée en tournant en dedans.

**Pas de bourrée détourné** [*pah duh boo-RAY day-toor-NAY*]. A term of the French School. Same as pas de bourrée dessous en tournant.

**Pas de bourrée devant** [*pah duh boo-RAY duh-VAHN*]. Pas de bourrée in front. Fifth position R foot back. Demi-plié and dégagé the R foot to the second position en l'air à la demi-hauteur. Bring the R foot to the fifth position front, rising on the demi-pointes, and immediately open the L foot to the second position, stepping on the demi-pointe. Bring the R foot in front of the L and lower both heels to the ground in the fifth position, demi-plié. The dégagé movement of this step may be started from the fifth position front or back. For a memory aid, *see* Pas de bourrée derrière.

**Pas de bourrée emboîté** [*pah duh boo-RAY ahn-bwah-TAY*]. Pas de bourrée "boxed." A term of the Russian School. *See* Emboîté sur les pointes.

**Pas de bourrée en arrière** [*pah duh boo-RAY ah na-RYEHR*]. Pas de bourrée backward. Fifth position R foot front. Demi-plié and dégagé the R foot to the fourth position front en l'air à la demi-hauteur. Bring the R foot to the fifth position front, rising on the demi-pointes, and immediately open the L foot to the fourth position back, stepping on the demi-pointe. Bring the R foot in front of the L and lower both heels to the floor in the fifth position or extend the L leg à la quatrième derrière à la demi-hauteur. May be taken croisé en arrière or effacé en arrière.

**Pas de bourrée en avant** [*pah duh boo-RAY ah na-VAHN*]. Pas de bourrée forward. Fifth position R foot back. Demi-plié and dégagé the R foot to the fourth position back en l'air à la demi-hauteur. Bring the R foot to the fifth position back, rising on the demi-pointes, and immediately open the L foot to the fourth position front, stepping on the demi-pointe. Bring the R foot in back of the L foot and lower both heels to the ground in demi-plié in the fifth position or extend the L leg forward à la quatrième devant à la demi-hauteur. May be taken croisé en avant or effacé en avant.

**Pas de bourrée en tournant en dedans** [*pah duh boo-RAY ahn toor-NAHN ahn duh-DAHN*]. Pas de bourrée, turning inward. The general construction of this step is the same as the pas de bourrée dessus en tournant.

**Pas de bourrée en tournant en dehors** [*pah duh boo-RAY ahn toor-NAHN ahn duh-AWR*]. Pas de bourrée, turning outward. The general construction of this step is the same as the pas de bourrée dessous en tournant.

**Pas de bourrée enveloppé en tournant** [*pah duh boo-RAY ahn-vuh-law-PAY ahn toor-NAHN*]. Pas de bourrée enveloped, turning. A term of the French School. Same as pas de bourrée dessus en tournant.

**Pas de bourrée jeté en tournant** [*pah duh boo-RAY zhuh-TAY ahn toor-NAHN*]. Pas de bourrée thrown, turning. A compound step consisting of a pas de bourrée dessus en tournant, making three-quarters of a turn, and a jeté en avant, completing the turn.

**Pas de bourrée piqué** [*pah duh boo-RAY pee-KAY*]. Pas de bourrée pricked. The free foot is picked up sharply sur le cou-de-pied or en retiré on each step. Pas de bourrée piqué may be done on the points or demi-pointes, dessous, dessus, en tournant en dedans and en tournant en dehors.

**Pas de bourrée piqué dessous** [*pah duh boo-RAY pee-KAY duh-SOO*]. Pas de bourrée piqué under. Fifth position croisé, R foot front. Fondu on R, raising L foot to retiré derrière. Piqué on the L point or demi-pointe, raising the R foot sharply to retiré devant. Step on the R point or demi-pointe to a small second position, raising the L foot to retiré devant. Coupé dessus on the L foot (croisé) with a good fondu, raising the R foot to retiré derrière. Pas de bourrée piqué may also be finished in the fifth position on the points or demi-pointes.

**Pas de bourrée renversé** [*pah duh boo-RAY rahn-vehr-SAY*]. Pas de bourrée upset. This is a pas de bourrée en tournant en dehors executed with a back-bend. *See* Renversé.

**Pas de bourrée suivi** [*pah duh boo-RAY swee-VEE*]. Pas de bourrée followed or connected. A term of the Russian School. This is a series of very small steps on the points. It may be done in all directions. There are two forms of pas de bourrée suivi, one done in the fifth position and one done in the first position. *See* Pas de bourrée couru en cinquième; Pas de bourrée couru en première.

**Pas de bourrée suivi en tournant** [*pah duh boo-RAY swee-VEE ahn toor-NAHN*]. Pas de bourrée connected, turning. This is a series of very small steps on the points in the fifth position, turning in place.

**Pas de bourrée suivi in fifth position** [*pah duh boo-RAY swee-VEE*]. Fifth position R foot front. Demi-plié and relevé to points. Step on the L point crossed behind the R foot, then close the R foot to the fifth position front; step to the right again on the L foot, and so on. Pas de bourrée suivi in fifth position may be taken in all directions. *See* Pas de bourrée couru en cinquième.

**Pas de bourrée suivi in first position (pas couru)** [*pah duh boo-RAY swee-VEE; pah koo-REW*]. This step is always executed without a turn-out (knees straight forward). It is done traveling forward or backward. *See* Pas de bourrée couru en première.

**Pas de chat, grand** [*grahn pah duh shah*]. Large cat's-step. The step owes its name to the likeness of the movement to a cat's leap. In the Cecchetti method pas de chat is done from fifth to fifth and travels obliquely forward. Fifth position R foot back. Raise the R toe in retiré to the side of the L knee and demi-plié on the L leg; spring upward and to the side on the R foot in a diagonal direction, bringing the L toe to the side of the R knee. The landing is made almost simultaneously; first the R foot lands in demi-plié, followed by the L foot, which closes in the fifth position front, bending the knee. If the pas de chat is petit, the jump is smaller and the free foot is raised sur le cou-de-pied instead of en retiré. *See* Saut de chat.

**Pas de chat, grand (Russian School)** [*grahn pah duh shah*]. This step is started from an auxiliary step such as a glissade or pas couru. After the preliminary step (to the right), the R leg is thrown forward as in grand jeté en avant (body effacé) with the L leg up and back. Quickly bend the R knee, bringing the R foot to the L knee, then land on the R foot in demi-plié and glide the L foot through the first position to the fourth position front in croisé, L leg in demi-plié. This pas de chat requires a long, high jump.

**Pas de chat russe, grand** [*grahn pah duh shah rewss*]. Large Russian pas de chat. Same as grand pas de chat (Russian School).

**Pas de chat (Russian School)** [*pah duh shah*]. In the Russian School, pas de chat is done in a different manner from the Cecchetti method. Fifth position croisé R foot back. Demi-plié and brush the R leg in a half-bent position à la quatrième derrière croisé (demi-hauteur). The L leg follows, being thrown back in a half-bent position in effacé to meet the R leg. There is a moment when both legs are in the air passing each other. The landing is made in demi-plié on the R leg, followed by the L leg, which passes forward into the fourth position croisé, body facing croisé. The L foot may also be closed in the fifth position. There should be a forward movement during the spring and the back should be arched when both feet are in the air.

**Pas de cheval** [*pah duh shuh-VAL*]. Horse's-step. This step is so called because it resembles the movement of a horse pawing the ground. From the fourth position devant pointe tendue, brush the pointed foot inward toward the knee of the supporting leg. Without stopping the movement, execute a développé, finishing pointe tendue à terre in the fourth position devant. The step may also be performed with a hop on the supporting foot as the working leg performs the développé and points on the floor. It is usually performed in a series on alternating feet on the points or demi-pointes.

**Pas de ciseaux** [*pah duh see-ZOH*]. Scissors step. A term of the Russian School. Pas de ciseaux is similar to a cabriole devant, except that the legs do not beat but pass over each other. Fourth position croisé derrière, R foot back, pointe tendue. Demi-plié on the L leg, thrusting the R leg forward in effacé with a grand battement, bending the torso back. Spring off the L, throwing it forward so that it passes the R in the air. The L leg, well extended, is immediately thrown backward through the first position into first arabesque, as the R leg descends in demi-plié.

**Pas de deux** [*pah duh duh*]. Dance for two.

**Pas de deux, grand** [*grahn pah duh duh*]. Grand dance for two. It differs from the simple pas de deux in that it has a definite structure. As a general rule the grand pas de deux falls into five parts: entrée, adage, variation for the danseuse, variation for the danseur, and the coda, in which both dancers dance together.

**Pas dégagé** [*pah day-ga-ZHAY*]. Disengaged or disengaging step. *See* Dégagé.

**Pas d'élévation** [*pah day-lay-va-SYAWN*]. *See* Élévation, pas d'.

**Pas de papillon** [*pah duh pa-pee-YAWN*]. Butterfly step. Same as jeté passé en arrière.

**Pas de poisson** [*pah duh pwah-SAWN*]. Fish step. Same as temps de poisson.

**Pas de polka** [*pah duh pawl-KA*]. Polka step. Fifth position R foot front. Temps levé on the L foot and execute a petit développé à la quatrième devant with the R leg. Step forward on the R foot and place the L foot slightly behind the R, then step forward on the R foot. Repeat on alternate feet. This step may be done sur les demi-pointes or sur les pointes traveling en avant, en arrière or in any direction.

**Pas de quatre** [*pah duh KA-truh*]. A dance for four. The most famous pas de quatre in ballet history took place in London on July 12, 1845, at a command performance for Queen Victoria, when the four greatest ballerinas of the nineteenth century, Marie Taglioni, Carlotta Grisi, Fanny Cerrito and Lucile Grahn, appeared together.

**Pas de trois** [*pah duh trwah*]. A dance for three. Similarly, a pas de cinq is a dance for five people; a pas de six is a dance for six people; etc.

**Pas de valse** [*pah duh valss*]. Waltz step. Done with a graceful swaying of the body with various arm movements. May be done facing or en tournant. The step is like a balancé, but the feet do not cross.

**Pas emboîté** [*pah ahn-bwah-TAY*]. "Boxed" step. *See* Emboîté.

**Pas failli** [*pah fah-YEE*]. Giving-way step. *See* Failli.

**Pas glissé** [*pah glee-SAY*]. Gliding step. Any step that glides on the floor. Example: battement glissé.

**Pas jeté** [*pah zhuh-TAY*]. Thrown or throwing step. *See* Jeté.

**Pas marché** [*pah mar-SHAY*]. Marching step. This is the dignified, classical walk of the ballerina and the premier danseur. The step is commenced with a petit développé R with a strongly arched instep, followed by a fondu on the supporting L leg. Step forward on the R foot in the fourth position croisé so that the toe reaches the ground first, then lower the R heel with the foot slightly turned out, transferring the weight forward. Repeat on alternate feet.

**Passé** [*pa-SAY*]. Passed. This is an auxiliary movement in which the foot of the working leg passes the knee of the supporting leg from one position to another (as, for example, in développé passé en avant) or one leg passes the other in the air (as in jeté passé en avant) or one foot is picked up and passes in back or in front of the supporting leg (as in chassé passé).

**Passé par terre** [*pa-SAY par tehr*]. Passed on the ground. This is an auxiliary movement in which the foot of the working leg is passed from the position pointe tendue in fourth devant to the position pointe tendue in fourth derrière, or vice versa.

**Passe-pied** [*pahss-PYAY*]. This is a term of the French School for a sort of petits jetés finished piqués à terre. Passe-pied is done devant, derrière and de côté on the point or demi-pointe. Fifth position R foot front; demi-plié and jump into the air, at the same time executing a dégagé with the R foot à la demi-hauteur to the fourth position front. Come to the ground on the L foot in demi-plié, pointing the R foot on the ground in the fourth position front. In this position jump into the air, dégagé the L foot to the fourth position front and land on the R foot in demi-plié. The movement is repeated with alternate feet as many times as desired.

**Passer la jambe** [*pa-SAY lah zhahnb*]. Pass the leg. The pointed foot of the extended leg is brought in to pass the side of the supporting knee and is then opened in a développé in the opposite direction or to the second position en l'air.

**Pas seul** [*pah suhl*]. Solo dance.

**Pas sissonne** [*pah see-SAWN*]. Sissonne step. *See* Sissonne.

**Pas tombé** [*pah tawn-BAY*]. Falling step. Pas tombé is used as a preparatory step. It is a movement falling forward or backward on one foot in a demi-plié, transferring the weight of the body. It is used with such steps as développé, ballonné and so on. *See* Sissonne tombée.

**Penché, penchée** [*pahn-SHAY*]. Leaning, inclining. As, for example, in arabesque penchée (*q.v.*).

**Petit, petite** [*puh-TEE, puh-TEET*]. Little, small. As, for example, in petit battement. (To find terms starting with "petit," look up the second word of the term.)

**Pied à demi** [*pyay a duh-MEE*]. Foot at the half. Another name for sur la demi-pointe. *See* Demi-pointes, sur les.

**Pied à pointe** [*pyay a pwent*]. Foot on the point. Another name for sur la pointe. *See* Pointes, sur les.

**Pied à quart** [*pyay a kar*]. Foot on the quarter-point. *See* Positions of the foot on the floor.

**Pied à terre** [*pyay a tehr*]. Foot on the ground. A term of the Cecchetti method for a position of the foot in which the entire base of the foot rests on the ground. *See* Plat, à.

**Pied à trois quarts** [*pyay a trwah kar*]. Foot on the three-quarter point. *See* Positions of the foot on the floor.

**Pied dans la main** [*pyay dahn lah men*]. Foot in the hand. A term of the French School. This is a class exercise done at the barre in which the dancer grasps the sole of the foot or heel from the inner side; the leg is then straightened and carried to the second position in the air, the foot still held with the hand. *See* Détiré.

**Pieds, cinq positions des** [*sen paw-zee-SYAWN day pyay*]. Five positions of the feet. See illustrations, p. 139. There are five basic positions of the feet in classical ballet, and every step or movement is begun and ended in one or another of these positions, which were established by Pierre Beauchamp, maître de ballet of the Académie Royale de Musique et de Danse from 1671 to 1687.

*First position (Première position):* In this position the feet form one line, heels touching one another.

*Second position (Seconde position):* The feet are on the same line but with a distance of about one foot between the heels.

*Third position (Troisième position):* In the third position one foot is in front of the other, heels touching the middle of the other foot.

*Fourth position (Quatrième position):* In the fourth position the placement of the feet is similar to that in the third position, the feet being parallel and separated by the length of one foot. This is the classical fourth position but it may also be done with the feet in the first position, only separated by the space of one foot. The former is known as quatrième position croisée (crossed fourth position), while the latter is called quatrième position ouverte (open fourth position). Today quatrième position croisée is done with the feet placed as in the fifth position, parallel and separated by the length of one foot, instead of the third position.

*Fifth position (Cinquième position):* In the fifth position, Cecchetti method, the feet are crossed so that the first joint of the big toe shows beyond either heel. In the French and Russian Schools the feet are completely crossed so that the heel of the front foot touches the toe of the back foot and vice versa.

**Pieds, positions des, à terre** [*paw-zee-SYAWN day pyay a tehr*]. When the entire base of both feet touches the ground the feet are said to be in a position à terre. All the positions described in the entry "Pieds, cinq positions des" are positions à terre.

**Pieds, positions des, en l'air** [*paw-zee-SYAWN day pyay ahn lehr*]. If either foot is placed in the second or fourth position pointe tendue and raised to the side in the second position or forward or backward in the fourth position so that the leg is at right angles to the hip of the supporting leg, the foot is said to be in the second or fourth position en l'air. Also termed à la hauteur, as in quatrième position à la hauteur.

**Pieds, positions des, en l'air (demi-position)** [*paw-zee-SYAWN day pyay ahn lehr (duh-MEE-paw-zee-SYAWN)*]. When a foot is raised in the second or fourth position to a position halfway between the position à terre and the same position en l'air, it is said to be raised in a position en l'air (demi-position). Also termed demi-hauteur, as in seconde position demi-hauteur.

**Pieds, positions des, pointe tendue** [*paw-zee-SYAWN day pyay pwent tahn-DEW*]. If, in the second or fourth positions, the heel of either foot is raised so that the foot rests on the tip of the toes, the foot is said to be in the second or fourth position pointe tendue. Also termed "piqué à terre."

**Piétiner** [*pyay-tee-NAY*]. To stamp the feet. A term of the French School applied to accented movements sur les pointes.

**Piqué** [*pee-KAY*]. Pricked, pricking. Executed by stepping directly on the point or demi-pointe of the working foot in any desired direction or position with the other foot raised in the air. As, for example, in piqué en arabesque, piqué développé and so on.

**Piqué à terre** [*pee-KAY a tehr*]. Piqué on the ground. This is a term of the French School to denote a position of the foot in the second or fourth position with the heel raised and only the tip of the toes touching the ground, the weight of the body being supported on the other foot. Piqué à terre is done devant, derrière or en seconde. Same as pointe tendue.

**Piqué ballonné** [*pee-KAY ba-law-NAY*]. Bouncing piqué. Stand on the R foot with the L foot sur le cou-de-pied derrière; piqué on the L point behind the R, extending the R foot to the second position at 45 degrees. Demi-plié on the L foot and cut the R foot behind the L calf. Repeat on alternate feet.

**Piqué détourné** [*pee-KAY day-toor-NAY*]. Piqué turned aside. Fifth position, R foot back. Demi-plié and dégagé the R foot to the second position at 45 degrees and step on the R point or demi-pointe; immediately step on the L point or demi-pointe crossed behind in the fifth position and pivot toward the back foot. The turn finishes with the L foot in the fifth position front.

**Piqué en arabesque** [*pee-KAY ah na-ra-BESK*]. Piqué in arabesque. Fifth position R foot front. Demi-plié and dégagé the R leg à la demi-hauteur and step forward directly onto the point of the R foot, raising the L leg in an arabesque position.

**Piqué en arrière** [*pee-KAY ah na-RYEHR*]. Piqué backward. Fifth position R foot back. Demi-plié and raise the R foot en raccourci derrière, or dégagé the R foot à la quatrième derrière demi-hauteur. Step directly onto the point or demi-pointe of the R foot with the L foot sur le cou-de-pied or en raccourci devant.

**Piqué en avant** [*pee-KAY ah na-VAHN*]. Piqué forward. Fifth position R foot front. Demi-plié and raise the R foot en raccourci devant or dégagé the R foot à la quatrième devant, demi-hauteur. Step directly onto the point or demi-pointe of the R foot with the L foot sur le cou-de-pied or en raccourci derrière.

**Piqué enveloppé** [*pee-KAY ahn-vuh-law-PAY*]. Piqué enveloped. A term of the French School. *See* Piqué tour en dehors; Tour dégagé.

**Piquer la pointe** [*pee-KAY lah pwent*]. To prod the toe. The working foot performs a battement dégagé to the second or fourth position, then strikes the floor lightly with the pointed toes. *See* Battement piqué, petit; Battement tendu jeté pointé.

**Piqué sur la pointe** [*pee-KAY sewr la pwent*]. *See* Piqué.

**Piqué tour** [*pee-KAY toor*]. Piqué, turning. This is a pirouette in which the dancer steps directly onto the point or demi-pointe with the raised leg sur le cou-de-pied devant or derrière, in attitude, arabesque or any given position. This turn is executed either en dedans or en dehors (see following entries).

**Piqué tour en dedans** [*pee-KAY toor ahn duh-DAHN*]. Piqué turning inward. Fifth position croisé R foot front; demi-plié and dégagé the R leg to the second position en l'air, demi-hauteur. Step onto the point or demi-pointe of the R foot, turning en dedans to the right with the L foot placed en raccourci derrière or sur le cou-de-pied derrière. After completing the turn, fall on the L foot in demi-plié (coupé dessous) with the R leg sur le cou-de-pied devant or extended in the fourth position en l'air, demi-hauteur. During the turn the L foot may be placed in front of the R leg instead of at the back. The turn may be single or double and may be done in a series traveling diagonally or in a circle. The head "spots."

**Piqué tour en dehors** [*pee-KAY toor ahn duh-AWR*]. Piqué turning outward. Fifth position R foot front; demi-plié and dégagé the L leg to the second position en l'air, demi-hauteur. Bring the L leg in front of the R leg and step directly onto the point or demi-pointe of the L foot, turning en dehors to the right with the R foot placed en raccourci devant or sur le cou-de-pied devant. After completing the turn, fall on the R foot in demi-plié (tombé) with the L leg extended in the second position en l'air, demi-hauteur. The movement is then continued to the same side. The turns may be single or double and the head "spots."

**Pirouette** [*peer-WET*]. Whirl or spin. A complete turn of the body on one foot, on point or demi-pointe. Pirouettes are performed en dedans, turning inward toward the supporting leg, or en dehors, turning outward in the direction of the raised leg. Correct body placement is essential in all kinds of pirouettes. The body must be well centered over the supporting leg with the back held strongly and the hips and shoulders aligned. The force of momentum is furnished by the arms, which remain immobile during the turn. The head is the last to move as the body turns away from the spectator and the first to arrive as the body comes around to the spectator, with the eyes focused at a definite point which must be at eye level. This use of the eyes while turning is called "spotting." Pirouettes may be performed in any given position, such as sur le cou-de-pied, en attitude, en arabesque, à la seconde, etc.

**Pirouette, grande** [*grahnd peer-WET*]. Large pirouette. This is a series of turns on one foot with the raised leg held in the second position en l'air, in attitude or arabesque, or in a combination of poses. The body turns en dehors and a relevé is made on the supporting foot with each turn. The series may also include small hopping turns in which the dancer pivots on the ball of the foot while quickly shifting the heel with tiny, sharp movements. The grande pirouette is concluded with multiple turns sur le cou-de-pied. It is usually performed to 16 or 32 measures of a galop. *See* Pirouette à la seconde, grande; Pirouette sautillée, grande.

**Pirouette, supported** [(supported) *peer-WET*]. This is a pirouette in which the dancer is supported and steadied by her male partner as she turns. There are several kinds of supported pirouettes, such as pirouettes en dehors, fouettés ronds de jambe en tournant (finger turns), pirouettes en dedans taken from a preparation enveloppé, and so on.

**Pirouette à la seconde, grande** [*grahnd peer-WET a lah suh-GAWND*]. Large pirouette in the second position. This pirouette is usually performed by male dancers. It is a series of turns on one foot with the free leg raised to the second position en l'air at 90 degrees. Demi-plié in the second position (R arm curved in front of the body, L arm in second); spring onto the L demi-pointe, throwing the R leg to the second position and turning en dehors. At the completion of the first turn, the supporting heel is lowered in demi-plié, then immediately pushes from the floor to demi-pointe, and the turn is repeated. After a series of 8 or 16 turns, grande pirouette is usually concluded with multiple pirouettes sur le cou-de-pied. The force for the first turn is taken by the R arm, which opens to the second position. The arms remain in the second position during the series of turns, then close in the first position for the concluding pirouettes. The head turns and the eyes "spot," providing additional force for the turns.

**Pirouette en arabesque** [*peer-WET ah na-ra-BESK*]. Pirouette in arabesque.
*En dedans:* Fourth position croisé R foot front with the weight on the R leg, which is in demi-plié. The R arm is curved in front of the body and the L arm is held in the second position. Push off with both heels (the L leg remains stretched) and relevé on the R foot, turning the body to face the right wall, at which time the first arabesque position is taken. One or two turns are executed, with the R arm providing the force. The eyes follow the R hand.
*En dehors:* Fourth position croisé R foot back. The L arm is extended to the second position, R arm curved in front of the body or extended forward. The center of weight is on the L leg with the R leg stretched in back. Push off with both heels (the R leg remains stretched) and relevé on the L leg, raising the R leg to the third Russian arabesque, and make a complete turn to the right. The L arm and hand give a push to the right while remaining in the arabesque position. The head remains immobile, with the eyes following the R hand.

**Pirouette en attitude** [*peer-WET ah na-tee-TEWD*]. Pirouette in attitude.

The turn is performed either en dedans or en dehors and the preparation is taken from the fourth position.

*En dedans:* Fourth position croisé R foot front; weight on the R leg, which is in demi-plié; L arm held in the second position, R arm curved in front of the waist. Push off with both heels and relevé on the R foot, establishing the pose attitude effacée immediately, then turn one or more turns to the right. The force is taken with the R arm, which is thrust to the side while the L arm swings above the head in the line of vision. The head does not "spot."

*En dehors:* Fourth position croisé R foot back, R arm extended forward (or curved in front of the waist), L arm extended to the side. Demi-plié and push off with both heels into a relevé on the L foot, establishing the pose attitude croisée derrière immediately, then turn one or more turns to the right. The head does not "spot."

**Pirouette en dedans** [*peer-WET ahn duh-DAHN*]. Pirouette, turning inward. The body turns toward the supporting leg; that is, if the turn is made on the right foot, the dancer will turn to the right. *See* Pirouette sur le cou-de-pied.

**Pirouette en dehors** [*peer-WET ahn duh-AWR*]. Pirouette, turning outward. The body turns toward the raised foot; that is, if the turn is made on the right foot, the dancer will turn to the left. *See* Pirouette sur le cou-de-pied.

**Pirouette from a grand plié** [*peer-WET; grahn plee-AY*]. This turn is used in adagio exercises in the classroom. When the extreme point of the plié is reached, the leg upon which the pirouette is to be done should be immediately extended and the desired number of turns executed on the demi-pointe, with the free foot sur le cou-de-pied. The turn is done en dedans or en dehors.

**Pirouette piquée** [*peer-WET pee-KAY*]. Pricked pirouette. A term of the French School. Same as piqué tour en dedans.

**Pirouette renversé** [*peer-WET rahn-vehr-SAY*]. Pirouette upset. This pirouette is performed en dedans with the raised leg held in retiré devant. Execute one or two pirouettes in this position, then, at the beginning of the last turn, bend the body to the side of the raised leg; at the end of the turn, bend the body forcefully to the side of the supporting leg, while throwing the raised leg in a développé à la seconde. *See* Renversé en écarté.

**Pirouette sautillée, grande** [*grahnd peer-WET soh-tee-YAY*]. Large hopping pirouette. A term of the Russian School. This pirouette is done with the supporting leg in demi-plié while turning en dehors with tiny hops on the whole foot, the heel barely leaving the floor. The working leg is held in the second position en l'air at 90 degrees.

**Pirouette sur le cou-de-pied** [*peer-WET sewr luh koo-duh-PYAY*]. Pirouette on the ankle. This is a complete turn of the body on point or demi-pointe with the free foot raised sur le cou-de-pied devant or retiré devant. The higher position with the foot pointed in front of the knee is usually used by girls, while boys usually keep the foot sur le cou-de-pied. The turn is done either en dedans or en dehors and may be single, double, triple, etc. The preparation for the turn is taken from the fifth, fourth or second position. As a rule, all pirouettes en dedans finish in front of the supporting leg, while all pirouettes en dehors finish behind the supporting leg.

*En dehors (from the fifth position):* Demi-plié in the fifth position R foot front with the R arm curved in front of the body and the L arm in the second position. Push off with both heels, relevé on the L foot with the R foot sur le cou-de-pied devant and make a complete turn to the right. The force for the turn is provided by the L arm, which comes in to meet the R arm in front of the waist. After one or more turns, finish in demi-plié in the fifth position R foot back, opening the arms slightly forward of the second position. The knees are then straightened.

*En dedans (from the fifth position):* Demi-plié in the fifth position R foot front with the R arm curved in front of the body and the L arm in the second position. Push off with both heels, relevé on the R foot and immediately bring the L foot sur le cou-de-pied devant, making a complete turn to the right. The force is provided by the L arm, which comes in to meet the R arm in front of the waist. After one or more turns, finish in demi-plié in the fifth position L foot front, opening the arms slightly forward of the second position.

*En dehors (from the fourth position):* There are two accepted stances for a pirouette en dehors from the fourth position. In one, both knees are bent in demi-plié with the weight equally distributed on both feet, while in the other the front knee is bent in demi-plié with the back leg stretched, the whole foot on the floor and the center of weight on the front leg. In the Russian School, the preparation with the weight on the forward leg is preferred. Fourth position croisé L foot front, R arm curved in front of the body and the L arm in the second position. Demi-plié on both legs, push off with both heels and relevé on the L foot, raising the R foot sur le cou-de-pied devant while making a complete turn to the right. The force for the turn is provided by the L arm, which comes in to meet the R arm in front of the waist. After one or more turns, finish in demi-plié in either the fourth or fifth position croisé, R foot back. The arms open slightly forward of the second position. If the pirouette is taken from the lunge position with the weight on the forward leg, the R arm is stretched forward and the L arm is held in the second position with both palms down. A quick demi-plié is taken on both feet with the center of weight over the front foot. The force for the turn is provided by the L arm.

*En dedans (from the fourth position):* Fourth position croisé R foot front with the weight on the R leg and the L leg stretched back with the whole foot on the floor. The R arm is curved in front of the body and the L arm is in the second position. Raise the back leg slightly and carry it to the second position en l'air at 45 degrees and open the R arm to the second position; immediately relevé on the R foot, bring the L foot sur le cou-de-pied devant and make a complete turn to the right. The L arm provides the force and both arms meet in front of the waist. Finish in demi-plié in the fifth position croisé L foot front.

In the Russian School when this turn is done on point, the working foot is brought directly to sur le cou-de-pied devant on the relevé.

*En dehors (from the second position):* This preparation is usually used by male dancers. Demi-plié in the second position with the R arm curved in front of the body and the L arm in the second position; push off with both heels and spring on the L demi-pointe, raising the R foot sur le cou-de-pied devant and making a complete turn to the right. The force for the turn is provided by the L arm, which comes in to meet the right in front of the waist. After one or more turns, finish in demi-plié in the fifth position R foot back. The arms open to slightly forward of the second position.

*En dedans (from the second position):* This is done in the same manner but the turn is done to the right on the R leg. Finish in demi-plié in the fifth position L foot front.

**Pistolet** [*peess-taw-LAY*]. "Pistol." Same as ailes de pigeon.

**Placé** [*pla-SAY*]. Placed. A term to describe the correct placing of the dancer's body, arms, legs and head in any of the dancing positions either à terre or en l'air.

**Place, sur** [*sewr plahss*]. In place. Term used to indicate that the dancer, in executing a step, stays in one spot—in other words, does not travel in any direction.

**Placement, placing.** A dancer is said to be well-placed when he or she has learned to hold body, head, arms and legs in their proper alignment to each other, has acquired the turn-out of the legs, a well-poised head, level hips and a stright spine in all steps and poses.

**Plané** [*pla-NAY*]. Soaring. As, for example, in temps plané. This term applies to such steps as the temps de poisson, in which the dancer tries to remain stationary in mid-air for a moment.

**Plat, à** [*a pla*]. On the flat. A term of the French School to denote that the entire sole of the foot rests flat on the floor. *See* Pied à terre.

**Plié** [*plee-AY*]. Bent, bending. A bending of the knee or knees. This is an exercise to render the joints and muscles soft and pliable and the tendons flexible and elastic, and to develop a sense of balance. There are two principal pliés: grand plié or full bending of the knees (the knees should be bent until the thighs are horizontal) and demi-plié or half-bending of the knees. Pliés are done at the bar and in the centre in all five positions of the feet. The third position is usually omitted. When a grand plié is executed in either the first, third or fourth position croisé (feet in the fifth position but separated by the space of one foot) or the fifth position, the heels always rise off the ground and are lowered again as the knees straighten. The bending movement should be gradual and free from jerks, and the knees should be at least half-bent before the heels are allowed to rise. The body should rise at the same speed at which it descended, pressing the heels into the floor. In the grand plié in the second position or the fourth position ouverte (feet in the first position but separated by the space of one foot) the heels do not rise off the ground. All demi-pliés are done without lifting the heels from the ground. In all pliés the legs must be well turned out from the hips, the knees open and well over the toes, and the weight of the body evenly distributed on both feet, with the whole foot grasping the floor.

**Plier** [*plee-AY*]. To bend. One of the seven movements in dancing.

**Pointes, sur les** [*sewr lay pwent*]. On the points. The raising of the body on the tips of the toes. Also used in the singular, "sur la pointe." First introduced in the late 1820s or early 1830s at the time of Taglioni. There are three ways of reaching the points, by piqué, relevé or sauté.

**Pointes, temps de** [*tahn duh pwent*]. See Temps de pointes.

**Pointe shoes.** The satin ballet shoes used by dancers when dancing sur les pointes. The ballet shoes of Marie Taglioni, the first major ballerina to dance on her points, were not blocked but were padded with cotton wool. Later (about 1862) the toes of the ballet slippers were stiffened (blocked) with glue and darned to give the dancer additional support. Today the toes of pointe shoes are reinforced with a box constructed of several layers of strong glue in between layers of material. Professional dancers usually darn the tip of the pointe shoe to obtain a better grip of the shoe on the floor and thus prevent slipping.

**Pointe tendue** [*pwent tahn-DEW*]. Point stretched. When the leg is extended with the heel raised and the instep forced outward so that only the tip of the toes rests on the floor, the position is said to be pointe tendue. See Dégagé; Piqué à terre.

**Poisson** [*pwa-SAWN*]. Fish. A position of the body in which the legs are crossed in the fifth position and held tightly together with the back arched. This pose is taken while jumping into the air or in double work when the danseuse is supported in a poisson position by her partner. See Fish dive; Temps de poisson.

**Polka.** A dance in 2/4 time which was first danced in Bohemia in the 1830s. It later spread from Prague throughout Europe and over into America. It became the national dance of the Czechs.

**Polka-mazurka.** A Polish dance in 3/4 time derived from the polka and from the mazurka.

**Polonaise.** A processional dance in 3/4 time with which the court ballets of the seventeenth century were opened. It may be seen today in such ballets as *The Sleeping Beauty* and *Swan Lake*. The polonaise is a march in which two steps are taken forward on the demi-pointes and then the third step is taken flat with the supporting knee bent in fondu and the other leg raised in front.

**Port de bras** [*pawr duh brah*]. Carriage of the arms. The term port de bras has two meanings: (1) A movement or series of movements made by passing the arm or arms through various positions. The passage of the arms from one position to another constitutes a port de bras. (2) A term for a group of exercises designed to make the arms move gracefully and harmoniously. In the Cecchetti method there are eight set exercises on port de bras.

In the execution of port de bras the arms should move from the shoulder and not from the elbow and the movement should be smooth and flowing. The arms should be softly rounded so that the points of the elbows are imperceptible and the hands must be simple, graceful and never flowery. The body and head should come into play and a suggestion of épaulement should be used. In raising the arms from one position to another the arms must pass through a position known in dancing as the gateway. This position corresponds to the fifth position en avant, Cecchetti method, or the first position, French and Russian Schools. In passing from a high position to a low one, the arms are generally lowered in a line with the sides. Exercises on port de bras can be varied to infinity by combining their basic elements according to the taste of the professor and the needs of the pupil.

**Port de bras, grand** [*grahn pawr duh brah*]. Large port de bras. This is a circular movement of the arms combined with cambré. There are several varieties of grand port de bras, of which the following is an example: Stand on the R foot in attitude croisée à terre. Lower the L toe to demi-pointe and demi-plié on both legs, bending the body and head forward. The rounded L arm almost touches the floor and the R arm is carried downward to meet the L arm. Lower the L heel to the floor and transfer the weight to the L foot, then rise upward with a circular movement to the left. The torso, head and arms swing to the left, then the body bends back and the R arm is raised above the head and the L arm extended to the side, R foot pointed forward. The body is then straightened and the circular movement completed by moving the R arm to the second position and the L arm above the head, head and torso inclined to the right. The dancer then does a demi-plié in the fourth position, lowering the arms to the fifth position en bas. The knees are then straightened and the dancer stands on the R foot in attitude croisée à terre.

**Porté, portée** [*pawr-TAY*]. Carried. Refers either to a step which is traveled in the air from one spot to another (such as assemblé dessus porté) or to the carrying of a danseuse by a danseur.

**Porteur** [*pawr-TUHR*]. Carrier. A term used during the latter half of the nineteenth century for a male ballet performer who did no dancing, but whose sole function was to support and lift the ballerina in various poses and leaps.

**Pose** [*pohz*]. Pose, posture. Any position held for any length of time such as an attitude or arabesque.

**Posé** [*poh-ZAY*]. Poised. A term of the Cecchetti method. This is a movement in which the dancer steps from one foot to the other with a petit développé onto the demi-pointe or point in any desired position. It is preceded by a fondu on the supporting leg and may be performed en avant, en arrière and de côté, in arabesque, in attitude, etc. *See* Piqué.

**Posé en tournant** [*poh-ZAY ahn toor-NAHN*]. Poised, turning. A term of the Cecchetti method. Same as piqué tour.

**Poser** [*poh-ZAY*]. To place. To place the foot on the ground. May be done en avant, en arrière, de côté, devant and derrière.

**Poser derrière** [*poh-ZAY deh-RYEHR*]. To place behind. To bring one foot in back of the other in the third or fifth position à terre.

**Poser devant** [*poh-ZAY duh-VAHN*]. To place in front. To bring one foot in front of the other in the third or the fifth position à terre.

**Position fermée** [*paw-zee-SYAWN fehr-MAY*]. Closed position. A position in which the feet touch each other. The first, third and fifth positions of the feet are positions fermées. *See* Fermé.

**Position ouverte** [*paw-zee-SYAWN oo-VEHRT*]. Open position. A position in which the feet are separated. The second and fourth positions of the feet are positions ouvertes. *See* Ouvert.

**Positions of the arms.** *See* Bras, positions des.

**Positions of the body, basic, Cecchetti method** (see illustration, p. 134). There are eight positions of the body in the Cecchetti method. These positions are in themselves a study in line and perspective and their precepts should be applied to other movements in dancing: (1) Croisé devant (crossed in front). (2) À la quatrième devant (to the fourth front). (3) Écarté (thrown wide apart, separated). (4) Effacé (shaded). (5) À la seconde (to the second). (6) Épaulé (shouldered). (7) À la quatrième derrière (to the fourth back). (8) Croisé derrière (crossed in back).

**Positions of the body, basic, Russian and French Schools** (see illustration, p. 136). In the Russian and French Schools there are eleven basic positions of the body. All these positions may be taken à terre or en l'air. They are as follows:
    (1) Croisé devant.   (2) Croisé derrière.
    (3) À la quatrième devant.   (4) À la quatrième derrière.
    (5) Écarté devant.   (6) Écarté derrière.
    (7) Effacé devant.   (8) Effacé derrière.
    (9) À la seconde.
    (10) Épaulé devant.   (11) Épaulé derrière.

**Positions of the foot on the floor.** There are five levels at which the foot may be placed on the floor. (1) Pied à terre, or foot on the ground. The entire sole of the foot rests on the ground. *See* Plat, à. (2) Pied à quart, or foot on the quarter-point. The heel is barely raised off the floor. (3) Pied à demi, or foot on the half-point. The dancer stands with the weight on the ball of the foot with the heel raised off the floor. (4) Pied à trois quarts, or foot on the three-quarter point. The dancer stands with the weight high on the ball of the foot and on the toes with the heel raised off the floor. (5) Sur la pointe, or on the full point. The dancer stands on the tips of the toes.

**Positions of the feet.** *See* Pieds, cinq positions des.

**Positions of the hand (Cecchetti method).** In the Cecchetti method there are three positions of the hand which are used during the exercises at the bar, the exercises in the centre and in arabesque.

(1) The position of the hand at the bar: The first and fourth fingers are somewhat curved while the second and third are held together and curved, so that the thumb rests on the first joint of the second finger and touches the inside first joint of the first finger. The wrist is curved inward and bent slightly downward to give a curved line of the arm from the shoulder to the fingertips. When this position is assumed during the initial exercises, the pupil learns to hold the fingers in a soft, natural manner and eliminates a common tendency of beginners to spread their fingers.

(2) The position of the hand during the exercises in the centre: The hand is held as above but with the second and third fingers less curved, so that all four fingers are open but not spread.

(3) The position of the hand in arabesque: The hand is held as in (2) but with the palm turned down and the wrist bent, so that the hand is turned in an outward direction from the wrist.

**Positions of the head (Cecchetti method).** In the Cecchetti method there are five principal positions of the head: (1) Head erect. (2) Head inclined to one side; this can be done to either side. (3) Head turned to one side; this can be either side. (4) Head raised. (5) Head lowered.

**Positions of the leg in the air.** *See* Angle of the leg in the air; Positions soulevées.

**Positions soulevées** [*paw-zee-SYAWN sool-VAY*]. Raised positions. This is a term of the French School and refers to the positions of the feet: pointe tendue and en l'air. The positions soulevées are as follows: From second position: piqué à terre, à la demi-hauteur, à la hauteur. From the fourth position: devant or derrière, piqué à terre, à la demi-hauteur, à la hauteur. These positions are taken en face, croisé or ouvert (effacé). *See* Pieds, positions des, en l'air; Pieds, positions des, pointe tendue.

**Premier, première** [*pruh-MYAY, pruh-MYEHR*]. First.

**Première, en** [*ahn pruh-MYEHR*]. In or through the first position.

**Préparation** [*pray-pay-ra-SYAWN*]. Preparation. The movement with which the dancer prepares for the execution of a step or turn.

**Promenade, en** [*ahn prawm-NAD*]. In a walk.

**Promenade, tour de** [*toor duh prawm-NAD*]. Turn in a walk. A term of the French School used to indicate that the dancer turns slowly in place on one foot by a series of slight movements of the heel to the required side while maintaining a definite pose such as an arabesque or attitude. The turn may be performed either en dedans or en dehors. In a pas de deux, the ballerina on point holds her pose and is slowly turned by her partner who walks around her holding her hand. *See* Tour lent.


**Quadrille** [*ka-DREE-yuh*]. (1) A French square dance of the early nineteenth century performed by two or four couples. (2) A division in the ranks of dancers in the Paris Opéra ballet (two of the lowest ranks being the premiers quadrilles and the seconds quadrilles). *See* Cadre; Défilé.

**Quarré (carré), en** [*ahn ka-RAY*]. In the shape of a square. Steps or exercises executed in a square formation, delineating three or four sides of a square.

**Quart** [*kar*]. Quarter, fourth part. As, for example, in un quart de tour.

**Quatre** [*KA-truh*]. Four.

**Quatrième** [*ka-tree-EM*]. Fourth.

**Quatrième croisée derrière** [*ka-tree-EM krwah-ZAY deh-RYEHR*]. A term of the French School. Same as croisé derrière.

**Quatrième croisée devant** [*ka-tree-EM krwah-ZAY duh-VAHN*]. A term of the French School. Same as croisé devant.

**Quatrième derrière, à la** [*a lah ka-tree-EM deh-RYEHR*]. To the fourth position back. A term implying that the foot is to be placed in the fourth position back à terre, or that a movement is to be made to the fourth position back en l'air. The position à la quatrième derrière is one of the eight directions of the body, Cecchetti method, in which the dancer stands facing the audience, the arms in the second position and either foot pointed in the fourth position back à terre or raised to the fourth position back en l'air. See illustration, p. 135.

**Quatrième derrière, grande** [*grahnd ka-tree-EM deh-RYEHR*]. Large fourth back. The fourth position back en l'air.

**Quatrième devant, à la** [*a lah ka-tree-EM duh-VAHN*]. To the fourth position front. A term implying that the foot is to be placed in the fourth position front à terre, or that a movement is to be made to the fourth position front en l'air. The position à la quatrième devant is one of the eight directions of the body, Cecchetti method, in which the dancer stands facing the audience, the arms in the second position and either foot pointed in the fourth position front à terre or raised to the fourth position front en l'air. See illustration, p. 134.

**Quatrième devant, grande** [*grahnd ka-tree-EM duh-VAHN*]. Large fourth front. The fourth position front en l'air.

**Quatrième ouverte derrière** [*ka-tree-EM oo-VEHRT deh-RYEHR*]. Open fourth position back. A term of the French School. Same as effacé derrière (Russian School).

**Quatrième ouverte devant** [*ka-tree-EM oo-VEHRT duh-VAHN*]. Open fourth position front. A term of the French School. Same as effacé devant (Russian School).

**Raccourci** [*ra-koor-SEE*]. Shortened. A term of the French School. (1) A position in which the thigh is raised to the second position en l'air, with the knee bent so that the pointed toe rests against the knee of the supporting leg. *See* Retiré. (2) A sharp bending movement of the knee, as in battement raccourci.

**Raccourci derrière** [*ra-koor-SEE deh-RYEHR*]. Shortened in back. A term of the French School. The pointed toe of the working foot is placed behind the supporting knee. *See* Retiré derrière.

**Raccourci devant** [*ra-koor-SEE duh-VAHN*]. Shortened in front. A term of the French School. The pointed toe of the working foot is placed in front of the supporting knee. *See* Retiré devant.

**Ramassé, ramassée** [*rà-ma-SAY*]. Picked up. As, for example, in entrechat cinq ramassé.

**Rat** [*ra*]. This is a slang term for a child dance student at the Paris Opéra. The term, coined early in the nineteenth century, was derived from the children's appearance: always in movement, with lean faces, and incessantly nibbling at food. The "petits rats" are the lowest rank of dancers in the cadre of the Paris Opéra ballet. *See* Défilé.

**Rebours, à** [*a ruh-BOOR*]. In reverse. Indicates that the direction of a step is to be reversed.

**Reculant, en** [*ahn ruh-kew-LAHN*]. Drawing back. A term of the French School implying that the working leg passes from front to back. As, for example, in assemblé en reculant.

**Régisseur** [*ray-zhee-SUHR*]. The stage manager of a ballet company. The régisseur restages and rehearses all the ballets in a company's repertoire.

**Relevé** [*ruhl-VAY*]. Raised. A raising of the body on the points or demi-pointes, point or demi-pointe. There are two ways to relevé. In the French School, relevé is done with a smooth, continuous rise while the Cecchetti method and the Russian School use a little spring. Relevé may be done in the first, second, fourth or fifth position, en attitude, en arabesque, devant, derrière, en tournant, passé en avant, passé en arrière and so on. Occasionally the term may refer to a lowering of the working foot from a position pointe tendue to the ground and re-raising it to the position pointe tendue, as in battement tendu relevé. In the Russian School the term relevé is also used to mean the slow raising of the stretched leg to 90° in any direction. *See* Battement relevé lent.

**Relevé (Cecchetti method)** [*ruhl-VAY*]. This is done with a slight spring from a demi-plié onto the three-quarter points or full points. During the spring, the toes are brought directly under the central line of balance or roughly to the same spot over which the insteps rested during the preparatory demi-plié.

**Relevé (French School)** [*ruhl-VAY*]. This is done with a smooth rise from a position à terre to the full points. The toes do not move from the spot at which the relevé began. The heels are then lowered by slowly descending through the demi-pointes. *See* Rise.

**Relevé (Russian School)** [*ruhl-VAY*]. This is done in the manner of the Cecchetti method and is termed "temps levé sur les pointes."

**Relevé d'adage de face en dedans** [*ruhl-VAY da-DAHZH duh fahss ahn duh-DAHN*]. Relevé of adage inward, facing forward. A term of the French School. Bring the R foot en raccourci derrière; demi-plié on the L foot, carrying the R leg backward to grande quatrième derrière.

Without stopping after the développé, immediately carry the R leg to grande seconde while the L foot rises sur la demi-pointe.

**Relevé d'adage de face en dehors** [*ruhl-VAY da-DAHZH duh fahss $\overline{ahn}$ duh-AWR*]. Relevé of adage outward, facing forward. A term of the French School. Fifth position R foot front. Bring the R foot en raccourci devant; demi-plié on the L foot, carrying the R leg forward to grande quatrième devant. Immediately carry the R leg to grande seconde while the L foot rises sur la demi-pointe.

**Relevé d'adage par quart de tour** [*ruhl-VAY da-DAHZH par kar duh toor*]. Relevé of adage by quarter-turns. A term of the French School. This exercise is done the same way as relevé d'adage de face but with a quarter-turn on the demi-pointe. The movement is done four times, turning a quarter-turn each time, so that a complete turn is made either en dehors or en dedans. The exercise may also be done with a half-turn or a full turn on each relevé.

**Relevé derrière** [*ruhl-VAY deh-RYEHR*]. Relevé in back. Fifth position R foot back. Demi-plié and spring onto the point or demi-pointe of the L foot, raising the R foot sur le cou-de-pied derrière or in retiré derrière. With a slight spring, lower both heels to the ground simultaneously in demi-plié in the fifth position R foot back. Relevé derrière may also be taken off one foot if the other is already raised.

**Relevé devant** [*ruhl-VAY duh-$\overline{VAHN}$*]. Relevé in front. Fifth position R foot front. Demi-plié, spring onto the point or demi-pointe of the L foot, raising the R foot sur le cou-de-pied devant or in retiré devant. With a slight spring, lower both heels to the ground simultaneously in demi-plié in the fifth position, R foot front. Relevé devant may be taken off one foot if the other is already raised. This step is also termed "sissonne simple sur la pointe" (Russian School).

**Relevé en arabesque** [*ruhl-VAY ah na-ra-BESK*]. Relevé in arabesque. A raising of the body sur la pointe or demi-pointe in an arabesque position. Stand in an arabesque position on the R foot. Demi-plié on the R leg and with a slight spring rise on the R point or demi-pointe, holding the arabesque position. With a slight spring lower the R heel to the ground with a demi-plié and continue the movement. Relevé in arabesque may start from the fifth position: demi-plié and with a slight spring (sissonne) rise on the R point or demi-pointe, turning the body and raising the L leg into an arabesque position. Lower the R heel to the ground in demi-plié, still holding the arabesque. The Russian School terms this "sissonne en arabesque sur la pointe."

**Relevé lent** [*ruhl-VAY $\overline{lahn}$*]. Slow raising. A term of the Russian School. *See* Battement relevé lent.

**Relevé passé en arrière** [*ruhl-VAY pa-SAY ah na-RYEHR*]. Relevé passed backward. Fifth position R foot front. Demi-plié and with a spring rise on the L point, raising the R foot in retiré devant. With a slight spring, lower both heels to the ground simultaneously in demi-plié in the fifth position R foot back.

**Relevé passé en avant** [*ruhl-VAY pa-SAY ah na-$\overline{VAHN}$*]. Relevé passed forward. Fifth position R foot back. Demi-plié and with a spring rise on the L point, raising the R foot in retiré derrière. With a slight spring, lower both heels to the ground simultaneously in demi-plié in the fifth position R foot front.

**Relever** [*ruhl-VAY*]. To raise, to lift. One of the seven movements in dancing.

**Relevé sur les pointes or demi-pointes (Cecchetti method)** [*ruhl-VAY sewr lay pwent* (or) *duh-mee-PWENT*]. Relevé on the points or half-points. Start in the first, second, fourth or fifth position. Demi-plié and with a slight spring, pushing off with the heels, rise on the points or demi-pointes; then with a slight spring lower the heels to the floor in the starting position in demi-plié. If the relevé is done in the fifth position the feet must be tightly closed at the moment of rising so that they give the impression of one foot. *See* Relevé (Cecchetti method); Sous-sus; Temps de cou-de-pied; Temps levé sur les pointes.

**Relevé sur les pointes or demi-pointes (French School)** [*ruhl-VAY sewr lay pwent* (or) *duh-mee-PWENT*]. In the French School, relevé is done by rising smoothly with a continuous movement onto the demi-pointes or full points and descending smoothly until the heels are lowered in the starting position. *See* Relevé (French School).

**Remontant, en** [*ahn ruh-mawn-TAHN*]. Going up. A term of the French School, generally applied to a traveling step. The working foot passes from front to back so that the dancer moves upstage. The opposite of en remontant is en descendant (*q.v*).

**Renversé, renversée** [*rahn-vehr-SAY*]. Upset, reversed. Of Spanish origin, this is the bending of the body during a turn in which the normal balance is upset but not the equilibrium. It applies to only three steps: a pirouette, a pas de bourrée en tournant and a détourné. The body bends from the waist, sideways and backward, the head following the movement of the body. Renversé may be performed en dehors and en dedans with either a relevé or a temps levé on the supporting foot. There are several varieties of renversé when performed en dehors. For renversé en dedans, *see* Pirouette renversée; Renversé en écarté.

**Renversé en dehors** [*rahn-vehr-SAY ahn duh-AWR*]. Renversé turning outward. This step consists of a grand rond de jambe en dehors ending in attitude croisée, then a pas de bourrée dessous en tournant with a renversé movement of the body. Fifth position croisé, R foot front. Step R croisé en avant into a demi-plié on R, raising the L foot sur le cou-de-pied derrière, bending the torso and head to the right (L arm second position, R arm curved in front of body). Immediately coupé dessous L (L arm curved in front of body, R arm second); relevé L, executing a grand rond de jambe en dehors, finishing in attitude croisée derrière (arms open to second position, then the R arm moves above the head and the L arm is curved in front of the body); fondu L, bending the torso to the left and back, forcing the legs to execute a pas de bourrée dessous en tournant (R arm moves downward to meet the L in the fifth position en bas) ending on the R foot with the torso and head bent to the right. The first two movements are done slowly with the pose in attitude held a moment, then a quick back-bend in pas de bourrée. Renversé en dehors may be performed sauté instead of relevé. There are various other preparatory steps, such as failli or coupé dessus, which may lead into renversé.

**Renversé en écarté** [*rahn-vehr-SAY ah nay-kar-TAY*]. Renversé thrown wide apart. Stand on the L leg in fourth Russian arabesque. Demi-plié and relevé on the L foot, bringing the R foot en tire-bouchon. At the same time the upper body bends forcefully to the right toward the raised knee. The body turns en dedans, then bends back. At the completion of the turn the L heel is placed firmly on the floor while the R leg immediately opens in the pose écarté derrière. *See* Pirouette renversée.

**Répéter** [*ray-pay-TAY*]. To rehearse or practice.

**Répétition** [*ray-pay-tee-SYAWN*]. Rehearsal.

**Répétition générale** [*ray-pay-tee-SYAWN zhay-nay-RAL*]. A term of the French School for dress rehearsal (usually attended by the press and an invited audience).

**Retiré** [*ruh-tee-RAY*]. Withdrawn. A position in which the thigh is raised to the second position en l'air with the knee bent so that the pointed toe rests in front of, behind or to the side of the supporting knee. *See* Raccourci.

**Retiré, battement** [*bat-MAHN ruh-tee-RAY*]. *See* Battement retiré.

**Retiré de côté** [*ruh-tee-RAY duh koh-TAY*]. Withdrawn to the side. The thigh is raised to the second position en l'air with the knee bent so that the pointed toe touches the side of the supporting knee.

**Retiré derrière** [*ruh-tee-RAY deh-RYEHR*]. Withdrawn in back. The thigh is raised to the second position en l'air with the knee bent so that the pointed toe is placed behind the supporting knee. *See* Raccourci derrière.

**Retiré devant** [*ruh-tee-RAY duh-VAHN*]. Withdrawn in front. The thigh is raised to the second position en l'air with the knee bent so that the pointed toe is placed in front of the supporting knee. *See* Raccourci devant.

**Retiré en l'air** [*ruh-tee-RAY ahn lehr*]. Withdrawn in the air. *See* Soubresaut, grand.

**Retiré sauté** [*ruh-tee-RAY soh-TAY*]. Retiré jumped. A drawing-up movement of one leg to pass behind or in front of the supporting leg while the supporting leg executes a temps levé.

**Retiré sauté en arrière** [*ruh-tee-RAY soh-TAY ah na-RYEHR*]. Retiré jumped backward. Fifth position R foot front. Draw the R foot up to the retiré position, at the same time executing a temps levé on the L foot. Come to the ground on the L foot in demi-plié and close the R foot in the fifth position back. The movement is then repeated on alternate feet.

**Retiré sauté en avant** [*ruh-tee-RAY soh-TAY ah na-V$\overline{AHN}$*]. Retiré jumped forward. Fifth position R foot back. Draw the R foot up to the retiré position, at the same time executing a temps levé on the L foot. Come to the ground on the L foot in demi-plié, then close the R foot in the fifth position front. The movement may then be repeated on alternate feet.

**Retombé, retombée** [*ruh-$\overline{tawn}$-BAY*]. Falling back. A term of the French School and the Cecchetti method. To fall back again to the original position.

**Révérence, grande** [*gr$\overline{ahn}$d ray-vay-R$\overline{AHN}$SS*]. Big reverence or curtsey. The elaborate curtsey performed by the female dancer to acknowledge the applause of the audience. It is also done at the end of a ballet class to show the respectful admiration of the pupils for their teacher. There are several types of révérence. Fifth position R foot back. Step to the right on the R foot, raising the L foot pointe tendue in second position and the arms to the second position; slide the L foot into a demi-plié in the fourth position derrière; transfer the weight to the L foot, straightening the knees as the R foot is stretched pointe tendue in the fourth position devant. As the L foot slides to the fourth position back into a demi-plié on both feet, the dancer bends forward and the arms drop to bras bas with the head lowered. When the weight is transferred to the back foot and the head and body straighten, the arms reopen to the second position. The R foot is then closed to the fifth position devant and the révérence may be repeated to the other side. The révérence may also be embellished with a petit battement sur le cou-de-pied (beating devant and derrière) before stepping on the L foot into the demi-plié in the fourth position derrière.

**Rise.** This is a smooth relevé from a position à terre through all the levels of the foot (quarter-point, half-point and three-quarter point). The toes do not move from the spot at which the rise began. *See* Relevé (French School).

**Rivoltade** [*ree-vawl-TAD*]. A French term derived from the Italian "rivoltare," to turn over. A male dancer's step in which the dancer places one leg in the air and then gives the impression that he jumps over it with the other leg. Raise the R leg up in front, spring into the air and bring the L leg over the top of the R leg (either straight or bent in retiré) while turning to the right. Land facing the opposite direction on the L leg with the R leg raised in back. Rivoltade may be executed from various preparations and ended in various poses such as first or third (Russian) arabesque.

**Rolling.** Dancers who do not have a good turn-out should not force their legs to turn out too much at first, as this usually results in rolling ankles. If the weight is on the inside of the feet, dancers call this rolling in; if the weight is on the outside of the feet, it is called rolling out. The toes and heels should be flat on the floor and the turn-out must come from the hip joints.

**Romantic ballet.** A style of ballet produced during the early nineteenth century in which the accent was on the conveyance of a mood to tell a story. Example of romantic ballets are *La Sylphide* and *Giselle*.

**Rond** [$\overline{rawn}$]. Round or circular.

**Rond de bras** [$\overline{rawn}$ $\underline{duh}$ brah]. Ronds de bras are circles of the arms.

**Rond de jambe** [$\overline{rawn}$ duh $\overline{zhahnb}$]. Round of the leg, that is, a circular movement of the leg. Ronds de jambe are used as an exercise at the bar, in the centre and in the adage, and are done à terre or en l'air. When used as a step, ronds de jambe are done en l'air and may be sauté or relevé. All are done clockwise (en dehors) and counterclockwise (en dedans).

**Rond de jambe à terre** [$\overline{rawn}$ duh $\overline{zhahnb}$ a tehr]. Rond de jambe on the ground. An exercise at the bar or in the centre in which one leg is made to describe a series of circular movements on the ground. Both legs must be kept perfectly straight and all movement must come from the hip, along with the arching and relaxing of the instep. The toe of the working foot does not rise off the ground and does not pass beyond the fourth position front (fourth position ouvert) or the fourth position back. This is an exercise to turn the legs out from the hips, to loosen the hips and to keep the toe well back and heel forward. There are two kinds of ronds de jambe à terre: those done en dedans (inward) and those done en dehors (outward).

The exercise at the bar is usually preceded by a preparation from the first or fifth position which is done on two introductory chords. Fifth position R foot front (L hand on bar, R arm in second position). Chord 1: demi-plié (lowering the R arm to the first position) and slide the R foot forward to the fourth position, pointe tendue (raising the R arm to the first position and inclining the head toward the bar). Chord 2: slide the R toe along the floor, describing an arc and finishing in the second position as the L knee straightens (the R arm opens to the second position and the head turns to the right). On the "upbeat" the R foot is drawn in an arc to the fourth position back (the head turns forward) and the dancer begins a series of ronds de jambe à terre en dehors. For ronds de jambe à terre en dedans, reverse the movements.

**Rond de jambe à terre, demi-** [*duh-mee-*$\overline{RAWN}$ duh $\overline{zhahnb}$ a tehr]. Half-rond de jambe on the ground. It may be executed either en dedans or en dehors. For en dehors, dégagé the working foot to the fourth position front and describe an arc on the floor finishing in the second position. For en dedans, reverse the movement.

**Rond de jambe à terre, demi-grand** [*duh-mee-*$\overline{GRAHN}$ $\overline{rawn}$ duh $\overline{zhahnb}$ a tehr]. Half-large rond de jambe on the ground. This is executed the same way as demi-rond de jambe à terre, except that it is performed with the supporting leg in fondu.

**Rond de jambe à terre en dedans** [$\overline{rawn}$ duh $\overline{zhahnb}$ a tehr $\overline{ahn}$ duh-$\overline{DAHN}$]. Rond de jambe on the ground, inward. First position; slide the R foot backward, gradually raising the heel, to the fourth position (ouvert) back, pointe tendue. With an inward sweep carry the foot along the ground through the second position, pointe tendue, to the fourth position (ouvert) front, pointe tendue. The foot is then brought backward to the first position, gradually lowering the heel. The complete half-circle traced by the inward sweep of the foot on the ground is termed rond de jambe à terre en dedans. In a series of ronds de jambe à terre, the strong accent occurs as the foot passes through the first position.

**Rond de jambe à terre en dedans, grand** [*grahn rawn duh zhahnb a tehr ahn duh-DAHN*]. Large rond de jambe on the ground, inward. Fifth position R foot back. Demi-plié and slide the R foot—straightening the knee—to the fourth position (ouvert) back, pointe tendue. With the L leg remaining in demi-plié, carry the R foot from the fourth position back, pointe tendue, to the second position, pointe tendue, to the fourth position (ouvert) front, pointe tendue. Close the R foot to the fifth position front, straightening the L knee.

**Rond de jambe à terre en dehors** [*rawn duh zhahnb a tehr ahn duh-AWR*]. Rond de jambe on the ground, outward. First position; slide the R foot forward, gradually raising the heel, to the fourth position (ouvert) front, pointe tendue. With an outward sweep carry the foot along the ground through the second position, pointe tendue, to the fourth position (ouvert) back, pointe tendue. The foot is then brought forward to the first position, gradually lowering the heel. The complete half-circle traced by the outward sweep of the foot on the ground is termed rond de jambe à terre en dehors. In a series of ronds de jambe à terre the strong accent occurs as the foot passes through the first position.

**Rond de jambe à terre en dehors, grand** [*grahn rawn duh zhahnb a tehr ahn duh-AWR*]. Large rond de jambe on the ground, outward. Fifth position R foot front. Demi-plié and slide the R foot—straightening the knee—to the fourth position (ouvert) front, pointe tendue. With the L leg remaining in demi-plié, carry the R foot from the fourth position front pointe tendue to the second position pointe tendue to the fourth position (ouvert) back, pointe tendue. Close the R foot to the fifth position back, straightening the L knee.

**Rond de jambe balancé** [*rawn duh zhahnb ba-lahn-SAY*]. Rocking rond de jambe. A term of the Cecchetti method. When the leg executes, quickly and successively, one grand rond de jambe en l'air en dehors, then one grand rond de jambe en l'air en dedans, or vice versa, the movement is termed rond de jambe balancé.

**Rond de jambe double** [*rawn duh zhahnb DOO-bluh*]. This is a term of the Russian School for a gargouillade. In this method, both legs execute a rond de jambe en l'air almost simultaneously, while the body is in the air. *En dehors:* Fifth position croisé R foot front. Demi-plié and spring upward and to the right, executing a double rond de jambe en l'air en dehors with the R leg; immediately execute a double rond de jambe en l'air en dehors with the L leg, beginning and ending it at the calf of the R leg. Land on the R leg in demi-plié and close the L leg to the fifth position front. *En dedans:* Fifth position R foot back. This is done in the same manner as en dehors, beginning with the back foot and executing both ronds de jambe en l'air en dedans. After the landing on the R leg, the L foot closes to the fifth position back.

**Rond de jambe en l'air** [*rawn duh zhahnb ahn lehr*]. Rond de jambe in the air. Ronds de jambe en l'air are done at the bar and in centre practice and may be single, or double, en dehors or en dedans. The toe of the working foot describes an oval, the extreme ends of which are the second position en l'air and the supporting leg. The thigh must be kept motionless and the hips well turned out, the whole movement being made by the leg below the knee. The thigh should also be held horizontal so that the pointed toe of the working foot passes at (approximately) the height of the supporting knee. Ronds de jambe en l'air may also be done with the leg extended to the second position en l'air (demi-position) and closed to the calf of the supporting leg. The accent of the movement comes when the foot is in the second position en l'air. The movement is done en dehors and en dedans.

**Rond de jambe en l'air (Cecchetti method)** [*rawn duh zhahnb ahn lehr*]. In the Cecchetti method, the path described by the pointed toe of the working leg resembles an isosceles triangle with an acute angle at its apex. After the leg is opened to the second position en l'air, the pointed toe is brought just in front of the supporting knee, then just behind it (or vice versa). It is then opened to the second position en l'air.

**Rond de jambe en l'air, double** [*DOO-bluh rawn duh zhahnb ahn lehr*]. Double rond de jambe en l'air. This is a double rond de jambe performed either sauté or relevé. It consists of two quick circles of the leg. The leg is extended in full after the second circle at 45 or 90 degrees.

**Rond de jambe en l'air en dedans** [*rawn duh zhahnb ahn lehr ahn duh-DAHN*]. Rond de jambe in the air, inward. The working leg is opened from the fifth position back to the second position en l'air. From here the toe describes an oval beginning with its forward arc, passing the knee of the supporting leg, through the backward arc, and finishing in the second position en l'air. The leg is then lowered to the fifth position front, or the movement may be repeated as many times as desired before lowering the leg.

**Rond de jambe en l'air en dedans, demi-grand** [*duh-mee-GRAHN rawn duh zhahnb ahn lehr ahn duh-DAHN*]. Half-large rond de jambe in the air, inward. From the fourth position back en l'air the leg is carried to the second position en l'air. The movement may also be started in the second position en l'air, from which position the leg is carried to the fourth position front en l'air.

**Rond de jambe en l'air en dedans, grand** [*grahn rawn duh zhahnb ahn lehr ahn duh-DAHN*]. Large rond de jambe in the air, inward. The movement is usually preceded by a développé à la quatrième derrière, from which position the leg is carried with a large movement through the second position en l'air to the fourth position front en l'air.

**Rond de jambe en l'air en dehors** [*rawn duh zhahnb ahn lehr ahn duh-*

*AWR*]. Rond de jambe in the air, outward. Ronds de jambe en l'air commence and end in the second position en l'air. To start the movement the working leg is opened from the fifth position front to the second position en l'air. From here the toe describes an oval beginning with its backward arc, passing the knee of the supporting leg, through the forward arc, and finishing in the second position en l'air. The leg may then be lowered into the fifth position back, or the movement may be repeated as many times as desired before lowering the leg.

**Rond de jambe en l'air en dehors, demi-grand** [*duh-mee-GRAHN rawn duh zhahnb ahn lehr ahn duh-AWR*]. Half a large rond de jambe in the air, outward. From the fourth position front en l'air the leg is carried to the second position en l'air. The movement may also be started in the second position en l'air, from which position the leg is carried to the fourth position back en l'air.

**Rond de jambe en l'air en dehors, grand** [*grahn rawn duh zhahnb ahn lehr ahn duh-AWR*]. Large rond de jambe in the air, outward. This is a large movement of the entire leg from the hip, done in a semicircle from front to back. It is usually preceded by a développé à la quatrième devant, from where the leg is carried with a sweeping movement through the second position en l'air to the fourth position back en l'air. This exercise is used at the bar and in the centre and is very useful for gaining balance and control.

**Rond de jambe en l'air en tournant** [*rawn duh zhahnb ahn lehr ahn toor-NAHN*]. Rond de jambe in the air, turning. This is an exercise of adage. A series of ronds de jambe en l'air either en dedans or en dehors is executed while a slow pivot (promenade) is made on the supporting leg.

**Rond de jambe en l'air relevé** [*rawn duh zhahnb ahn lehr ruhl-VAY*]. Rond de jambe in the air, raised. This rond de jambe is executed on the point or demi-pointe, en dehors or en dedans, and may be single or double.

**Rond de jambe en l'air relevé, double** [*DOO-bluh rawn duh zhahnb ahn lehr ruhl-VAY*]. Double rond de jambe in the air, raised. This consists of two circles in the air. The working leg is extended to the second position en l'air after the completion of the second circle.

**Rond de jambe en l'air relevé en dedans** [*rawn duh zhahnb ahn lehr ruhl-VAY ahn duh-DAHN*]. Rond de jambe in the air inward, raised. Fifth position R foot back. Demi-plié and spring onto the point or demi-pointe of the L foot, opening the R leg to the second position en l'air, à la hauteur or à la demi-hauteur. Execute a rond de jambe en l'air en dedans. With a slight spring, lower both heels to the ground in demi-plié in the fifth position R foot front. A double rond de jambe en l'air may be executed instead of the single rond de jambe en l'air.

**Rond de jambe en l'air relevé en dehors** [*rawn duh zhahnb ahn lehr ruhl-VAY ahn duh-AWR*]. Rond de jambe in the air outward, raised. Fifth position R foot front. Demi-plié and spring onto the point or demi-pointe of the L foot, opening the R leg to the second position en l'air, à la hauteur or à la demi-hauteur. Execute a rond de jambe en l'air en dehors. With a slight spring, lower both heels to the ground in demi-plié in the fifth position R foot back. A double rond de jambe en l'air may be executed instead of the single rond de jambe en l'air.

**Rond de jambe en l'air sauté** [*rawn duh zhahnb ahn lehr soh-TAY*]. Rond de jambe in the air, jumping. From a demi-plié the dancer jumps into the air, performs a rond de jambe en l'air with the working leg and lands on the supporting leg as the working leg extends à la seconde en l'air. The rond de jambe is done either en dedans or en dehors and may be single or double.

**Rond de jambe en l'air sauté, double** [*DOO-bluh rawn duh zhahnb ahn lehr soh-TAY*]. Double rond de jambe in the air, jumping. This step is performed exactly like rond de jambe en l'air sauté, the only difference being that two ronds de jambe are performed in the air before the supporting leg descends to the floor.

**Rond de jambe en l'air sauté en dedans** [*rawn duh zhahnb ahn lehr soh-TAY ahn duh-DAHN*]. Rond de jambe in the air inward, jumping. Fifth position R foot back. Demi-plié and spring into the air, thrusting the R leg to the second position en l'air and executing a rond de jambe en l'air en dedans. Land in demi-plié on the L leg, the R leg opening to the second position en l'air. This rond de jambe may also be done with a sissonne ouverte to the second position at 45 degrees before the jump (temps levé).

**Rond de jambe en l'air sauté en dehors** [*rawn duh zhahnb ahn lehr soh-TAY ahn duh-AWR*]. Rond de jambe in the air outward, jumping. Fifth position R foot front. Demi-plié and spring into the air, thrusting the R leg to the second position en l'air and executing a rond de jambe en l'air en dehors. Land in demi-plié on the L leg, the R leg opening to the second position en l'air. This rond de jambe may also be done with a sissonne ouverte to the second position at 45 degrees before the jump (temps levé).

**Rond de jambe en tournant, fouetté** [*fweh-TAY rawn duh zhahnb ahn toor-NAHN*]. Rond de jambe turning and whipped. *See* Fouetté rond de jambe en tournant.

**Rond de jambe fermé** [*rawn duh zhahnb fehr-MAY*]. Closed rond de jambe. If, after completing one or more ronds de jambe en l'air sauté or relevé, the working leg is closed to the fifth position with an assemblé, the rond de jambe is said to be closed, or fermé.

**Rond de jambe jeté, grand** [*grahn rawn duh zhahnb zhuh-TAY*]. Large rond de jambe thrown. A term of the Russian School. This is an exercise for the hip joint performed at the bar. It is usually preceded by a rond de jambe à terre which gives the necessary impetus for the vigorous forward thrust of the leg. It may also be done consecutively as an exercise in itself. It is performed en dedans and en dehors.

**Rond de jambe jeté en dedans, grand** [*grahn rawn duh zhahnb zhuh-TAY ahn duh-DAHN*]. Large rond de jambe thrown inward. From the fourth position front, pointe tendue, the leg is forcefully thrown backward with a passé par terre through the first position and raised in back in a turned-out, half-bent position at 45 degrees. The leg immediately stretches out and describes a circle forward at 90 degrees, then is carefully lowered to the fourth position front, pointe tendue. The arms, shoulders and torso remain motionless.

**Rond de jambe jeté en dehors, grand** [*grahn rawn duh zhahnb zhuh-TAY ahn duh-AWR*]. Large rond de jambe thrown outward. From the fourth position back, pointe tendue, the leg is forcefully thrown forward with a passé par terre through the first position and raised in front in a turned-out, half-bent position at 45 degrees. The leg immediately stretches out and describes a circle backward at the height of 90 degrees, then is carefully lowered to the fourth position back, pointe tendue.

**Rond de jambe ouvert** [*rawn duh zhahnb oo-VEHR*]. Open rond de jambe. If, after completing one or more ronds de jambe en l'air, the working leg is left in the second position en l'air while the other foot descends to the floor, the rond de jambe is said to be open, or ouvert.

**Rond de jambe par terre** [*rawn duh zhahnb par tehr*]. Rond de jambe along the ground. Same as rond de jambe à terre.

**Rond de jambe piqué** [*rawn duh zhahnb pee-KAY*]. Rond de jambe pricked. This is an exercise at the bar. Instead of sliding the foot along the floor in rond de jambe à terre, the foot is placed pointe tendue in the fourth position front, in the second position and in the fourth position back, or vice versa, with a tapping movement.

**Rond de jambe relevé, grand** [*grahn rawn duh zhahnb ruhl-VAY*]. Large rond de jambe raised. The working leg describes a semicircle in the air at 90 degrees, either en dedans or en dehors, while the supporting leg does a relevé.

**Rond de jambe retombé (Cecchetti method)** [*rawn duh zhahnb ruh-tawn-BAY*]. Rond de jambe, falling back. Fifth position R foot back. Demi-plié and relevé on the L point, opening the R leg to the second position en l'air. Execute a rond de jambe en dedans en l'air and tombé on the R foot in the fifth position front. Immediately raise the L foot to a small attitude derrière with the body bending forward. The step may then be repeated with the other foot.

**Rond de jambe sauté, grand** [*grahn rawn duh zhahnb soh-TAY*]. Large rond de jambe jumped. The working leg describes a semicircle in the air at 90 degrees, either en dedans or en dehors, while the supporting leg does a temps levé.

**Rond de jambe soulevé** [*rawn duh zhahnb sool-VAY*]. Rond de jambe raised. A term of the French School. Fifth position R foot front. In one sweeping movement raise the R leg à la quatrième devant à la demi-hauteur, open the leg to the second position à la demi-hauteur and close the leg to the first position. The R leg is raised again and the movement repeated. Rond de jambe soulevé is done en dedans by reversing the movement.

**Royale** [*rwah-YAL*]. Royal. A changement in which the calves are beaten together before the feet change position. Also termed "changement battu." Fifth position R foot front. Demi-plié in preparation for a small spring into the air, opening both legs slightly. Quickly close the legs and beat the calves of the legs together, open slightly to the side, and come to the ground in demi-plié in the fifth position R foot back.

**Royale double** [*rwah-YAL DOO-bluh*]. Double royale. This is like an entrechat six finished or commenced in the second position.

**Royale fermée** [*rwah-YAL fehr-MAY*]. Closed royale. This is like an entrechat quatre commenced in the second position and finished in the fifth position. It is usually preceded by an échappé sauté. From a demi-plié in the second position, spring into the air, beat the L leg in front, beat the R leg in front, then execute a changement and land in demi-plié in the fifth position. Also termed "entrechat cinq fermé."

**Royale ouverte** [*rwah-YAL oo-VEHRT*]. Open royale. This is like an entrechat quatre commenced in the fifth position and finished in the second position. Demi-plié in the fifth position R foot front; spring into the air, beat the L leg front, beat the R leg front, then open both legs and land in demi-plié in the second position. Also termed "entrechat cinq ouvert."

**Russian School.** The Russian School was founded in St. Petersburg in 1738 by the French dancer Jean-Baptiste Landé. The French influence continued under such great teachers as Charles Le Picq, Charles Didelot, Christian Johannsen, Jules Perrot, Arthur Saint-Léon and Marius Petipa.

In 1885 Virginia Zucchi, a famous Italian ballerina, appeared in St. Petersburg and created a sensation with her forceful and brilliant Italian technique which differed from the soft, graceful elegance of the French technique prevalent in Russia until then. Other Italian dancers such as Enrico Cecchetti arrived in Russia and continued to astound the Russians with their amazing dexterity, brilliant pirouettes, tours and fouettés. The Russian dancers rapidly absorbed everything the Italians had to teach and incorporated it into the Russian system. Thus, the Russian School of Ballet is a development of the French and Italian Schools.

During the 1920s the Russian ballerina and teacher Agrippina Vaganova developed a planned instructional system which later became known to the whole world as the Vaganova system. This system has become the basic method of the entire Soviet choreographic school.

**Salle, autour de la** [*oh-TOOR duh lah sal*]. Round the room. A term of the Cecchetti method. This term indicates that a series of turns or steps is to be performed in a circle around the stage. *See* Manège, en.

**Saut** [*soh*]. Jump. A jump off both feet, landing with the feet in the same position.

**Saut de basque (French and Russian Schools)** [*soh duh bask*]. Basque jump. A traveling step in which the dancer turns in the air with one foot drawn up to the knee of the other leg. Fifth position R foot front. Demi-plié with R foot retiré devant; step on the R foot in demi-plié to the second position, turning en dedans one half-turn and thrusting the L leg to the second position en l'air; push off the floor with the R foot and complete the turn, traveling to the side of the extended leg and landing on the L foot in fondu with the R leg bent in retiré devant. Both legs should be fully turned out during the jump. Saut de basque may also be performed with a double turn in the air. *See* Jeté en tournant en avant, grand (Cecchetti method).

**Saut de basque battu** [*soh duh bask ba-TEW*]. Saut de basque beaten. Saut de basque may be done with single, double or triple beats while the body is turning in the air. To execute a triple beat, thrust the L leg to the second position en l'air; the R follows to beat the L leg three times, the first beat being in front of the L leg, the second behind, and the third in front, where it stays on the L knee in raccourci devant for the landing.

**Saut de chat** [*soh duh shah*]. Cat's jump. A term of the French School. This is similar to the Italian pas de chat. The working foot, instead of being raised to the side of the knee, is raised in raccourci derrière. After the jump in the air, during which both knees and feet are drawn up, the landing is made in fondu on the foot which was raised first, with the other foot in raccourci devant. The raised foot is then closed in demi-plié in the fifth position front. If the saut de chat is petit, the jump is smaller and the free foot is raised sur le cou-de-pied. *See* Pas de chat, grand.

**Saut de flèche** [*soh duh flesh*]. Arrow jump. *See* Temps de flèche.

**Saut de l'ange** [*soh duh lahnzh*]. Angel's jump, angel's step. A term of the French School. *See* Temps de l'ange.

**Sauté, sautée** [*soh-TAY*]. Jumped, jumping. When this term is added to the name of a step, the movement is performed while jumping. As, for example, échappé sauté. Note: In all jumping movements the tips of the toes should be the first to reach the ground after the jump, then the sole of the foot followed by the heel. In rising from the ground the foot moves in the reverse order.

**Sauter** [*soh-TAY*]. To jump. One of the seven movements in dancing.

**Sautillé, sautillée** [*soh-tee-YAY*]. Hopped, hopping. When this term is added to the name of a step, the movement is performed with hops. As, for example, grande pirouette sautillée.

**Scène** [*sen*]. Stage; scenery, scene.

**Scène d'action** [*sen dak-SYAWN*]. Action scene. A mimed scene introduced in the ballet d'action in the nineteenth century.

**Seconde, à la** [*ah la suh-GAWND*]. To the second. A term to imply that the foot is to be placed in the second position, or that a movement is to be made to the second position en l'air. As, for example, in grand battement à la seconde. A la seconde is one of the eight directions of the body, Cecchetti method. See illustration, p. 135.

**Seconde, en** [$\overline{ahn}$ suh-G$\overline{AWN}$D]. In second. In the second position.

**Seconde, grande** [$\overline{grahnd}$ suh-G$\overline{AWN}$D]. Large second. The second position en l'air.

**Sept** [set]. Seven.

**Serré, serrée** [seh-RAY]. Tight, close. As, for example, in petits battements serrés.

**Serrer les reins** [seh-RAY lay $\overline{ren}$]. To tighten the loins. A term used in ballet teaching to indicate that the body should be erect and the torso well lifted, with the buttocks and abdominal muscles tightened.

**Sickling.** This term is used for a fault in which the dancer turns his or her foot in from the ankle, thereby breaking the straight line of the leg.

**Side practice.** Side practice, or bar exercises, is a series of exercises with which every ballet lesson begins. These exercises are essential for developing the muscles correctly, to turn out the legs from the hips and to gain control and suppleness of both muscles and joints. *See* Exercices à la barre.

**Simple** [$\overline{SEN}$-pluh]. Simple, ordinary, single. As, for example, in sissonne simple.

**Sissonne** [see-SAWN]. Sissonne is named for the originator of the step. It is a jump from both feet onto one foot with the exception of sissonne fermée, sissonne tombée and sissonne fondue, which finish on two feet. Sissonne may be performed petite or grande. The petites sissonnes are sissonne simple, sissonne fermée, sissonne ouverte at 45 degrees and sissonne tombée at 45 degrees. The grandes sissonnes are sissonne ouverte at 90 degrees, sissonne renversée and sissonne soubresaut.

**Sissonne à la seconde** [see-SAWN a lah suh-G$\overline{AWN}$D]. Sissonne to the second (position). A term of the French School. *See* Sissonne fermée dessous; Sissonne fermée dessus.

**Sissonne battue** [see-SAWN ba-TEW]. Sissonne beaten. Sissonne simple, ouverte and fermée can be beaten.

**Sissonne changée en arrière** [see-SAWN sh$\overline{ahn}$-ZHAY ah na-RYEHR]. Sissonne changed, backward. This is a term of the Cecchetti method. Fifth position R foot back. Demi-plié and spring upward and backward into the air; come to the ground on the L foot in demi-plié with the R leg in the fourth position front in the air. As soon as the L foot comes to the ground, close the R foot to the fifth position front in demi-plié.

**Sissonne changée en avant** [see-SAWN sh$\overline{ahn}$-ZHAY ah na-V$\overline{AHN}$]. Sissonne changed, forward. This is a term of the Cecchetti method. Fifth position R foot front. Demi-plié and spring upward and forward into the air; come to the ground on the L foot in demi-plié with the R leg in the fourth position back en l'air. As soon as the L foot comes to the ground, close the R foot to the fifth position back in demi-plié.

**Sissonne doublée** [*see-SAWN doo-BLAY*]. Sissonne doubled. A term of the French School. This is a compound step consisting of a sissonne ouverte de côté, a coupé and an assemblé. The step may be done either dessus or dessous. According to the coupé and assemblé used, sissonne doublée if done in a series can be made to travel in one direction or to alternate sides. Also called "sissonne retombée" (Cecchetti method).

**Sissonne doublée battue** [*see-SAWN doo-BLAY ba-TEW*]. Sissonne doubled, beaten. This compound step consists of a sissonne ouverte de côté with the beat of an entrechat trois, cinq or sept, finished with the leg in the second position en l'air; a coupé dessus or dessous; and an assemblé battu either dessus or dessous. *See* Sissonne doublée.

**Sissonne doublée dessous** [*see-SAWN doo-BLAY duh-SOO*]. Sissonne doubled, under. Fifth position R foot front. Demi-plié and spring into the air, executing a sissonne ouverte de côté. The R leg then executes a coupé dessous, followed by an assemblé dessous with the L leg.

**Sissonne doublée dessus** [*see-SAWN doo-BLAY duh-SEW*]. Sissonne doubled, over. This is the reverse of the sissonne doublée dessous and consists of a sissonne ouverte de côté executed with the back foot, followed by a coupé dessus and an assemblé dessus.

**Sissonne en arabesque sur la pointe (Russian School)** [*see-SAWN ah na-ra-BESK sewr la pwent*]. Same as relevé en arabesque.

**Sissonne en descendant** [*see-SAWN ahn day-sahn-DAHN*]. Sissonne coming down. A term of the French School. Same as sissonne fermée en avant.

**Sissonne en remontant** [*see-SAWN ahn ruh-mawn-TAHN*]. Sissonne going up. A term of the French School. Same as sissonne fermée en arrière.

**Sissonne fermée** [*see-SAWN fehr-MAY*]. Closed sissonne. A step of low elevation performed to a quick tempo. This sissonne finishes on two feet with the working foot gliding along the floor into the demi-plié in the fifth position. It may be performed en avant, en arrière and de côté in all directions, such as croisé, effacé, écarté, etc. The French School terms this step "faux entrechat cinq ramassé."

**Sissonne fermée battue** [*see-SAWN fehr-MAY ba-TEW*]. Sissonne closed and beaten. This step can be taken en avant or en arrière. It consists of a sissonne fermée with the beat of an entrechat quatre and is also known as "entrechat cinq ramassé." When executed de côté it is performed with a royale.

**Sissonne fermée battue en arrière** [*see-SAWN fehr-MAY ba-TEW ah na-RYEHR*]. Sissonne closed and beaten, backward. Fifth position R foot back. Demi-plié and spring upward and backward into the air, beating the L leg behind the R leg and then opening the L leg to the fourth position devant low to the floor. Land in demi-plié on the R foot and immediately close the L foot in demi-plié in the fifth position front.

This sissonne may be done en arrière, croisé en arrière or effacé en arrière.

**Sissonne fermée battue en avant** [*see-SAWN fehr-MAY ba-TEW ah na-VAHN*]. Sissonne closed and beaten, forward. Fifth position R foot front. Demi-plié and spring upward and forward into the air, beating the L leg in front of the R leg and then opening the L leg to the fourth position derrière low to the floor. Land in demi-plié on the R foot and immediately close the L foot in demi-plié in the fifth position back. This sissonne may be done en avant, croisé en avant or effacé en avant.

**Sissonne fermée de côté** [*see-SAWN fehr-MAY duh koh-TAY*]. Sissonne closed, traveled to the side. This sissonne is performed dessus, dessous or without change of feet.

**Sissonne fermée dessous** [*see-SAWN fehr-MAY duh-SOO*]. Sissonne closed, under. Fifth position R foot front. Demi-plié and spring into the air, traveling to the left and opening the R foot to the second position low to the floor. Come to the ground on the L foot in demi-plié and glide the R toe along the floor to finish in demi-plié in the fifth position back.

**Sissonne fermée dessus** [*see-SAWN fehr-MAY duh-SEW*]. Sissonne closed, over. Fifth position R foot back. Demi-plié and spring into the air, traveling to the left and opening the R foot to the second position low to the floor. Come to the ground on the L foot in demi-plié and immediately glide the R toe along the floor to finish in demi-plié in the fifth position front.

**Sissonne fermée en arrière** [*see-SAWN fehr-MAY ah na-RYEHR*]. Sissonne closed, traveled backward. Fifth position R foot back. Demi-plié and spring into the air, traveling backward either croisé en arrière or effacé en arrière, and opening the L foot to the fourth position front low to the floor. Come to the ground on the R foot in demi-plié and immediately glide the L toe along the floor to finish in a demi-plié in the fifth position front, either croisé or effacé.

**Sissonne fermée en avant** [*see-SAWN fehr-MAY ah na-VAHN*]. Sissonne closed, traveled forward. Fifth position R foot front. Demi-plié and spring into the air, traveling forward either croisé en avant or effacé en avant and opening the L foot to the fourth position back low to the floor. Come to the ground on the R foot in demi-plié and immediately glide the L toe along the floor to finish in demi-plié in the fifth position back, either croisé or effacé.

**Sissonne fondue** [*see-SAWN fawn-DEW*]. Sissonne sinking. This sissonne is performed in the same way as sissonne fermée but with a higher jump and with the leg raised to 90 degrees. In closing the step, the second foot does not glide over the floor but is softly placed down in demi-plié in the fifth position or placed sur le cou-de-pied. It may be performed en avant, en arrière, de côté and in all the directions.

**Sissonne ouverte, grande** [*grahnd see-SAWN oo-VEHRT*]. Big open sissonne. This sissonne is usually performed with high elevation and is done from a demi-plié on both feet and finished on one foot with the other leg raised in the desired pose, such as attitude, arabesque à la seconde, etc. It is performed en avant, en arrière, de côté, en tournant and is done with a développé or a grand battement at 90 degrees.

**Sissonne ouverte, petite** [*puh-TEET see-SAWN oo-VEHRT*]. Small open sissonne. This sissonne is performed with low elevation. It is finished on one foot and is done with a développé or battement at 45 degrees. In the Russian School the opening of the leg must take place through the position sur le cou-de-pied.

**Sissonne ouverte battue** [*see-SAWN oo-VEHRT ba-TEW*]. Open sissonne with a beat. This may be performed with the beat of an entrechat trois, cinq or sept.

**Sissonne ouverte de côté** [*see-SAWN oo-VEHRT duh koh-TAY*]. Sissonne opened sideways. Fifth position R foot front. Demi-plié, spring upward and sideways (left) into the air, opening the R leg to the second position en l'air either à la hauteur or à la demi-hauteur. Come to the ground on the L foot in demi-plié, holding the R leg in the air. May also be executed with the R foot back.

**Sissonne ouverte en arrière** [*see-SAWN oo-VEHRT ah na-RYEHR*]. Sissonne opened backward. Fifth position R foot front. Demi-plié and spring upward and backward into the air, opening the R leg à la quatrième devant, either à la hauteur or à la demi-hauteur. Come to the ground on the L foot in demi-plié, holding the R leg in the air. May be executed en arrière, croisé en arrière or effacé en arrière.

**Sissonne ouverte en avant** [*see-SAWN oo-VEHRT ah na-VAHN*]. Sissonne opened forward. Fifth position R foot front. Demi-plié, spring upward and forward into the air, opening the L leg à la quatrième derrière, either à la hauteur or à la demi-hauteur. Come to the ground on the R foot in demi-plié, holding the L leg in the air. May be executed en avant, croisé en avant or effacé en avant.

**Sissonne ouverte en développé** [*see-SAWN oo-VEHRT ahn dayv-law-PAY*]. Sissonne opened in développé. This is done the same way as sissonne ouverte, but instead of opening the leg with a straight knee, the leg is opened in développé. May be done en avant, en arrière, de côté and en tournant.

**Sissonne ouverte en tournant** [*see-SAWN oo-VEHRT ahn toor-NAHN*]. Open sissonne, turning. Fifth position croisée R foot front. Demi-plié, spring into the air, turning en dehors or en dedans; come to the ground in fondu on the L foot, opening the R leg with or without a développé to the desired pose at 45 or 90 degrees.

**Sissonne ouverte sur la pointe (Russian School)** [*see-SAWN oo-VEHRT sewr lah pwent*]. Open sissonne on the point. This is a relevé on the point and may be done petite or grande.

*Petite sissonne ouverte sur la pointe:* Fifth position R foot front. Demi-plié and spring on the point of the L foot, opening the R leg through sur le cou-de-pied (devant or derrière) to the second position at 45 degrees. Come down in demi-plié in the fifth position on both legs at the same time. The working leg may also be opened croisé, effacé or écarté, either devant or derrière.

*Grande sissonne ouverte sur la pointe:* This is done in the same manner, opening the working leg to second position at 90 degrees by means of a développé. The working leg may also be opened croisé, effacé or écarté, either devant or derrière. This grande sissonne is also performed in attitude croisée, attitude effacée and first, second, third and fourth arabesque, raising the working leg to 90 degrees by means of a battement.

**Sissonne passée derrière** [*see-SAWN pa-SAY deh-RYEHR*]. Sissonne passed in back. Fifth position R foot front. Demi-plié, spring upward into the air with knees and toes extended. Come to the ground in demi-plié on the L foot with the R foot sur le cou-de-pied derrière.

**Sissonne passée devant** [*see-SAWN pa-SAY duh-VAHN*]. Sissonne passed in front. Fifth position R foot back. Demi-plié, spring upward into the air with knees and toes extended. Come to the ground in demi-plié on the L foot with the R foot sur le cou-de-pied devant.

**Sissonne renversée** [*see-SAWN rahn-vehr-SAY*]. Sissonne upset. A term of the Russian School. From the fifth position croisé, execute a sissonne ouverte en avant into attitude croisée, then immediately do a pas de bourrée en dehors, bending the body in renversé.

**Sissonne retombée** [*see-SAWN ruh-tawn-BAY*]. Sissonne, falling back. A term of the Cecchetti method. Same as sissonne doublée.

**Sissonne simple** [*see-SAWN SEN-pluh*]. Simple sissonne. This sissonne is done sur place, devant, derrière, passée devant and passée derrière, and may be executed en face or en tournant. This term is used in the Russian and French Schools; the step consists of a spring from the fifth position, landing with one foot sur le cou-de-pied. The Cecchetti method terms this "temps levé."

**Sissonne simple battue** [*see-SAWN SEN-pluh ba-TEW*]. Simple sissonne beaten. When sissonne simple is done with a beat it changes its name and is called "entrechat trois" or "entrechat cinq" according to the number of times the feet are changed or beaten in the air.

**Sissonne simple derrière** [*see-SAWN SEN-pluh deh-RYEHR*]. Simple sissonne in back. Fifth position R foot back. Demi-plié, spring upward into the air with knees and toes extended. Come to the ground in demi-plié on the L foot with the R foot sur le cou-de-pied derrière.

**Sissonne simple détournée** [*see-SAWN SEN-pluh day-toor-NAY*]. Simple sissonne turned aside. This is a sissonne simple en tournant turning in the direction of the back foot. Fifth position R foot back; demi-plié; spring into the air, making a complete turn to the right (en dehors). Land in demi-plié on the L foot with the R foot sur le cou-de-pied derrière or devant.

**Sissonne simple devant** [*see-SAWN SEN-pluh duh-VAHN*]. Simple sissonne in front. Fifth position R foot front. Demi-plié, spring upward into the air with knees and toes extended. Come to the ground in demi-plié on the L foot with the R foot sur le cou-de-pied devant.

**Sissonne simple en tournant** [*see-SAWN SĒN-pluh ahn toor-NĀHN*]. Simple sissonne, turning. Fifth position R foot front. Demi-plié; spring into the air, making a complete turn to the right (en dehors). Land in demi-plié on the L foot with the R foot sur le cou-de-pied devant. The turn may also be done en dedans: Fifth position R foot back; demi-plié; and spring into the air, making a complete turn to the left (en dedans). Land in demi-plié on the L foot with the R foot sur le cou-de-pied devant. Called "temps levé en tournant" in the Cecchetti method.

**Sissonne simple sur la pointe (Russian School)** [*see-SAWN SĒN-pluh sewr lah pwent*]. Simple sissonne on the point. This is a relevé on the point of one foot with the working foot raised sur le cou-de-pied or retiré. For the execution of this step devant, *see* Relevé devant. For derrière, *see* Relevé derrière. For passée en avant, *see* Relevé passé en avant. For passée en arrière, *see* Relevé passé en arrière.

**Sissonne soubresaut** [*see-SAWN soo-bruh-SOH*]. Sissonne with a sudden jump or jerk. A term of the Russian School. Same as temps de poisson.

**Sissonne sur la pointe (Russian School)** [*see-SAWN sewr lah pwent*]. Sissonne on the point. In the Russian School the term sissonne, when done on point, is used like the Cecchetti method term "relevé." It is a spring from demi-plié onto point from both feet to one foot. *See* Sissonne ouverte sur la pointe; Sissonne simple sur la pointe.

**Sissonne tombante** [*see-SAWN tawn-BĀHNT*]. Sissonne, falling. A term of the Cecchetti method. Same as sissonne tombée.

**Sissonne tombée** [*see-SAWN tawn-BAY*]. Sissonne, falling. This is a compound step consisting of a sissonne simple and a tombé. Fifth position R foot front. Execute a sissonne simple devant. Immediately upon landing on the L foot, fall forward in demi-plié on the R foot in the fourth position front, either croisé or effacé. Sissonne tombée may also be performed to the fourth position back or to the second position. Also called "sissonne tombante."

**Six** [*seess*]. Six.

**Soubresaut** [*soo-bruh-SOH*]. Sudden spring or bound. A term of the French and Russian Schools. A springing jump from both feet usually performed traveling forward in either a croisé or effacé direction and landing on both feet. From demi-plié in the fifth position, spring into the air with well-crossed legs, extended knees and feet pointed. Land simultaneously on both feet in demi-plié in the fifth position with the same foot in the front that started the jump. In the Russian School, the body inclines forward before the jump and then forcefully bends back at the height of the jump so that the legs are behind.

**Soubresaut, grand** [*grahn soo-bruh-SOH*]. Large soubresaut. A jump with both feet from the fifth position with the knees bent and the feet drawn up, toes pointed. The position in mid-air should be the same as a grand plié in the fifth position.

**Soubresaut sur la pointe** [*soo-bruh-SOH sewr lah pwent*]. Soubresaut on the point. This is a term of the French School. It is a tiny hop taken on the point. The jumps are very small and are done in demi-plié on point without straightening the knee between the jumps. They are done with a strongly held heel, keeping the arch and ankle tense. They may be done in attitude, arabesque, etc. *See* Temps levé sur les pointes (Russian School).

**Soulevé, soulevée** [*sool-VAY*]. Raised. As in rond de jambe soulevé.

**Sous-sus** [*soo-SEW*]. Under-over. A term of the Cecchetti method. Sous-sus is a relevé in the fifth position performed sur place or traveled forward, backward or to the side. The dancer springs onto the points or demi-pointes, drawing the feet and legs tightly together. *See* Relevé sur les pointes; Temps de cou-de-pied. *See* Sus-sous.

**Soutenu, soutenue** [*soot-NEW*]. Sustained. As, for example, in assemblé soutenu.

**Soutenu en tournant** [*soot-NEW ahn toor-NAHN*]. Sustained in turning. *See* Assemblé soutenu en tournant en dedans.

**Spotting.** This is a term given to the movement of the head and focusing of the eyes in pirouettes, déboulés, fouetté ronds de jambe en tournant and so on. In these turns the dancer chooses a spot in front and as the turn is made away from the spot, the head is the last to leave and the first to arrive as the body completes the turn. This rapid movement or snap of the head gives the impression that the face is always turned forward and prevents the dancer from becoming dizzy. *See* Pirouette.

**Step.** A step is used in classical ballet as a connecting movement to transfer the weight from one leg to the other. It is usually preceded by a fondu on the supporting leg and the foot taking the step is pointed before being placed on the floor. The step can begin with a stretched leg or with a développé.

**Stretching.** Dancers do many varied stretching exercises before leaving the bar to further loosen the muscles. *See* Détiré; Limbering.

**Suite, de** [*duh sweet*]. Continuously. Indicates that a step or movement is to be repeated several times. As, for example, in assemblés de suite.

**Sujet** [*sew-ZHEH*]. A term used in French ballet for a soloist. There are both petits and grands sujets. *See* Défilé.

**Supporting leg.** A term used by dancers and teachers for the leg which supports the body so that the working leg is free to execute a given movement.

**Sur** [*sewr*]. On, upon. As, for example, in sur les pointes.

**Sus-sous** [*sew-SOO*]. Over-under. A term of the French and Russian Schools. Same as Sous-sus.

**Tableau** [*ta-BLOH*]. Picture. A striking or artistic grouping that forms a large picture on the stage.

**Talon** [*ta-LAWN*]. Heel.

**Taqueté** [*tak-TAY*]. Pegged. A term used to indicate a dance sur les pointes consisting of quick, little steps in which the points strike the floor sharply in a staccato manner. Steps of taqueterie include piqué, emboîté sur les pointes, pas de bourrée and so on.

**Tarantella** [*tah-rahn-TEL-lah*]. A fast Italian dance in 6/8 time.

**Temps** [*tahn*]. Time, step, movement. A part of a step or movement in which no transfer of weight takes place. A temps is a section of a pas.

**Temps collé** [*tahn kaw-LAY*]. Adhering movement. *See* Collé; Temps de poisson.

**Temps de ciseaux** [*tahn duh see-ZOH*]. Scissors movement. Same as pas de ciseaux.

**Temps de cou-de-pied** [*tahn duh koo-duh-PYAY*]. Movement of the instep. This is an equal pulling up in the fifth position of both feet onto the points or demi-pointes. The feet are well crossed so that the front foot hides the back one. *See* Relevé sur les pointes.

**Temps de cuisse** [*tahn duh kweess*]. Thigh movement. A compound step consisting of a battement dégagé and a sissonne fermée. The working foot executes a battement dégagé on the upbeat of the measure in preparation for a sissonne fermée in the required direction. The step is traveled slightly and the feet must close sharply. It may be executed dessous, dessus, en avant and en arrière. There are several variations of the temps de cuisse dessous and dessus in which the body may be turned in any given direction.

**Temps de cuisse dessous** [*tahn duh kweess duh-SOO*]. Temps de cuisse under. Fifth position R foot front. Demi-plié and execute a battement dégagé to the second position with the R foot. Immediately slide the R foot to the fifth position back in demi-plié. Spring off both feet, using the insteps only and traveling slightly to the left. Come to the ground on the L foot in demi-plié with the R foot extended à la seconde demi-hauteur, then slide the R foot to the fifth position back, bending the knee.

**Temps de cuisse dessus** [*tahn duh kweess duh-SEW*]. Temps de cuisse over. Fifth position R foot back. Demi-plié and execute a battement dégagé to the second position with the R foot. Immediately slide the R foot to the fifth position front in demi-plié. Spring off both feet, using the insteps only and traveling slightly to the left. Come to the ground on the L foot in demi-plié with the R foot à la seconde demi-hauteur, then slide the R foot to the fifth position front, bending the knee.

**Temps de cuisse en arrière** [*tahn duh kweess ah na-RYEHR*]. Temps de cuisse backward. Fifth position R foot front. Demi-plié and execute a battement dégagé to the second position with the R foot. Immediately close the R foot to the fifth position back in demi-plié. Spring off both feet, traveling backward. Come to the ground on the R foot in demi-plié with the L foot extended to the fourth position front, low to the floor, then slide the L foot to the fifth position front in demi-plié.

**Temps de cuisse en avant** [*tahn duh kweess ah na-VAHN*]. Temps de cuisse forward. Fifth position R foot back. Demi-plié and execute a battement dégagé to the second position with the R foot. Immediately close the R foot to the fifth position front in demi-plié. Spring off both feet, traveling forward. Come to the ground on the R foot in demi-plié with the L foot extended to the fourth position back, low to the floor, then slide the L foot to the fifth position back in demi-plié.

**Temps de flèche** [*tahn duh flesh*]. Arrow movement. This step is so named because the first leg acts as a kind of bow and the second leg the arrow. There are several variations of this step. (1) From demi-plié in the fifth position, the front leg (the bow) executes a grand battement a la quatrième devant and is then brought back to the knee (raccourci) with a spring into the air as the second leg (the arrow) does a quick développé through it. The dancer then alights in fondu on the first leg. (2) From a demi-plié in the fifth position, perform a grand battement with the front leg, then a second battement with the back leg before the first leg alights. The legs pass each other in the air. (3) From a demi-plié in the fifth position R foot back, execute an enveloppé with the R leg while springing into the air; as the pointed toe of the R foot comes in to the knee of the L leg, quickly raise the L knee and développé the L leg effacé devant while alighting on the R leg in fondu.

**Temps de l'ange** [*tahn duh lahnzh*]. Angel's step. This step is very similar to the temps de poisson, but the legs are bent as in attitude with the knees slightly open. The back is well arched with the head back and the arms en couronne. The step is plané and the landing is made on the same spot as where the step started.

**Temps d'élévation** [*tahn day-lay-va-SYAWN*]. Step of elevation. This term is applied to all movements which involve a jump or spring. These include changements, soubresauts, jetés, sissonnes and so on.

**Temps de pointe détourné** [*tahn duh pwent day-toor-NAY*]. Toe movement, turned aside. A term of the French School. From a demi-plié in the fifth position the dancer springs into a relevé on the points, pivoting toward the rear foot and finishing the turn with the rear foot in front. *See* Détourné.

**Temps de pointe en descendant** [*tahn duh pwent ahn day-sahn-DAHN*]. Toe movement, coming down. A term of the French School. Same as piqué en avant.

**Temps de pointe en remontant** [*tahn duh pwent ahn ruh-mawn-TAHN*]. Toe movement, going up. A term of the French School. Same as piqué en arrière.

**Temps de pointes** [*tahn duh pwent*]. Movement(s) on the points (toes), pointe work. A term of the French School. These include piqué, relevé, etc. (*qq.v*).

**Temps de poisson** [*tahn duh pwah-SAWN*]. Fish step or movement. This is a form of soubresaut in which the dancer jumps with the back arched. The legs, which are well extended, are behind and held close together with the pointed feet crossed so as to represent a fish's tail. Fifth position croisé R foot front. Demi-plié and spring upward and forward into the air, turning the body effacé. As the body rises in the air, the legs are thrown upward in back of the body with the back well arched and the arms en couronne. The landing is made in fondu on the R foot with the L leg extended back in the air. To repeat the temps de poisson it is usual to perform a chassé passé in the direction croisé en avant with the L foot, followed by an assemblé dessus R, to bring the feet into the fifth position. Also known as "pas de poisson," "sissonne soubresaut" and "temps collé."

**Temps levé** [*tahn luh-VAY*]. Time raised, or raising movement. A term of the Cecchetti method. This is a hop from one foot with the other raised in any position. The instep is fully arched when leaving the ground and the spring must come from the pointing of the toe and the extension of the leg after the demi-plié. In the Cecchetti method the term also means a spring from the fifth position, raising one foot sur le cou-de-pied. In the Russian and French Schools this latter step is termed "sissonne simple."

**Temps levé chassé** [*tahn luh-VAY sha-SAY*]. Temps levé chased. A term of the Cecchetti method. Same as chassé en avant (Russian and French Schools).

**Temps levé en arabesque** [*tahn luh-VAY ah na-ra-BESK*]. Temps levé in an arabesque position. From an arabesque or attitude on the R foot, demi-plié and spring into the air, holding the arabesque or attitude position. Come to the ground in demi-plié on the R foot in the same position.

**Temps levé en tournant** [*tahn luh-VAY ahn toor-NAHN*]. Temps levé, turning. A term of the Cecchetti method. Same as sissonne simple en tournant.

**Temps levé sauté** [*tahn luh-VAY soh-TAY*]. Temps levé jumped. A term of the Russian School. This is a jump from both feet ending in the same position. From the first position, demi-plié, push off with the heels and jump into the air, pointing the toes and straightening the knees. Land in demi-plié in the first position. Temps levé sauté may be performed in the first, second, fourth and fifth positions of the feet. It may also be performed on one foot with the other foot held in a position taken before the jump.

**Temps levé sur la pointe** [*tahn luh-VAY sewr lah pwent*]. This is a small jump close to the floor on the point of one foot with the other leg raised in any pose at 45 degrees or in an arabesque at 90 degrees. The foot of the supporting leg is held taut and the knee remains slightly bent in the jump. It may be done in a series, in place, traveling forward or backward, or turning in place. It may also be done with the free leg executing ballonné or rond de jambe en l'air en dehors. *See* Soubresaut sur la pointe.

**Temps levé sur le cou-de-pied derrière** [*tahn luh-VAY sewr luh koo-duh-PYAY deh-RYEHR*]. Temps levé on the back of the ankle. Raise the R foot to the position sur le cou-de-pied derrière; demi-plié on the L foot; spring upward into the air off the L foot; come to the ground on the L foot in demi-plié.

**Temps levé sur le cou-de-pied devant** [*tahn luh-VAY sewr luh koo-duh-PYAY duh-VAHN*]. Temps levé on the front of the ankle. Raise the R foot to the position sur le cou-de-pied devant with the instep fully arched and the toe pointing downward; demi-plié on the L foot; spring upward into the air off the L foot; come to the ground on the L foot in demi-plié.

**Temps levé sur les pointes (Russian School)** [*tahn luh-VAY sewr lay pwent*]. Temps levé on the points. This is done in the first, second, fourth and fifth positions. Demi-plié, push off from the heels with a slight spring, straightening the knees and rising on the points; with a slight spring, lower the heels to the floor in demi-plié. *See* Relevé sur les pointes or demi-pointes (Cecchetti method).

**Temps lié** [*tahn lyay*]. Connected movement. Temps lié, an exercise used in centre practice, is composed of a series of steps and arm movements based on the fourth, fifth and second positions. A very valuable exercise for the achievement of a soft demi-plié, it teaches control and balance in transmitting the weight of the body from one position to another with a smooth, rhythmical movement. It is widely used in the Russian School, starting in the beginner's classes and gradually increasing in difficulty. The movement is done en avant and en arrière and may be done sauté, with développé at 90 degrees, with pirouettes and sur les pointes.

**Temps lié, grand** [*grahn tahn lyay*]. Big connected movement. Grand temps lié is done raising the legs 90 degrees. Fifth position R foot front, facing croisé. Demi-plié on the L leg and développé the R leg to croisé devant, raising the arms from bras bas to the gateway. Piqué on the R demi-pointe en attitude croisée en l'air. Coupé dessous on the L foot, bringing the R foot to retiré devant, body en face, and lowering the L arm down in front of the diaphragm. Développé the R leg to the second position, opening the L arm to the second position. Step on the R demi-pointe, raising the L leg into the second position en l'air. Demi-plié on the R leg and bring the L foot to retiré devant, or close the L foot to the fifth position croisé and demi-plié, lowering the arms to bras bas. Repeat the movement to the other side. Grand temps lié may also be done en arrière.

**Temps lié par terre** [*tahn lyay par tehr*]. Connected movement on the ground. Same as temps lié simple (en avant or en arrière).

**Temps lié sauté** [*tahn lyay soh-TAY*]. Connected movement, jumped. This temps lié is executed with a sissonne simple taken each time from the fifth position, then followed by a piqué on demi-pointe into attitude or à la seconde, and finished with an assemblé to close in the fifth position.

**Temps lié sauté en tournant** [*tahn lyay soh-TAY ahn toor-NAHN*]. Connected movement, jumped and turned. This is a temps lié sauté performed with a sissonne simple en tournant before stepping into each position.

**Temps lié simple en arrière** [*tahn lyay SEN-pluh ah na-RYEHR*]. Simple connected movement, traveling backward. Fifth position croisé L foot back, arms bras bas. Demi-plié and glide the pointed toe of the L foot into the fourth position croisé derrière. Demi-plié in the fourth position, then shift the weight onto the L foot, straightening the knees and raising the R foot pointe tendue croisé devant. Close the R foot to the fifth position front in demi-plié, body en face. Slide the pointed toe of the L foot to the second position, leaving the R foot in demi-plié; shift the weight onto the L foot demi-plié, straighten the knees and point the R foot in the second position, then slide the R foot into the fifth position croisé derrière and demi-plié. Repeat the whole movement to the other side. The arms and head are moved as in temps lié simple en avant.

**Temps lié simple en avant** [*tahn lyay SEN-pluh ah na-VAHN*]. Simple connected movement, traveling forward. Fifth position croisé R foot front, arms bras bas. Demi-plié and glide the pointed toe of the R foot into the fourth position croisé and raise the arms to the gateway. Demi-plié in the fourth position, then shift the weight onto the R foot, straightening both knees and raising the L foot pointe tendue croisé derrière and the arms en attitude, L arm high. Close the L foot to the fifth position back in demi-plié, body en face, and lower the L arm in front of the waist. Slide the pointed toe of the R foot to the second position, leaving the L foot in demi-plié; shift the weight onto the R foot in demi-plié, straighten the knees opening the L arm to the second position and turning the head to the left. With pointed toes, slide the L foot into the fifth position croisé devant and demi-plié, lowering the arms to bras bas. Repeat the whole movement to the other side.

**Temps lié sur les pointes** [*tahn lyay sewr lay pwent*]. Connected movement on the points. Fifth position croisé, R foot front, with the arms held in the position bras bas. Demi-plié, sliding the R foot forward pointe tendue and raising the arms to the gateway. Step onto the R point, drawing the L foot to the fifth position back on point, and raise the arms en attitude, L arm high. Lower the heels and demi-plié, turning the body en face and bringing the L arm down in front of the diaphragm. Slide the R foot to the second position pointe tendue, leaving the L leg in demi-plié and opening the L arm to the second position. Step onto the R point, drawing the L foot to the fifth position front on point and turning the body croisé. Lower the heels and demi-plié, dropping the arms to bras bas. The head moves in proper épaulement (toward the shoulder on the same side as the leg that is in the front). Temps lié sur les pointes may also be done en arrière.

**Temps plané** [*tahn pla-NAY*]. Time soared, soaring movement. *See* Plané.

**Temps relevé** [*tahn ruhl-VAY*]. Lifting movement. A term of the Russian School. This is an exercise done at the bar or in the centre. It is often used as a preparation for another movement. When it serves as preparation for a pirouette, the working leg does the développé forward, then is whipped to second position and to sur le cou-de-pied while the supporting leg remains in demi-plié. The dancer immediately does a relevé and turns in a pirouette en dehors. Temps relevé may be performed en dedans or en dehors at 45 to 90 degrees.

**Temps relevé, grand** [*grahn tahn ruhl-VAY*]. Large lifting movement. This is performed in the same manner as petit temps relevé with the développé performed at 90 degrees.

**Temps relevé, petit** [*puh-TEE tahn ruhl-VAY*]. Small lifting movement. *En dehors:* Fifth position R foot front. Demi-plié and développé the R leg to the fourth position front at 45 degrees. Without stopping the movement, carry the R leg to the second position at 45 degrees, rising simultaneously on the L demi-pointe. *En dedans:* This is done in the same manner but starting with the R foot back and reversing the movement.

**Tendu, tendue** [*tahn-DEW*]. Stretched. As, for example, in battement tendu.

**Terminé, terminée** [*tehr-mee-NAY*]. Ended. Example: pirouette sur le cou-de-pied terminée en attitude.

**Terre, à** [*a tehr*]. On the ground. This term indicates: (1) that the entire base of the supporting foot or feet touches the ground; (2) that the foot usually raised in a pose is to remain on the ground with the toes extended. Example: arabesque à terre.

**Terre, par** [*par tehr*]. Along the ground. Same as à terre. As, for example, in rond de jambe par terre.

**Terre à terre** [*tehr a tehr*]. Ground to ground. Term used to indicate that in the execution of a step the feet barely leave the ground, as in glissade.

**Tête** [*tet*]. Head.

**Tights.** Same as maillot (*q.v.*).

**Tire-bouchon, en** [*ahn teer-boo-SHAWN*]. Like a corkscrew. A term of the Russian School. This is a position in which the leg is raised so that the thigh is in the second position and the tip of the pointed toe touches the knee of the supporting leg. A pirouette in this position, when done with a renversé movement, gives the impression of a corkscrew. *See* Pirouette renversée.

**Tiroirs, faire les** [*fehr lay teer-WAHR*]. To act like the drawers of a chest. Indicates that two opposite lines of dancers are to cross each other and cross back again to their original positions.

**Tombant** [*tawn-BAHN*]. Falling. Same as tombé.

**Tombé, tombée** [*tawn-BAY*]. Falling. This is a movement in which the dancer, with the working leg raised in the air, falls forward, backward or sideways into a fondu on the working leg.

**Tonnelet** [*tawn-LEH*]. Literally, a cask. A short cask-shaped skirt stretched over a hoop-shaped frame worn by male dancers during the eighteenth century.

**Tour** [*toor*]. Turn. A turn of the body. *See* Pirouette.

**Tour, petit** [*puh-TEE toor*]. Little turn. A term of the Cecchetti method. Petits tours are a series of turns done on the points or demi-pointes, making a half-turn on each foot with the feet close together. The turns should be done evenly and with great speed, aided by small movements of the arms and the spotting of the head. Petits tours are usually performed en diagonale or in a circle (autour de la salle).

**Tour chaîné** [*toor sheh-NAY*]. Tours chaînés are turns in a chain. *See* Chaînés; Déboulés.

**Tour chaîné déboulé** [*toor sheh-NAY day-boo-LAY*]. Tours chaînés déboulés are literally "a chain of turns, rolling like a ball." A term of the French School. *See* Chaînes; Déboulés; Tours, petits.

**Tour de basque** [*toor duh bask*]. Basque turn. This is a type of pas de basque performed en tournant either sur les demi-pointes or sur les pointes. Fifth position R foot front. Demi-plié and execute a demi-rond de jambe en l'air en dehors at 45 degrees with the R leg; spring onto the R point or demi-pointe and immediately close the L foot in the fifth position front and pivot to the right. Finish facing front with the R foot front and execute a coupé dessous with the L foot, extending the R foot forward. *See* Pas de basque sur les pointes; Tour glissade en tournant (sur les pointes).

**Tour de force** [*toor duh fawrss*]. An arresting, vital step; a feat of technical skill such as a series of brilliant pirouettes or a combination of outstanding jumps and beats.

**Tour dégagé** [*toor day-ga-ZHAY*]. Disengaged turn. A term of the Russian School. These tours are performed en dedans and en dehors starting from a preparation dégagé. *See* Piqué tour en dedans; Piqué tour en dehors.

**Tour de reins** [*toor duh rēn*]. Turn of the back. This is a series of coupé-jeté en tournant done en manège. The dancer contracts his back muscles and leans toward the centre of the circle at an acute angle. The angle is obtained through the speed and continuity of the step which demands good elevation and a well-arched back. The tempo has an unusual accent and the step actually becomes jeté-coupé instead of coupé-jeté. The jeté may be performed in attitude or arabesque. *See* Coupé-jeté en tournant.

**Tour en dedans** [*toor āhn duh-DAHN*]. Inward turn. A turn in which the dancer turns to the side of the supporting leg; that is, if the turn is done on the R foot, the turn will be to the right. *See* Pirouette en dedans.

**Tour en dehors** [*toor āhn duh-AWR*]. Outward turn. A turn in which the dancer turns to the side of the working leg; that is, if the turn is done on the L foot, the turn will be to the right. *See* Pirouette en dehors.

**Tour en l'air** [*toor ahn lehr*]. Turn in the air. This is essentially a male dancer's step although contemporary choreographers use this tour for girls. It is a turn in the air in which the dancer rises straight into the air from a demi-plié, makes a complete turn and lands in the fifth position with the feet reversed. The turn may be single, double or triple according to the ability of the dancer. Fifth position R foot front. Demi-plié and push off the floor into the air, turning en dehors (to the right). Land in demi-plié in the fifth position, R foot back. The arms assist and the head must spot as in pirouettes. Tour en l'air may also be finished in various poses such as attitude, arabesque, grande seconde or on one knee. It may also be done in a series.

**Tour en l'air avec chute allongée** [*toor ahn lehr a-VEK shewt a-lawn-ZHAY*]. Turn in the air with an outstretched fall. This is a double tour en l'air in which the dancer, before the end of the movement, inclines his body in the direction of the turn and falls sideways to the floor in a horizontal position.

**Tour glissade en tournant (sur les pointes)** [*toor glee-SAD ahn toor-NAHN sewr lay pwent*]. Glissade, turning on the points. A term of the Russian School. Same as pas de basque sur les pointes.

**Tour-hanche** [*toor-AHNSH*]. "Hip turn." This was a mechanical device of the eighteenth century designed for achieving a turn-out. The feet were fixed in a turned-out position in this device which did not turn out the leg at the hip joints but only at the ankles and knee joints. Therefore it did not fulfill the purpose for which it was designed.

**Tour jeté** [*toor zhuh-TAY*]. This is a corruption of the term "grand jeté dessus en tournant." *See* Jeté dessus en tournant, grand (French School); Jeté en tournant en arrière, grand (Cecchetti method); Jeté entrelacé (Russian School).

**Tour lent** [*toor lahn*]. Slow turn. A term of the Russian School. A slow turn, used in adagio, performed on the whole sole of the foot. It is done either en dehors or en dedans by a slight movement of the heel in the required direction. These turns are done in all poses such as attitude, arabesque, à la seconde, and also with a change from one position to another during the turn. The entire body must remain immobile while turning. In a pas de deux, the girl does a supported tour lent sur la pointe while the boy walks around her in a promenade. *See* Promenade, tour de.

**Tournant, en** [*ahn toor-NAHN*]. Turning. Indicates that the body is to turn while executing a given step. As, for example, in assemblé en tournant.

**Tourner** [*toor-NAY*]. To turn around. One of the seven movements in dancing.

**Tour piqué en dedans** [*toor pee-KAY ahn duh-DAHN*]. Pricked turn, inward. Same as piqué tour en dedans.

**Tour piqué en dehors** [*toor pee-KAY ahn duh-AWR*]. Pricked turn, outward. Same as piqué tour en dehors.

**Tour posé** [*toor poh-ZAY*]. Poised turn. A term of the Cecchetti method. Same as Piqué tour.

**Tour sauté** [*toor soh-TAY*]. Jumping turn. Tours sautés are done with the supporting leg in demi-plié, the other leg raised in grande seconde, in arabesque or attitude. The dancer does a series of quick little hops, pivoting on the ball of the foot and shifting the heel with each little hop, turning either en dehors or en dedans. The head "spots." Tours sautés are often combined with pirouettes à la seconde and pirouettes sur le cou-de-pied to make up the many variations of grande pirouette. *See* Pirouette, grande.

**Tour sautillé** [*toor soh-tee-YAY*]. Hopping turn. A term of the Russian School. These turns are done with a series of tiny hops turning in demi-plié on the supporting foot with the heel barely leaving the floor. The turns are done en dedans in first and second arabesque and attitude effacée and en dehors in third and fourth arabesque and attitude croisée.

**Travesti, en** [*ahn tra-ves-TEE*]. In disguise. A term applied to a female dancer dressed as a man and taking a man's part.

**Trois** [*trwah*]. Three. As, for example, in entrechat trois.

**Troisième** [*trwah-ZYEM*]. Third. As, for example, in troisième arabesque.

**Turn-out.** This is the ability of the dancer to turn his or her feet and legs out from the hip joints to a 90-degree position. This turn-out, or en-dehors, is one of the essential principles of the classical dance, giving the dancer freedom of movement in every direction.

**Tutu** [*tew-TEW*]. This is the short classical ballet skirt made of many layers of tarlatan or net. The romantic tutu is the long skirt reaching below the calf.

**Un, une** [*uhn, ewn*]. One; a.

**Vaganova, Agrippina** [*ah-gree-PEE-nah vah-GAH-naw-vah*]. The greatest Russian teacher of her day (1879–1951). She was a graduate of the St. Petersburg Imperial Ballet School, where she studied under Ivanov, Vazem, Gerdt, Legat and others. She was accepted into the corps de ballet of the Maryinski Theatre in 1897 and became a ballerina in 1915. She left the stage in 1917 to devote herself to teaching. In 1921 she became a teacher at the Leningrad State Ballet School (formerly the Imperial Ballet School, St. Petersburg) and began developing the instructional system that later became known to the world as the Vaganova system. In 1934 she became head of the Leningrad Choreographic Technicum and published her textbook *Fundamentals of the Classic Dance*. Vaganova's method has become the basic method of the entire Soviet choreographic school. This method is still being developed by Vaganova's followers.

**Valse** [*vals*]. Waltz. *See* Pas de valse.

**Variation** [*va-rya-SYAWN*]. Variation. A solo dance in a classic ballet.

**Virtuoso.** A performer with great technical ability.

**Volé, volée** [*vaw-LAY*]. Flown, flying. As, for example, in brisé volé.

**Volée, de** [*duh vaw-LAY*]. In flight. Indicates that a specific step is to be done with a flying or soaring movement. As, for example, in entrechat cinq de volée.

**Voyagé** [*vwah-yah-ZHAY*]. Traveled, traveling. Indicates that the dancer while holding a specific pose, generally en arabesque, progresses on the supporting foot by a series of small jumps, landing on the ball of the foot (in demi-plié) with the heel slightly raised. The heel is placed down with a slight fondu.

**Waltz.** A ballroom dance in 3/4 time. It was first introduced in a ballet by Pierre Gardel in his *La Dansomanie* of 1800.

**Warm-up.** This is the term used by dancers for the exercises they perform in the wings before going on stage for a performance. These are usually bar exercises plus stretching and limbering. Dancers always warm up as a precaution against injury to the muscles and tendons and to make sure that the body is pliable and ready for the strain to be placed upon it.

**Working leg.** A term used by dancers and teachers to denote the leg that is executing a given movement while the weight of the body is on the supporting leg.

**Wrapped position.** This term of the Russian School refers to a position sur le cou-de-pied in which the foot is wrapped around the ankle. *See* Cou-de-pied, sur le (Russian School).

# *Illustrations*

*Audience*

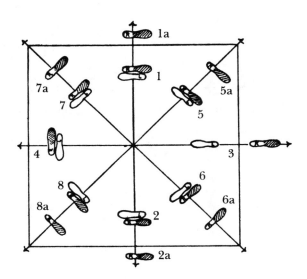

## DIAGRAMMATIC FLOOR PLAN:
## DIRECTIONS OF BODY AND FEET

This plan shows the directions of the body and feet when using the right foot. When the left foot is used the directions croisé and effacé are reversed.

1. De face.
1a. En avant.
2. De face.
2a. En arrière.
3. À la seconde, or de côté.
4. Facing de côté.
5. Facing effacé or ouvert.

5a. Effacé or ouvert en avant.
6. Facing effacé or ouvert.
6a. Effacé or ouvert en arrière.
7. Facing croisé.
7a. Croisé en avant.
8. Facing croisé.
8a. Croisé en arrière.

First arabesque.

Second arabesque.

Third arabesque.

Fourth arabesque.

Fifth arabesque.

ARABESQUES: CECCHETTI METHOD
*(see p. 2)*

Arabesque ouverte.

Arabesque croisée.

**ARABESQUES: FRENCH SCHOOL**
*(see p. 3)*

First arabesque.

Second arabesque.

Third arabesque.

Fourth arabesque.

**ARABESQUES: RUSSIAN SCHOOL**
*(see p. 3)*

Attitude effacée (Cecchetti).

Attitude effacée (Russian).

Attitude épaulée.

Attitude croisée derrière (Cecchetti).

Attitude croisée derrière (Russian).

Attitude croisée devant.

## ATTITUDES
*(see p. 9)*

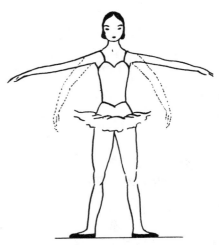

First position of the arms (and feet).

Second position of the arms (and feet). The dotted lines show the demi-seconde position of the arms.

Third position of the arms (and feet).

Fourth position en avant of the arms (with the feet in the fourth position croisée).

**POSITIONS DES BRAS: CECCHETTI METHOD**
*(see p. 23)*

Fourth position en haut of the arms
(with the feet in the fourth position
croisée).

Fifth position en bas of the arms
(with the feet in the fifth position).

Fifth position en avant of the arms
(with the feet in the fifth position).

Fifth position en haut of the arms
(with the feet in the fifth position).

Bras au repos.

First position of the arms.

Second position of the arms.

Third position of the arms.

Fourth position of the arms.

Fifth position of the arms.

**POSITIONS DES BRAS: FRENCH SCHOOL**
*(see p. 24)*

Preparatory position.

First position of the arms.

Second position of the arms.

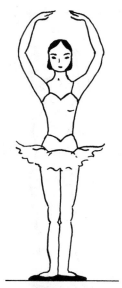

Third position of the arms.

**POSITIONS DES BRAS: RUSSIAN SCHOOL**
*(see p. 25)*

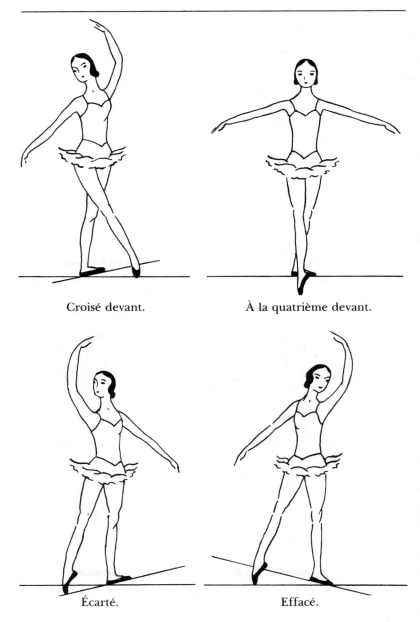

Croisé devant.

À la quatrième devant.

Écarté.

Effacé.

**BASIC POSITIONS OF THE BODY:
CECCHETTI METHOD**
*(see p. 91)*

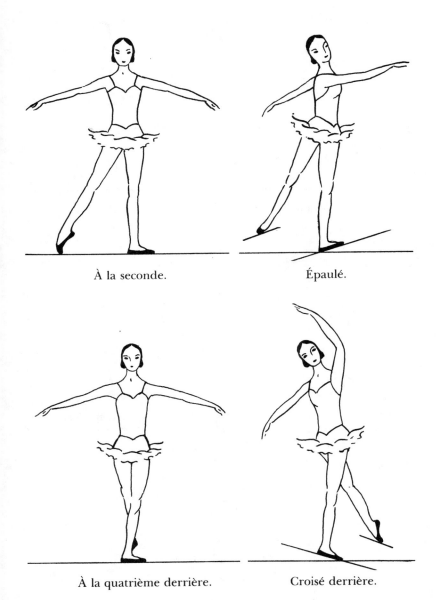

À la seconde.                                    Épaulé.

À la quatrième derrière.                         Croisé derrière.

Croisé devant.

Croisé derrière.

À la quatrième devant.

À la quatrième derrière.

À la seconde.

**BASIC POSITIONS OF THE BODY:**
**RUSSIAN AND FRENCH SCHOOLS**
(*see p.* 91)

Écarté devant.                    Écarté derrière.

Effacé devant.                    Effacé derrière.

Épaulé devant.                    Épaulé derrière.

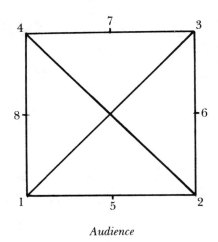

*Audience*

**FIXED POINTS OF THE PRACTICE ROOM OR STAGE:
CECCHETTI METHOD**
*(see p. 52)*

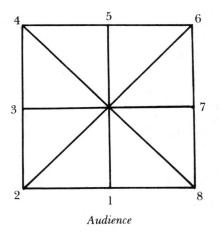

*Audience*

**FIXED POINTS OF THE PRACTICE ROOM OR STAGE:
RUSSIAN SCHOOL (VAGANOVA)**
*(see p. 52)*

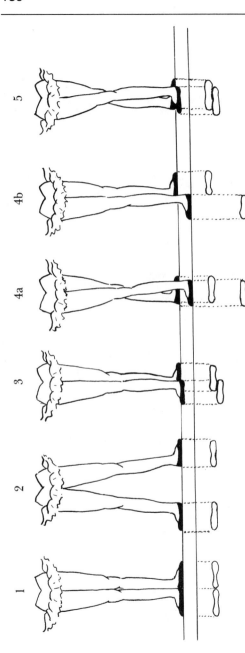

## CINQ POSITIONS DES PIEDS
(*see p. 82*)

1. First position of the feet.
2. Second position of the feet.
3. Third position of the feet.
4a. Fourth position of the feet. This position may also be done with the feet placed in the third position, parallel and separated by the length of one foot.
4b. Fourth position ouverte of the feet.
5. Fifth position of the feet (Cecchetti). In the Russian and French Schools the feet are completely crossed toe to heel.

# A CATALOG OF SELECTED
# DOVER BOOKS
## IN ALL FIELDS OF INTEREST

# A CATALOG OF SELECTED DOVER
# BOOKS IN ALL FIELDS OF INTEREST

CONCERNING THE SPIRITUAL IN ART, Wassily Kandinsky. Pioneering work by father of abstract art. Thoughts on color theory, nature of art. Analysis of earlier masters. 12 illustrations. 80pp. of text. 5⅜ x 8½. 0-486-23411-8

CELTIC ART: The Methods of Construction, George Bain. Simple geometric techniques for making Celtic interlacements, spirals, Kells-type initials, animals, humans, etc. Over 500 illustrations. 160pp. 9 x 12. (Available in U.S. only.) 0-486-22923-8

AN ATLAS OF ANATOMY FOR ARTISTS, Fritz Schider. Most thorough reference work on art anatomy in the world. Hundreds of illustrations, including selections from works by Vesalius, Leonardo, Goya, Ingres, Michelangelo, others. 593 illustrations. 192pp. 7⅛ x 10¼. 0-486-20241-0

CELTIC HAND STROKE-BY-STROKE (Irish Half-Uncial from "The Book of Kells"): An Arthur Baker Calligraphy Manual, Arthur Baker. Complete guide to creating each letter of the alphabet in distinctive Celtic manner. Covers hand position, strokes, pens, inks, paper, more. Illustrated. 48pp. 8¼ x 11. 0-486-24336-2

EASY ORIGAMI, John Montroll. Charming collection of 32 projects (hat, cup, pelican, piano, swan, many more) specially designed for the novice origami hobbyist. Clearly illustrated easy-to-follow instructions insure that even beginning papercrafters will achieve successful results. 48pp. 8¼ x 11. 0-486-27298-2

BLOOMINGDALE'S ILLUSTRATED 1886 CATALOG: Fashions, Dry Goods and Housewares, Bloomingdale Brothers. Famed merchants' extremely rare catalog depicting about 1,700 products: clothing, housewares, firearms, dry goods, jewelry, more. Invaluable for dating, identifying vintage items. Also, copyright-free graphics for artists, designers. Co-published with Henry Ford Museum & Greenfield Village. 160pp. 8¼ x 11. 0-486-25780-0

THE ART OF WORLDLY WISDOM, Baltasar Gracian. "Think with the few and speak with the many," "Friends are a second existence," and "Be able to forget" are among this 1637 volume's 300 pithy maxims. A perfect source of mental and spiritual refreshment, it can be opened at random and appreciated either in brief or at length. 128pp. 5⅜ x 8½. 0-486-44034-6

JOHNSON'S DICTIONARY: A Modern Selection, Samuel Johnson (E. L. McAdam and George Milne, eds.). This modern version reduces the original 1755 edition's 2,300 pages of definitions and literary examples to a more manageable length, retaining the verbal pleasure and historical curiosity of the original. 480pp. 5³⁄₁₆ x 8¼. 0-486-44089-3

ADVENTURES OF HUCKLEBERRY FINN, Mark Twain, Illustrated by E. W. Kemble. A work of eternal richness and complexity, a source of ongoing critical debate, and a literary landmark, Twain's 1885 masterpiece about a barefoot boy's journey of self-discovery has enthralled readers around the world. This handsome clothbound reproduction of the first edition features all 174 of the original black-and-white illustrations. 368pp. 5⅜ x 8½. 0-486-44322-1

STICKLEY CRAFTSMAN FURNITURE CATALOGS, Gustav Stickley and L. & J. G. Stickley. Beautiful, functional furniture in two authentic catalogs from 1910. 594 illustrations, including 277 photos, show settles, rockers, armchairs, reclining chairs, bookcases, desks, tables. 183pp. 6½ x 9¼. 0-486-23838-5

AMERICAN LOCOMOTIVES IN HISTORIC PHOTOGRAPHS: 1858 to 1949, Ron Ziel (ed.). A rare collection of 126 meticulously detailed official photographs, called "builder portraits," of American locomotives that majestically chronicle the rise of steam locomotive power in America. Introduction. Detailed captions. xi+ 129pp. 9 x 12. 0-486-27393-8

AMERICA'S LIGHTHOUSES: An Illustrated History, Francis Ross Holland, Jr. Delightfully written, profusely illustrated fact-filled survey of over 200 American lighthouses since 1716. History, anecdotes, technological advances, more. 240pp. 8 x 10¾. 0-486-25576-X

TOWARDS A NEW ARCHITECTURE, Le Corbusier. Pioneering manifesto by founder of "International School." Technical and aesthetic theories, views of industry, economics, relation of form to function, "mass-production split" and much more. Profusely illustrated. 320pp. 6⅛ x 9¼. (Available in U.S. only.) 0-486-25023-7

HOW THE OTHER HALF LIVES, Jacob Riis. Famous journalistic record, exposing poverty and degradation of New York slums around 1900, by major social reformer. 100 striking and influential photographs. 233pp. 10 x 7⅞. 0-486-22012-5

FRUIT KEY AND TWIG KEY TO TREES AND SHRUBS, William M. Harlow. One of the handiest and most widely used identification aids. Fruit key covers 120 deciduous and evergreen species; twig key 160 deciduous species. Easily used. Over 300 photographs. 126pp. 5⅜ x 8½. 0-486-20511-8

COMMON BIRD SONGS, Dr. Donald J. Borror. Songs of 60 most common U.S. birds: robins, sparrows, cardinals, bluejays, finches, more—arranged in order of increasing complexity. Up to 9 variations of songs of each species.
Cassette and manual 0-486-99911-4

ORCHIDS AS HOUSE PLANTS, Rebecca Tyson Northen. Grow cattleyas and many other kinds of orchids—in a window, in a case, or under artificial light. 63 illustrations. 148pp. 5⅜ x 8½. 0-486-23261-1

MONSTER MAZES, Dave Phillips. Masterful mazes at four levels of difficulty. Avoid deadly perils and evil creatures to find magical treasures. Solutions for all 32 exciting illustrated puzzles. 48pp. 8¼ x 11. 0-486-26005-4

MOZART'S DON GIOVANNI (DOVER OPERA LIBRETTO SERIES), Wolfgang Amadeus Mozart. Introduced and translated by Ellen H. Bleiler. Standard Italian libretto, with complete English translation. Convenient and thoroughly portable—an ideal companion for reading along with a recording or the performance itself. Introduction. List of characters. Plot summary. 121pp. 5¼ x 8½. 0-486-24944-1

FRANK LLOYD WRIGHT'S DANA HOUSE, Donald Hoffmann. Pictorial essay of residential masterpiece with over 160 interior and exterior photos, plans, elevations, sketches and studies. 128pp. 9¼ x 10¾. 0-486-29120-0

THE CLARINET AND CLARINET PLAYING, David Pino. Lively, comprehensive work features suggestions about technique, musicianship, and musical interpretation, as well as guidelines for teaching, making your own reeds, and preparing for public performance. Includes an intriguing look at clarinet history. "A godsend," *The Clarinet,* Journal of the International Clarinet Society. Appendixes. 7 illus. 320pp. 5⅜ x 8½. 0-486-40270-3

HOLLYWOOD GLAMOR PORTRAITS, John Kobal (ed.). 145 photos from 1926-49. Harlow, Gable, Bogart, Bacall; 94 stars in all. Full background on photographers, technical aspects. 160pp. 8⅜ x 11¼. 0-486-23352-9

THE RAVEN AND OTHER FAVORITE POEMS, Edgar Allan Poe. Over 40 of the author's most memorable poems: "The Bells," "Ulalume," "Israfel," "To Helen," "The Conqueror Worm," "Eldorado," "Annabel Lee," many more. Alphabetic lists of titles and first lines. 64pp. 5 3/16 x 8¼. 0-486-26685-0

PERSONAL MEMOIRS OF U. S. GRANT, Ulysses Simpson Grant. Intelligent, deeply moving firsthand account of Civil War campaigns, considered by many the finest military memoirs ever written. Includes letters, historic photographs, maps and more. 528pp. 6⅛ x 9¼. 0-486-28587-1

ANCIENT EGYPTIAN MATERIALS AND INDUSTRIES, A. Lucas and J. Harris. Fascinating, comprehensive, thoroughly documented text describes this ancient civilization's vast resources and the processes that incorporated them in daily life, including the use of animal products, building materials, cosmetics, perfumes and incense, fibers, glazed ware, glass and its manufacture, materials used in the mummification process, and much more. 544pp. 6 1/8 x 9 1/4. (Available in U.S. only.) 0-486-40446-3

RUSSIAN STORIES/RUSSKIE RASSKAZY: A Dual-Language Book, edited by Gleb Struve. Twelve tales by such masters as Chekhov, Tolstoy, Dostoevsky, Pushkin, others. Excellent word-for-word English translations on facing pages, plus teaching and study aids, Russian/English vocabulary, biographical/critical introductions, more. 416pp. 5⅜ x 8½. 0-486-26244-8

PHILADELPHIA THEN AND NOW: 60 Sites Photographed in the Past and Present, Kenneth Finkel and Susan Oyama. Rare photographs of City Hall, Logan Square, Independence Hall, Betsy Ross House, other landmarks juxtaposed with contemporary views. Captures changing face of historic city. Introduction. Captions. 128pp. 8¼ x 11. 0-486-25790-8

NORTH AMERICAN INDIAN LIFE: Customs and Traditions of 23 Tribes, Elsie Clews Parsons (ed.). 27 fictionalized essays by noted anthropologists examine religion, customs, government, additional facets of life among the Winnebago, Crow, Zuni, Eskimo, other tribes. 480pp. 6⅛ x 9¼. 0-486-27377-6

TECHNICAL MANUAL AND DICTIONARY OF CLASSICAL BALLET, Gail Grant. Defines, explains, comments on steps, movements, poses and concepts. 15-page pictorial section. Basic book for student, viewer. 127pp. 5⅜ x 8½. 0-486-21843-0

THE MALE AND FEMALE FIGURE IN MOTION: 60 Classic Photographic Sequences, Eadweard Muybridge. 60 true-action photographs of men and women walking, running, climbing, bending, turning, etc., reproduced from rare 19th-century masterpiece. vi + 121pp. 9 x 12. 0-486-24745-7

ANIMALS: 1,419 Copyright-Free Illustrations of Mammals, Birds, Fish, Insects, etc., Jim Harter (ed.). Clear wood engravings present, in extremely lifelike poses, over 1,000 species of animals. One of the most extensive pictorial sourcebooks of its kind. Captions. Index. 284pp. 9 x 12. 0-486-23766-4

1001 QUESTIONS ANSWERED ABOUT THE SEASHORE, N. J. Berrill and Jacquelyn Berrill. Queries answered about dolphins, sea snails, sponges, starfish, fishes, shore birds, many others. Covers appearance, breeding, growth, feeding, much more. 305pp. 5¼ x 8¼. 0-486-23366-9

ATTRACTING BIRDS TO YOUR YARD, William J. Weber. Easy-to-follow guide offers advice on how to attract the greatest diversity of birds: birdhouses, feeders, water and waterers, much more. 96pp. 5³⁄₁₆ x 8¼. 0-486-28927-3

MEDICINAL AND OTHER USES OF NORTH AMERICAN PLANTS: A Historical Survey with Special Reference to the Eastern Indian Tribes, Charlotte Erichsen-Brown. Chronological historical citations document 500 years of usage of plants, trees, shrubs native to eastern Canada, northeastern U.S. Also complete identifying information. 343 illustrations. 544pp. 6½ x 9¼. 0-486-25951-X

STORYBOOK MAZES, Dave Phillips. 23 stories and mazes on two-page spreads: Wizard of Oz, Treasure Island, Robin Hood, etc. Solutions. 64pp. 8¼ x 11.
0-486-23628-5

AMERICAN NEGRO SONGS: 230 Folk Songs and Spirituals, Religious and Secular, John W. Work. This authoritative study traces the African influences of songs sung and played by black Americans at work, in church, and as entertainment. The author discusses the lyric significance of such songs as "Swing Low, Sweet Chariot," "John Henry," and others and offers the words and music for 230 songs. Bibliography. Index of Song Titles. 272pp. 6½ x 9¼. 0-486-40271-1

MOVIE-STAR PORTRAITS OF THE FORTIES, John Kobal (ed.). 163 glamor, studio photos of 106 stars of the 1940s: Rita Hayworth, Ava Gardner, Marlon Brando, Clark Gable, many more. 176pp. 8⅜ x 11¼. 0-486-23546-7

YEKL and THE IMPORTED BRIDEGROOM AND OTHER STORIES OF YIDDISH NEW YORK, Abraham Cahan. Film Hester Street based on *Yekl* (1896). Novel, other stories among first about Jewish immigrants on N.Y.'s East Side. 240pp. 5⅜ x 8½. 0-486-22427-9

SELECTED POEMS, Walt Whitman. Generous sampling from *Leaves of Grass*. Twenty-four poems include "I Hear America Singing," "Song of the Open Road," "I Sing the Body Electric," "When Lilacs Last in the Dooryard Bloom'd," "O Captain! My Captain!"–all reprinted from an authoritative edition. Lists of titles and first lines. 128pp. 5³⁄₁₆ x 8¼. 0-486-26878-0

SONGS OF EXPERIENCE: Facsimile Reproduction with 26 Plates in Full Color, William Blake. 26 full-color plates from a rare 1826 edition. Includes "The Tyger," "London," "Holy Thursday," and other poems. Printed text of poems. 48pp. 5¼ x 7.
0-486-24636-1

THE BEST TALES OF HOFFMANN, E. T. A. Hoffmann. 10 of Hoffmann's most important stories: "Nutcracker and the King of Mice," "The Golden Flowerpot," etc. 458pp. 5⅜ x 8½. 0-486-21793-0

THE BOOK OF TEA, Kakuzo Okakura. Minor classic of the Orient: entertaining, charming explanation, interpretation of traditional Japanese culture in terms of tea ceremony. 94pp. 5⅜ x 8½. 0-486-20070-1

FRENCH STORIES/CONTES FRANÇAIS: A Dual-Language Book, Wallace Fowlie. Ten stories by French masters, Voltaire to Camus: "Micromegas" by Voltaire; "The Atheist's Mass" by Balzac; "Minuet" by de Maupassant; "The Guest" by Camus, six more. Excellent English translations on facing pages. Also French-English vocabulary list, exercises, more. 352pp. 5⅜ x 8½. 0-486-26443-2

CHICAGO AT THE TURN OF THE CENTURY IN PHOTOGRAPHS: 122 Historic Views from the Collections of the Chicago Historical Society, Larry A. Viskochil. Rare large-format prints offer detailed views of City Hall, State Street, the Loop, Hull House, Union Station, many other landmarks, circa 1904-1913. Introduction. Captions. Maps. 144pp. 9⅜ x 12¼. 0-486-24656-6

OLD BROOKLYN IN EARLY PHOTOGRAPHS, 1865-1929, William Lee Younger. Luna Park, Gravesend race track, construction of Grand Army Plaza, moving of Hotel Brighton, etc. 157 previously unpublished photographs. 165pp. 8⅞ x 11¾. 0-486-23587-4

THE MYTHS OF THE NORTH AMERICAN INDIANS, Lewis Spence. Rich anthology of the myths and legends of the Algonquins, Iroquois, Pawnees and Sioux, prefaced by an extensive historical and ethnological commentary. 36 illustrations. 480pp. 5⅜ x 8½. 0-486-25967-6

AN ENCYCLOPEDIA OF BATTLES: Accounts of Over 1,560 Battles from 1479 B.C. to the Present, David Eggenberger. Essential details of every major battle in recorded history from the first battle of Megiddo in 1479 B.C. to Grenada in 1984. List of Battle Maps. New Appendix covering the years 1967-1984. Index. 99 illustrations. 544pp. 6½ x 9¼. 0-486-24913-1

SAILING ALONE AROUND THE WORLD, Captain Joshua Slocum. First man to sail around the world, alone, in small boat. One of great feats of seamanship told in delightful manner. 67 illustrations. 294pp. 5⅜ x 8½. 0-486-20326-3

ANARCHISM AND OTHER ESSAYS, Emma Goldman. Powerful, penetrating, prophetic essays on direct action, role of minorities, prison reform, puritan hypocrisy, violence, etc. 271pp. 5⅜ x 8½. 0-486-22484-8

MYTHS OF THE HINDUS AND BUDDHISTS, Ananda K. Coomaraswamy and Sister Nivedita. Great stories of the epics; deeds of Krishna, Shiva, taken from puranas, Vedas, folk tales; etc. 32 illustrations. 400pp. 5⅜ x 8½. 0-486-21759-0

MY BONDAGE AND MY FREEDOM, Frederick Douglass. Born a slave, Douglass became outspoken force in antislavery movement. The best of Douglass' autobiographies. Graphic description of slave life. 464pp. 5⅜ x 8½. 0-486-22457-0

FOLLOWING THE EQUATOR: A Journey Around the World, Mark Twain. Fascinating humorous account of 1897 voyage to Hawaii, Australia, India, New Zealand, etc. Ironic, bemused reports on peoples, customs, climate, flora and fauna, politics, much more. 197 illustrations. 720pp. 5⅜ x 8½. 0-486-26113-1

THE PEOPLE CALLED SHAKERS, Edward D. Andrews. Definitive study of Shakers: origins, beliefs, practices, dances, social organization, furniture and crafts, etc. 33 illustrations. 351pp. 5⅜ x 8½. 0-486-21081-2

THE MYTHS OF GREECE AND ROME, H. A. Guerber. A classic of mythology, generously illustrated, long prized for its simple, graphic, accurate retelling of the principal myths of Greece and Rome, and for its commentary on their origins and significance. With 64 illustrations by Michelangelo, Raphael, Titian, Rubens, Canova, Bernini and others. 480pp. 5⅜ x 8½. 0-486-27584-1

PSYCHOLOGY OF MUSIC, Carl E. Seashore. Classic work discusses music as a medium from psychological viewpoint. Clear treatment of physical acoustics, auditory apparatus, sound perception, development of musical skills, nature of musical feeling, host of other topics. 88 figures. 408pp. 5⅜ x 8½. 0-486-21851-1

LIFE IN ANCIENT EGYPT, Adolf Erman. Fullest, most thorough, detailed older account with much not in more recent books, domestic life, religion, magic, medicine, commerce, much more. Many illustrations reproduce tomb paintings, carvings, hieroglyphs, etc. 597pp. 5⅜ x 8½. 0-486-22632-8

SUNDIALS, Their Theory and Construction, Albert Waugh. Far and away the best, most thorough coverage of ideas, mathematics concerned, types, construction, adjusting anywhere. Simple, nontechnical treatment allows even children to build several of these dials. Over 100 illustrations. 230pp. 5⅜ x 8½. 0-486-22947-5

THEORETICAL HYDRODYNAMICS, L. M. Milne-Thomson. Classic exposition of the mathematical theory of fluid motion, applicable to both hydrodynamics and aerodynamics. Over 600 exercises. 768pp. 6⅛ x 9¼. 0-486-68970-0

OLD-TIME VIGNETTES IN FULL COLOR, Carol Belanger Grafton (ed.). Over 390 charming, often sentimental illustrations, selected from archives of Victorian graphics—pretty women posing, children playing, food, flowers, kittens and puppies, smiling cherubs, birds and butterflies, much more. All copyright-free. 48pp. 9¼ x 12¼. 0-486-27269-9

PERSPECTIVE FOR ARTISTS, Rex Vicat Cole. Depth, perspective of sky and sea, shadows, much more, not usually covered. 391 diagrams, 81 reproductions of drawings and paintings. 279pp. 5⅜ x 8½. 0-486-22487-2

DRAWING THE LIVING FIGURE, Joseph Sheppard. Innovative approach to artistic anatomy focuses on specifics of surface anatomy, rather than muscles and bones. Over 170 drawings of live models in front, back and side views, and in widely varying poses. Accompanying diagrams. 177 illustrations. Introduction. Index. 144pp. 8⅜ x11¼. 0-486-26723-7

GOTHIC AND OLD ENGLISH ALPHABETS: 100 Complete Fonts, Dan X. Solo. Add power, elegance to posters, signs, other graphics with 100 stunning copyright-free alphabets: Blackstone, Dolbey, Germania, 97 more—including many lower-case, numerals, punctuation marks. 104pp. 8⅛ x 11. 0-486-24695-7

THE BOOK OF WOOD CARVING, Charles Marshall Sayers. Finest book for beginners discusses fundamentals and offers 34 designs. "Absolutely first rate . . . well thought out and well executed."–E. J. Tangerman. 118pp. 7¾ x 10⅝. 0-486-23654-4

ILLUSTRATED CATALOG OF CIVIL WAR MILITARY GOODS: Union Army Weapons, Insignia, Uniform Accessories, and Other Equipment, Schuyler, Hartley, and Graham. Rare, profusely illustrated 1846 catalog includes Union Army uniform and dress regulations, arms and ammunition, coats, insignia, flags, swords, rifles, etc. 226 illustrations. 160pp. 9 x 12. 0-486-24939-5

WOMEN'S FASHIONS OF THE EARLY 1900s: An Unabridged Republication of "New York Fashions, 1909," National Cloak & Suit Co. Rare catalog of mail-order fashions documents women's and children's clothing styles shortly after the turn of the century. Captions offer full descriptions, prices. Invaluable resource for fashion, costume historians. Approximately 725 illustrations. 128pp. 8⅜ x 11¼. 0-486-27276-1

HOW TO DO BEADWORK, Mary White. Fundamental book on craft from simple projects to five-bead chains and woven works. 106 illustrations. 142pp. 5⅜ x 8.
0-486-20697-1

THE 1912 AND 1915 GUSTAV STICKLEY FURNITURE CATALOGS, Gustav Stickley. With over 200 detailed illustrations and descriptions, these two catalogs are essential reading and reference materials and identification guides for Stickley furniture. Captions cite materials, dimensions and prices. 112pp. 6½ x 9¼. 0-486-26676-1

EARLY AMERICAN LOCOMOTIVES, John H. White, Jr. Finest locomotive engravings from early 19th century: historical (1804–74), main-line (after 1870), special, foreign, etc. 147 plates. 142pp. 11⅜ x 8¼. 0-486-22772-3

LITTLE BOOK OF EARLY AMERICAN CRAFTS AND TRADES, Peter Stockham (ed.). 1807 children's book explains crafts and trades: baker, hatter, cooper, potter, and many others. 23 copperplate illustrations. 140pp. 4⅝ x 6.
0-486-23336-7

VICTORIAN FASHIONS AND COSTUMES FROM HARPER'S BAZAR, 1867–1898, Stella Blum (ed.). Day costumes, evening wear, sports clothes, shoes, hats, other accessories in over 1,000 detailed engravings. 320pp. 9⅜ x 12¼.
0-486-22990-4

THE LONG ISLAND RAIL ROAD IN EARLY PHOTOGRAPHS, Ron Ziel. Over 220 rare photos, informative text document origin ( 1844) and development of rail service on Long Island. Vintage views of early trains, locomotives, stations, passengers, crews, much more. Captions. 8⅞ x 11¾. 0-486-26301-0

VOYAGE OF THE LIBERDADE, Joshua Slocum. Great 19th-century mariner's thrilling, first-hand account of the wreck of his ship off South America, the 35-foot boat he built from the wreckage, and its remarkable voyage home. 128pp. 5⅜ x 8½.
0-486-40022-0

TEN BOOKS ON ARCHITECTURE, Vitruvius. The most important book ever written on architecture. Early Roman aesthetics, technology, classical orders, site selection, all other aspects. Morgan translation. 331pp. 5⅜ x 8½. 0-486-20645-9

THE HUMAN FIGURE IN MOTION, Eadweard Muybridge. More than 4,500 stopped-action photos, in action series, showing undraped men, women, children jumping, lying down, throwing, sitting, wrestling, carrying, etc. 390pp. 7⅞ x 10⅝.
0-486-20204-6 Clothbd.

TREES OF THE EASTERN AND CENTRAL UNITED STATES AND CANADA, William M. Harlow. Best one-volume guide to 140 trees. Full descriptions, woodlore, range, etc. Over 600 illustrations. Handy size. 288pp. 4½ x 6⅜. 0-486-20395-6

GROWING AND USING HERBS AND SPICES, Milo Miloradovich. Versatile handbook provides all the information needed for cultivation and use of all the herbs and spices available in North America. 4 illustrations. Index. Glossary. 236pp. 5⅜ x 8½.
0-486-25058-X

BIG BOOK OF MAZES AND LABYRINTHS, Walter Shepherd. 50 mazes and labyrinths in all—classical, solid, ripple, and more—in one great volume. Perfect inexpensive puzzler for clever youngsters. Full solutions. 112pp. 8⅛ x 11. 0-486-22951-3

PIANO TUNING, J. Cree Fischer. Clearest, best book for beginner, amateur. Simple repairs, raising dropped notes, tuning by easy method of flattened fifths. No previous skills needed. 4 illustrations. 201pp. 5⅜ x 8½. 0-486-23267-0

HINTS TO SINGERS, Lillian Nordica. Selecting the right teacher, developing confidence, overcoming stage fright, and many other important skills receive thoughtful discussion in this indispensible guide, written by a world-famous diva of four decades' experience. 96pp. 5⅜ x 8½. 0-486-40094-8

THE COMPLETE NONSENSE OF EDWARD LEAR, Edward Lear. All nonsense limericks, zany alphabets, Owl and Pussycat, songs, nonsense botany, etc., illustrated by Lear. Total of 320pp. 5⅜ x 8½. (Available in U.S. only.) 0-486-20167-8

VICTORIAN PARLOUR POETRY: An Annotated Anthology, Michael R. Turner. 117 gems by Longfellow, Tennyson, Browning, many lesser-known poets. "The Village Blacksmith," "Curfew Must Not Ring Tonight," "Only a Baby Small," dozens more, often difficult to find elsewhere. Index of poets, titles, first lines. xxiii + 325pp. 5⅝ x 8¼. 0-486-27044-0

DUBLINERS, James Joyce. Fifteen stories offer vivid, tightly focused observations of the lives of Dublin's poorer classes. At least one, "The Dead," is considered a masterpiece. Reprinted complete and unabridged from standard edition. 160pp. 5 3/16 x 8¼. 0-486-26870-5

GREAT WEIRD TALES: 14 Stories by Lovecraft, Blackwood, Machen and Others, S. T. Joshi (ed.). 14 spellbinding tales, including "The Sin Eater," by Fiona McLeod, "The Eye Above the Mantel," by Frank Belknap Long, as well as renowned works by R. H. Barlow, Lord Dunsany, Arthur Machen, W. C. Morrow and eight other masters of the genre. 256pp. 5⅜ x 8½. (Available in U.S. only.) 0-486-40436-6

THE BOOK OF THE SACRED MAGIC OF ABRAMELIN THE MAGE, translated by S. MacGregor Mathers. Medieval manuscript of ceremonial magic. Basic document in Aleister Crowley, Golden Dawn groups. 268pp. 5⅜ x 8½. 0-486-23211-5

THE BATTLES THAT CHANGED HISTORY, Fletcher Pratt. Eminent historian profiles 16 crucial conflicts, ancient to modern, that changed the course of civilization. 352pp. 5⅜ x 8½. 0-486-41129-X

NEW RUSSIAN-ENGLISH AND ENGLISH-RUSSIAN DICTIONARY, M. A. O'Brien. This is a remarkably handy Russian dictionary, containing a surprising amount of information, including over 70,000 entries. 366pp. 4½ x 6⅛. 0-486-20208-9

NEW YORK IN THE FORTIES, Andreas Feininger. 162 brilliant photographs by the well-known photographer, formerly with *Life* magazine. Commuters, shoppers, Times Square at night, much else from city at its peak. Captions by John von Hartz. 181pp. 9¼ x 10¾. 0-486-23585-8

INDIAN SIGN LANGUAGE, William Tomkins. Over 525 signs developed by Sioux and other tribes. Written instructions and diagrams. Also 290 pictographs. 111pp. 6⅛ x 9¼. 0-486-22029-X

ANATOMY: A Complete Guide for Artists, Joseph Sheppard. A master of figure drawing shows artists how to render human anatomy convincingly. Over 460 illustrations. 224pp. 8⅜ x 11¼. 0-486-27279-6

MEDIEVAL CALLIGRAPHY: Its History and Technique, Marc Drogin. Spirited history, comprehensive instruction manual covers 13 styles (ca. 4th century through 15th). Excellent photographs; directions for duplicating medieval techniques with modern tools. 224pp. 8⅜ x 11¼. 0-486-26142-5

DRIED FLOWERS: How to Prepare Them, Sarah Whitlock and Martha Rankin. Complete instructions on how to use silica gel, meal and borax, perlite aggregate, sand and borax, glycerine and water to create attractive permanent flower arrangements. 12 illustrations. 32pp. 5⅜ x 8½. 0-486-21802-3

EASY-TO-MAKE BIRD FEEDERS FOR WOODWORKERS, Scott D. Campbell. Detailed, simple-to-use guide for designing, constructing, caring for and using feeders. Text, illustrations for 12 classic and contemporary designs. 96pp. 5⅜ x 8½. 0-486-25847-5

THE COMPLETE BOOK OF BIRDHOUSE CONSTRUCTION FOR WOODWORKERS, Scott D. Campbell. Detailed instructions, illustrations, tables. Also data on bird habitat and instinct patterns. Bibliography. 3 tables. 63 illustrations in 15 figures. 48pp. 5¼ x 8½. 0-486-24407-5

SCOTTISH WONDER TALES FROM MYTH AND LEGEND, Donald A. Mackenzie. 16 lively tales tell of giants rumbling down mountainsides, of a magic wand that turns stone pillars into warriors, of gods and goddesses, evil hags, powerful forces and more. 240pp. 5⅜ x 8½. 0-486-29677-6

THE HISTORY OF UNDERCLOTHES, C. Willett Cunnington and Phyllis Cunnington. Fascinating, well-documented survey covering six centuries of English undergarments, enhanced with over 100 illustrations: 12th-century laced-up bodice, footed long drawers (1795), 19th-century bustles, 19th-century corsets for men, Victorian "bust improvers," much more. 272pp. 5⅝ x 8¼. 0-486-27124-2

ARTS AND CRAFTS FURNITURE: The Complete Brooks Catalog of 1912, Brooks Manufacturing Co. Photos and detailed descriptions of more than 150 now very collectible furniture designs from the Arts and Crafts movement depict davenports, settees, buffets, desks, tables, chairs, bedsteads, dressers and more, all built of solid, quarter-sawed oak. Invaluable for students and enthusiasts of antiques, Americana and the decorative arts. 80pp. 6½ x 9¼. 0-486-27471-3

WILBUR AND ORVILLE: A Biography of the Wright Brothers, Fred Howard. Definitive, crisply written study tells the full story of the brothers' lives and work. A vividly written biography, unparalleled in scope and color, that also captures the spirit of an extraordinary era. 560pp. 6⅛ x 9¼. 0-486-40297-5

THE ARTS OF THE SAILOR: Knotting, Splicing and Ropework, Hervey Garrett Smith. Indispensable shipboard reference covers tools, basic knots and useful hitches; handsewing and canvas work, more. Over 100 illustrations. Delightful reading for sea lovers. 256pp. 5⅜ x 8½. 0-486-26440-8

FRANK LLOYD WRIGHT'S FALLINGWATER: The House and Its History, Second, Revised Edition, Donald Hoffmann. A total revision–both in text and illustrations–of the standard document on Fallingwater, the boldest, most personal architectural statement of Wright's mature years, updated with valuable new material from the recently opened Frank Lloyd Wright Archives. "Fascinating"–*The New York Times*. 116 illustrations. 128pp. 9¼ x 10¾. 0-486-27430-6

PHOTOGRAPHIC SKETCHBOOK OF THE CIVIL WAR, Alexander Gardner. 100 photos taken on field during the Civil War. Famous shots of Manassas Harper's Ferry, Lincoln, Richmond, slave pens, etc. 244pp. 10⅝ x 8¼. 0-486-22731-6

FIVE ACRES AND INDEPENDENCE, Maurice G. Kains. Great back-to-the-land classic explains basics of self-sufficient farming. The one book to get. 95 illustrations. 397pp. 5⅜ x 8½. 0-486-20974-1

A MODERN HERBAL, Margaret Grieve. Much the fullest, most exact, most useful compilation of herbal material. Gigantic alphabetical encyclopedia, from aconite to zedoary, gives botanical information, medical properties, folklore, economic uses, much else. Indispensable to serious reader. 161 illustrations. 888pp. 6½ x 9¼. 2-vol. set. (Available in U.S. only.)     Vol. I: 0-486-22798-7     Vol. II: 0-486-22799-5

HIDDEN TREASURE MAZE BOOK, Dave Phillips. Solve 34 challenging mazes accompanied by heroic tales of adventure. Evil dragons, people-eating plants, blood-thirsty giants, many more dangerous adversaries lurk at every twist and turn. 34 mazes, stories, solutions. 48pp. 8¼ x 11.     0-486-24566-7

LETTERS OF W. A. MOZART, Wolfgang A. Mozart. Remarkable letters show bawdy wit, humor, imagination, musical insights, contemporary musical world; includes some letters from Leopold Mozart. 276pp. 5⅜ x 8½.     0-486-22859-2

BASIC PRINCIPLES OF CLASSICAL BALLET, Agrippina Vaganova. Great Russian theoretician, teacher explains methods for teaching classical ballet. 118 illustrations. 175pp. 5⅜ x 8½.     0-486-22036-2

THE JUMPING FROG, Mark Twain. Revenge edition. The original story of The Celebrated Jumping Frog of Calaveras County, a hapless French translation, and Twain's hilarious "retranslation" from the French. 12 illustrations. 66pp. 5⅜ x 8½.
0-486-22686-7

BEST REMEMBERED POEMS, Martin Gardner (ed.). The 126 poems in this superb collection of 19th- and 20th-century British and American verse range from Shelley's "To a Skylark" to the impassioned "Renascence" of Edna St. Vincent Millay and to Edward Lear's whimsical "The Owl and the Pussycat." 224pp. 5⅜ x 8½.
0-486-27165-X

COMPLETE SONNETS, William Shakespeare. Over 150 exquisite poems deal with love, friendship, the tyranny of time, beauty's evanescence, death and other themes in language of remarkable power, precision and beauty. Glossary of archaic terms. 80pp. 5³⁄₁₆ x 8¼.     0-486-26686-9

HISTORIC HOMES OF THE AMERICAN PRESIDENTS, Second, Revised Edition, Irvin Haas. A traveler's guide to American Presidential homes, most open to the public, depicting and describing homes occupied by every American President from George Washington to George Bush. With visiting hours, admission charges, travel routes. 175 photographs. Index. 160pp. 8¼ x 11.     0-486-26751-2

THE WIT AND HUMOR OF OSCAR WILDE, Alvin Redman (ed.). More than 1,000 ripostes, paradoxes, wisecracks: Work is the curse of the drinking classes; I can resist everything except temptation; etc. 258pp. 5⅜ x 8½.     0-486-20602-5

SHAKESPEARE LEXICON AND QUOTATION DICTIONARY, Alexander Schmidt. Full definitions, locations, shades of meaning in every word in plays and poems. More than 50,000 exact quotations. 1,485pp. 6½ x 9¼. 2-vol. set.
Vol. 1: 0-486-22726-X     Vol. 2: 0-486-22727-8

SELECTED POEMS, Emily Dickinson. Over 100 best-known, best-loved poems by one of America's foremost poets, reprinted from authoritative early editions. No comparable edition at this price. Index of first lines. 64pp. 5³⁄₁₆ x 8¼.   0-486-26466-1

THE INSIDIOUS DR. FU-MANCHU, Sax Rohmer. The first of the popular mystery series introduces a pair of English detectives to their archnemesis, the diabolical Dr. Fu-Manchu. Flavorful atmosphere, fast-paced action, and colorful characters enliven this classic of the genre. 208pp. 5³⁄₁₆ x 8¼.     0-486-29898-1

THE MALLEUS MALEFICARUM OF KRAMER AND SPRENGER, translated by Montague Summers. Full text of most important witchhunter's "bible," used by both Catholics and Protestants. 278pp. 6⅝ x 10. 0-486-22802-9

SPANISH STORIES/CUENTOS ESPAÑOLES: A Dual-Language Book, Angel Flores (ed.). Unique format offers 13 great stories in Spanish by Cervantes, Borges, others. Faithful English translations on facing pages. 352pp. 5⅜ x 8½. 0-486-25399-6

GARDEN CITY, LONG ISLAND, IN EARLY PHOTOGRAPHS, 1869–1919, Mildred H. Smith. Handsome treasury of 118 vintage pictures, accompanied by carefully researched captions, document the Garden City Hotel fire (1899), the Vanderbilt Cup Race (1908), the first airmail flight departing from the Nassau Boulevard Aerodrome (1911), and much more. 96pp. 8⅞ x 11¾. 0-486-40669-5

OLD QUEENS, N.Y., IN EARLY PHOTOGRAPHS, Vincent F. Seyfried and William Asadorian. Over 160 rare photographs of Maspeth, Jamaica, Jackson Heights, and other areas. Vintage views of DeWitt Clinton mansion, 1939 World's Fair and more. Captions. 192pp. 8⅞ x 11. 0-486-26358-4

CAPTURED BY THE INDIANS: 15 Firsthand Accounts, 1750-1870, Frederick Drimmer. Astounding true historical accounts of grisly torture, bloody conflicts, relentless pursuits, miraculous escapes and more, by people who lived to tell the tale. 384pp. 5⅜ x 8½. 0-486-24901-8

THE WORLD'S GREAT SPEECHES (Fourth Enlarged Edition), Lewis Copeland, Lawrence W. Lamm, and Stephen J. McKenna. Nearly 300 speeches provide public speakers with a wealth of updated quotes and inspiration–from Pericles' funeral oration and William Jennings Bryan's "Cross of Gold Speech" to Malcolm X's powerful words on the Black Revolution and Earl of Spenser's tribute to his sister, Diana, Princess of Wales. 944pp. 5⅜ x 8⅜. 0-486-40903-1

THE BOOK OF THE SWORD, Sir Richard F. Burton. Great Victorian scholar/adventurer's eloquent, erudite history of the "queen of weapons"–from prehistory to early Roman Empire. Evolution and development of early swords, variations (sabre, broadsword, cutlass, scimitar, etc.), much more. 336pp. 6⅛ x 9¼. 0-486-25434-8

AUTOBIOGRAPHY: The Story of My Experiments with Truth, Mohandas K. Gandhi. Boyhood, legal studies, purification, the growth of the Satyagraha (nonviolent protest) movement. Critical, inspiring work of the man responsible for the freedom of India. 480pp. 5⅜ x 8½. (Available in U.S. only.) 0-486-24593-4

CELTIC MYTHS AND LEGENDS, T. W. Rolleston. Masterful retelling of Irish and Welsh stories and tales. Cuchulain, King Arthur, Deirdre, the Grail, many more. First paperback edition. 58 full-page illustrations. 512pp. 5⅜ x 8½. 0-486-26507-2

THE PRINCIPLES OF PSYCHOLOGY, William James. Famous long course complete, unabridged. Stream of thought, time perception, memory, experimental methods; great work decades ahead of its time. 94 figures. 1,391pp. 5⅜ x 8½. 2-vol. set. Vol. I: 0-486-20381-6 Vol. II: 0-486-20382-4

THE WORLD AS WILL AND REPRESENTATION, Arthur Schopenhauer. Definitive English translation of Schopenhauer's life work, correcting more than 1,000 errors, omissions in earlier translations. Translated by E. F. J. Payne. Total of 1,269pp. 5⅜ x 8½. 2-vol. set. Vol. 1: 0-486-21761-2 Vol. 2: 0-486-21762-0

CATALOG OF DOVER BOOKS

MAGIC AND MYSTERY IN TIBET, Madame Alexandra David-Neel. Experiences among lamas, magicians, sages, sorcerers, Bonpa wizards. A true psychic discovery. 32 illustrations. 321pp. 5⅜ x 8½. (Available in U.S. only.) 0-486-22682-4

THE EGYPTIAN BOOK OF THE DEAD, E. A. Wallis Budge. Complete reproduction of Ani's papyrus, finest ever found. Full hieroglyphic text, interlinear transliteration, word-for-word translation, smooth translation. 533pp. 6½ x 9¼.
0-486-21866-X

HISTORIC COSTUME IN PICTURES, Braun & Schneider. Over 1,450 costumed figures in clearly detailed engravings—from dawn of civilization to end of 19th century. Captions. Many folk costumes. 256pp. 8⅜ x 11¾. 0-486-23150-X

MATHEMATICS FOR THE NONMATHEMATICIAN, Morris Kline. Detailed, college-level treatment of mathematics in cultural and historical context, with numerous exercises. Recommended Reading Lists. Tables. Numerous figures. 641pp. 5⅜ x 8½.
0-486-24823-2

PROBABILISTIC METHODS IN THE THEORY OF STRUCTURES, Isaac Elishakoff. Well-written introduction covers the elements of the theory of probability from two or more random variables, the reliability of such multivariable structures, the theory of random function, Monte Carlo methods of treating problems incapable of exact solution, and more. Examples. 502pp. 5⅜ x 8½. 0-486-40691-1

THE RIME OF THE ANCIENT MARINER, Gustave Doré, S. T. Coleridge. Doré's finest work; 34 plates capture moods, subtleties of poem. Flawless full-size reproductions printed on facing pages with authoritative text of poem. "Beautiful. Simply beautiful."—*Publisher's Weekly.* 77pp. 9¼ x 12. 0-486-22305-1

SCULPTURE: Principles and Practice, Louis Slobodkin. Step-by-step approach to clay, plaster, metals, stone; classical and modern. 253 drawings, photos. 255pp. 8⅛ x 11.
0-486-22960-2

THE INFLUENCE OF SEA POWER UPON HISTORY, 1660–1783, A. T. Mahan. Influential classic of naval history and tactics still used as text in war colleges. First paperback edition. 4 maps. 24 battle plans. 640pp. 5⅜ x 8½. 0-486-25509-3

THE STORY OF THE TITANIC AS TOLD BY ITS SURVIVORS, Jack Winocour (ed.). What it was really like. Panic, despair, shocking inefficiency, and a little heroism. More thrilling than any fictional account. 26 illustrations. 320pp. 5⅜ x 8½.
0-486-20610-6

ONE TWO THREE . . . INFINITY: Facts and Speculations of Science, George Gamow. Great physicist's fascinating, readable overview of contemporary science: number theory, relativity, fourth dimension, entropy, genes, atomic structure, much more. 128 illustrations. Index. 352pp. 5⅜ x 8½. 0-486-25664-2

DALÍ ON MODERN ART: The Cuckolds of Antiquated Modern Art, Salvador Dalí. Influential painter skewers modern art and its practitioners. Outrageous evaluations of Picasso, Cézanne, Turner, more. 15 renderings of paintings discussed. 44 calligraphic decorations by Dalí. 96pp. 5⅜ x 8½. (Available in U.S. only.) 0-486-29220-7

ANTIQUE PLAYING CARDS: A Pictorial History, Henry René D'Allemagne. Over 900 elaborate, decorative images from rare playing cards (14th–20th centuries): Bacchus, death, dancing dogs, hunting scenes, royal coats of arms, players cheating, much more. 96pp. 9¼ x 12¼. 0-486-29265-7

MAKING FURNITURE MASTERPIECES: 30 Projects with Measured Drawings, Franklin H. Gottshall. Step-by-step instructions, illustrations for constructing handsome, useful pieces, among them a Sheraton desk, Chippendale chair, Spanish desk, Queen Anne table and a William and Mary dressing mirror. 224pp. 8⅛ x 11¼.
0-486-29338-6

NORTH AMERICAN INDIAN DESIGNS FOR ARTISTS AND CRAFTSPEOPLE, Eva Wilson. Over 360 authentic copyright-free designs adapted from Navajo blankets, Hopi pottery, Sioux buffalo hides, more. Geometrics, symbolic figures, plant and animal motifs, etc. 128pp. 8⅜ x 11. (Not for sale in the United Kingdom.) 0-486-25341-4

THE FOSSIL BOOK: A Record of Prehistoric Life, Patricia V. Rich et al. Profusely illustrated definitive guide covers everything from single-celled organisms and dinosaurs to birds and mammals and the interplay between climate and man. Over 1,500 illustrations. 760pp. 7½ x 10⅛. 0-486-29371-8

VICTORIAN ARCHITECTURAL DETAILS: Designs for Over 700 Stairs, Mantels, Doors, Windows, Cornices, Porches, and Other Decorative Elements, A. J. Bicknell & Company. Everything from dormer windows and piazzas to balconies and gable ornaments. Also includes elevations and floor plans for handsome, private residences and commercial structures. 80pp. 9⅜ x 12¼. 0-486-44015-X

WESTERN ISLAMIC ARCHITECTURE: A Concise Introduction, John D. Hoag. Profusely illustrated critical appraisal compares and contrasts Islamic mosques and palaces–from Spain and Egypt to other areas in the Middle East. 139 illustrations. 128pp. 6 x 9. 0-486-43760-4

CHINESE ARCHITECTURE: A Pictorial History, Liang Ssu-ch'eng. More than 240 rare photographs and drawings depict temples, pagodas, tombs, bridges, and imperial palaces comprising much of China's architectural heritage. 152 halftones, 94 diagrams. 232pp. 10¾ x 9⅞. 0-486-43999-2

THE RENAISSANCE: Studies in Art and Poetry, Walter Pater. One of the most talked-about books of the 19th century, *The Renaissance* combines scholarship and philosophy in an innovative work of cultural criticism that examines the achievements of Botticelli, Leonardo, Michelangelo, and other artists. "The holy writ of beauty."–Oscar Wilde. 160pp. 5⅜ x 8½. 0-486-44025-7

A TREATISE ON PAINTING, Leonardo da Vinci. The great Renaissance artist's practical advice on drawing and painting techniques covers anatomy, perspective, composition, light and shadow, and color. A classic of art instruction, it features 48 drawings by Nicholas Poussin and Leon Battista Alberti. 192pp. 5⅜ x 8½.
0-486-44155-5

THE MIND OF LEONARDO DA VINCI, Edward McCurdy. More than just a biography, this classic study by a distinguished historian draws upon Leonardo's extensive writings to offer numerous demonstrations of the Renaissance master's achievements, not only in sculpture and painting, but also in music, engineering, and even experimental aviation. 384pp. 5⅜ x 8½. 0-486-44142-3

WASHINGTON IRVING'S RIP VAN WINKLE, Illustrated by Arthur Rackham. Lovely prints that established artist as a leading illustrator of the time and forever etched into the popular imagination a classic of Catskill lore. 51 full-color plates. 80pp. 8⅜ x 11. 0-486-44242-X

HENSCHE ON PAINTING, John W. Robichaux. Basic painting philosophy and methodology of a great teacher, as expounded in his famous classes and workshops on Cape Cod. 7 illustrations in color on covers. 80pp. 5⅜ x 8½. 0-486-43728-0

# CATALOG OF DOVER BOOKS

LIGHT AND SHADE: A Classic Approach to Three-Dimensional Drawing, Mrs. Mary P. Merrifield. Handy reference clearly demonstrates principles of light and shade by revealing effects of common daylight, sunshine, and candle or artificial light on geometrical solids. 13 plates. 64pp. 5⅜ x 8½. 0-486-44143-1

ASTROLOGY AND ASTRONOMY: A Pictorial Archive of Signs and Symbols, Ernst and Johanna Lehner. Treasure trove of stories, lore, and myth, accompanied by more than 300 rare illustrations of planets, the Milky Way, signs of the zodiac, comets, meteors, and other astronomical phenomena. 192pp. 8⅜ x 11.

0-486-43981-X

JEWELRY MAKING: Techniques for Metal, Tim McCreight. Easy-to-follow instructions and carefully executed illustrations describe tools and techniques, use of gems and enamels, wire inlay, casting, and other topics. 72 line illustrations and diagrams. 176pp. 8¼ x 10⅞. 0-486-44043-5

MAKING BIRDHOUSES: Easy and Advanced Projects, Gladstone Califf. Easy-to-follow instructions include diagrams for everything from a one-room house for bluebirds to a forty-two-room structure for purple martins. 56 plates; 4 figures. 80pp. 8¾ x 6⅜. 0-486-44183-0

LITTLE BOOK OF LOG CABINS: How to Build and Furnish Them, William S. Wicks. Handy how-to manual, with instructions and illustrations for building cabins in the Adirondack style, fireplaces, stairways, furniture, beamed ceilings, and more. 102 line drawings. 96pp. 8¾ x 6⅜. 0-486-44259-4

THE SEASONS OF AMERICA PAST, Eric Sloane. From "sugaring time" and strawberry picking to Indian summer and fall harvest, a whole year's activities described in charming prose and enhanced with 79 of the author's own illustrations. 160pp. 8¼ x 11. 0-486-44220-9

THE METROPOLIS OF TOMORROW, Hugh Ferriss. Generous, prophetic vision of the metropolis of the future, as perceived in 1929. Powerful illustrations of towering structures, wide avenues, and rooftop parks—all features in many of today's modern cities. 59 illustrations. 144pp. 8¼ x 11. 0-486-43727-2

THE PATH TO ROME, Hilaire Belloc. This 1902 memoir abounds in lively vignettes from a vanished time, recounting a pilgrimage on foot across the Alps and Apennines in order to "see all Europe which the Christian Faith has saved." 77 of the author's original line drawings complement his sparkling prose. 272pp. 5⅜ x 8½.

0-486-44001-X

THE HISTORY OF RASSELAS: Prince of Abissinia, Samuel Johnson. Distinguished English writer attacks eighteenth-century optimism and man's unrealistic estimates of what life has to offer. 112pp. 5⅜ x 8½. 0-486-44094-X

A VOYAGE TO ARCTURUS, David Lindsay. A brilliant flight of pure fancy, where wild creatures crowd the fantastic landscape and demented torturers dominate victims with their bizarre mental powers. 272pp. 5⅜ x 8½. 0-486-44198-9